PERFECT
BRIGHTNESS
H*of*OPE

PERFECT BRIGHTNESS *of* HOPE

A LATTER-DAY SAINT'S JOURNEY THROUGH ALCOHOL AND DRUG ADDICTION

PHIL SIMKINS

CFI
AN IMPRINT OF CEDAR FORT, INC.
SPRINGVILLE, UTAH

ISBN 13: 978-1-4621-1083-4

Published by CFI, an imprint of Cedar Fort, Inc.
2373 W. 700 S., Springville, UT 84663
Distributed by Cedar Fort, Inc., www.cedarfort.com
First published in 2002 by Maasai Publishing

LIBRARY OF CONGRESS CATALOGING-IN-PUBLICATION DATA

S., Phil, author.
A perfect brightness of hope : a Latter-day Saint's journey through alcohol and drug addiction / Philip H. Simkins.
     pages cm
Includes bibliographical references and index.
Summary: The biography of an alcoholic member of the Church of Jesus Christ of Latter-day Saints.
ISBN 978-1-4621-1083-4 (alk. paper)
1. S., Phil. 2. Alcoholics Anonymous. 3. Alcoholism--Religious aspects--Church of Jesus Christ of Latter-day Saints. 4. Recovering alcoholics--United States--Biography. 5. Mormons--United States--Biography. I. Title.

HV5068.S2 2012
362.29092--dc23
[B]

2012035004

Cover design by Angela Olsen
Cover design © 2012 by Lyle Mortimer
Edited and typeset by Whitney A. Lindsley

Printed in the United States of America

10 9 8 7 6 5 4 3 2 1

To all whose lives are affected by alcoholism and addiction. More especially, to my first family whose lives were so altered and for whom I will always need forgiveness. And finally—to the addict in all of us.

In memory of

Deanne Sue Giles

Patty Reber

Steve Honeyman

Praise for

PERFECT BRIGHTNESS
OF HOPE

The following are testimonials from readers who benefitted from reading Perfect Brightness of Hope. *I hope that you, like them, will also find comfort as you read this book.*

Just wanted to thank you for your powerful book. I work in a library and saw your book and thought it sounded interesting. Wow! It really has the power to change lives. I have passed it on to several people including my bishop, who said a lot of what he deals with is addiction problems and would find it useful. I have never had an alcohol addiction, but I recognize some other addictive behavior in my life. Your book has helped me to realize that we all have challenges to overcome and that we all need to at some point turn our will over to God and enlist His help in overcoming whatever weaknesses we have in life. Indeed, perhaps those weaknesses are given to us to bring us to God. It has also helped me to realize that we all have a story, we all have struggles, and that we should never judge another person because most of us are desperately trying to do the best we can with what we have been dealt in life. We all make poor choices at times and must suffer the consequences of our own actions, but it is wonderful to think that no matter what has happened in the past, our Savior is reaching out to us with open arms waiting to help us. I just wanted you to know you made a difference to me. I understand others better, and in talking to other people I have found that there are so many shattered lives because of problems of addiction and abuse. It is much more prevalent in society than many people realize. I would like to be someone who can help others. Thanks for helping me do that better and for sharing your story.

NANCY B.

Your story is amazing . . . This book is applicable to any and all addictions, which makes the book far reaching to its readership. I hope and pray it will help many, many people.

LINDA E.

Words can't adequately describe the feelings generated from vicariously living your experience, yet I have a few to help us both reflect. Often I was deeply moved, which required setting the book aside to personally reflect on the feelings generated in order to progress in my own life. I can honestly say that your testimony has touched me deeply, and helped me to look at my own addictions of various sorts. . . . [Your] book holds awesome power for those willing to use it as a means to crawl out of their darkness into the light . . .

The tale of your journey into, through, and then out of darkness was illuminating, and therefore rewarding. Mere words will only convey the value of that experience in a limited way. Know that it is the spirit behind the words that will resonate with the kindred spirits you wish to touch.

MARK E.

It is a great book and very helpful to families who have alcoholics with whom they need to deal with and [understand what they're going through]. We certainly do appreciate the book and have enjoyed reading it.

RICHARD B.

Thank you very much for the book. I just started reading it this morning on the twenty-five-mile ride to work on our employee van . . . I was enjoying the emotion, family sharing, wisdom, and honesty of "The Carrot and the Donkey" chapter so much, I was disappointed to realize that we were here already. My dad also drank too much, but he loved our family intensely and worked hard, often with multiple jobs, to support us. It seemed that he never lost work or abused us, though my brothers and sister also experienced the overheard arguments and feared for the possible divorce, which never occurred. . . . Your book definitely has my interest and I will continue reading. . . . I was "at" the basketball game with the winning shot, followed by the referee's call. I "saw" you floating down the irrigation canal. . And you have already explained the at-first-innocent "problem(s)/solution" of a young kid, feeling lonely and on the outside, discovering the powerful and instant remedy of alcohol for reducing loneliness and being left out, always picked last, etc. This reminds me of what I often, to my embarrassment, forget . . .

BOB H.

I read your book over last weekend. I was moved in many ways (from gut-wrenching despair. . . . wanting to yell at you, to elation and wanting to celebrate with you) by your book. Thank you for exerting the considerable effort to write it. Thanks for your fearless openness and candor. Thanks for caring about everyone else that suffers similar afflictions. I'm the bishop of a ward in Heber, [Utah,] and as soon as I finished the book I gave it to a member of my ward who continues to struggle with alcohol (successful businessman, loving husband, good dad, but . . . well, you know). I hope it can inspire him to abandon his will to Father and begin the healing process. I'm certain that I am now equipped to provide better counsel, with more understanding, to my ward family members. May the Lord continue to bless you for being so willing to share.

ROB L.

I was cheering for you every time you beat your addictions and then sad for you when you were overtaken by them. I could really relate. I've fought being a chocoholic off and on and finally gave it up for good seven months ago. I feel like I am a compassionate person, yet when I read the book I gained a whole different perspective on the power of addictive substances on our behavior. I would like there to be more people at church with the smell of cigarettes on their clothes and liquor on their breath. I think sometimes that we expect everyone who walks in the door to be perfect and that is not what church is about. I liked how you said that those of us who stay away from church need to be fed spiritually. I think that is important. I wish they would give your book to new missionaries to give them some insight into how an alcoholic thinks when in the middle of the addiction.

Thanks for putting your life out there for all of us to read about and learn from. Very inspirational, and it really helped me to be less judgmental.

JEANNE P.

Your book is a strength to me and it will be a strength to many people seeking the Atonement. I will always remember you and the feeling I felt when I read your book. Thank you!

MILINDA T.

I have finished reading your book and have such strong emotions about it. I admit, as did Steve Young, that I was not very informed about addiction. I am saddened by the fact that I didn't know about your struggles, although I don't know if I could have helped in any way. I wish I could have.

You have a beautiful ability to write, express yourself and engage the reader in what you were thinking and experiencing. I have a son and a son-in-law who teaches seminary; and if they feel as strongly as you have felt, I have not heard them express it. I especially loved your powerful testimony of the love of our Heavenly Father and the Atonement of the Savior and the way you expressed it.

I can only imagine the hours of time spent recalling, reliving, and writing this book. I am grateful that you wrote it. Reading your book has had a tremendous effect on me, and I believe I can be more helpful and compassionate with anyone who might need my help. I will recommend it heartily to everyone I talk to.

Many tears fell while I was reading your book, but I finished with a feeling of hope and happiness for you and your family. I'm grateful I had the opportunity to share these experiences with you. I am trying to be more grateful for my family and my life.

BONNIE B.

Already I am reexamining my own attitudes about a family member who is an alcoholic. My own lack of support, stemming from my fear of him, needs to be changed. You and I can talk about this more later. Phil, your courage in writing and publishing the book is a blessing to countless people. Never doubt that you have <u>saved lives</u>. All the best to you and your family.

DEB H.

I am so grateful for your book. I took it with me on a short, two-day trip. I couldn't put it down until I had finished it before returning home. By the way, I am a volunteer seminary teacher. I now wish that we had been able to spend some time when you were at my office. As a stake president, we deal with compulsive behaviors often. Your experience gave me a much-needed perspective.

RICHARD E.

I read your book about six months ago; it changed my life. I have never been able to grieve properly over my addiction because I felt that I had to beat it. It was not until your book that I understood how to turn my will over to the Lord. I have been attending the ARP [Addiction Recovery Program] for pornography and have been sober for twenty-two weeks. Your book inspires me, and I am looking forward to reading it again. I gave it to my brother so he would have a better understanding of what I am going through; it was great. I need to have my wife read it next. Maybe it will help save my marriage.

DAMON D.

I just finished reading your book . . . It was so inspirational. My son . . . was part of the drug court program [at a treatment center]. He told me he had met you at the meeting at [the center], and he had read your book twice, because it meant so much to him [and] was a lot like his life. He wanted me to read it . . . He is now in . . . jail . . . may be thrown out of drug court, and has other charges pending. He considers you book and the NA blue book his sources of hope, and his faith in God. I am trying to be as supportive as I can in Louisiana, but he is all alone in Utah with no family. He does have a sponsor . . . who has been wonderful help to me for moral support. All I can do from here is go to Al-Anon meetings, which I do regularly, went to an NA meeting, and read all I can get my hands on. Do not know what the outcome of this jail time will be, but I do believe [my son] has the strength to recover in the NA program.

Your book has meant a lot to me and to [my son], and I am so glad he had me read it. And I intend to read it again. Thanks so much for writing it and sharing your life with us. . .

Dottie W.

What a wonderful book.

My wife and I were called as Church service missionaries to serve in the LDS Addiction Recovery Program. As new missionaries, we were . . . given a copy of the book.

This will be a most valuable treasure in our library.

We have been presenting information on the LDS Addiction Recovery Program to members of our Stake and have recommended your book as a "must read"

I am encouraging every bishop in the stake to get a copy of the book and to have a copy for every Priesthood and Relief Society leader. They need to understand what the addict is going through, and I have found nothing better to give than insight than your book. . . .

Again, thank you for keeping a journal. Thank you for turning to the Lord, so that this book could be published as a success story. This will give insight to the non addict and HOPE to those still trapped in the chains of addiction.

David H.

Thank you for sharing your book about your life with me. It helped me to understand addictions and weaknesses much better. I can feel you have a special mission to help others overcome their addictions and weaknesses and to come unto Jesus Christ. . . .

LaRae C.

I am also an alcoholic Mormon. I just got my first DUI a few weeks ago and am lucky to be alive. I can relate with everything you've said and have the same uncontrollable feelings toward alcohol. I can't control my drinking. I thought I was the only alcoholic Mormon out there. I look forward to reading the rest of your book.

DEWEY

I just "cryingly" finished your book. Your story and testimony has impacted my life greatly. . . .

ROBERT W.

$\mathscr{C}$ONTENTS

ACKNOWLEDGMENTS

THIS BOOK IS DEDICATED TO MY PARENTS, WHO, ALTHOUGH now living beyond the veil, continue to touch my life daily with their legacy of love.

I offer heartfelt thanks to Steve Young for providing a special foreword and endorsement for this book. I am grateful to Dr. Stephen R. Covey for his endorsement of this book.

My wife, Vickie Lee, provided her special touch by drawing each of the book's original sketches. I am grateful for her love and her belief in me throughout much of the living and all of the writing of this book. She is truly an angel to me.

Over the forty-two years that I have lived and written this story, many individuals have cared, helped, read, edited, and given advice. Because the list is too long to recite, I will simply say, "Thanks to all of you. I am deeply grateful."

$\mathscr{F}$OREWORD

S EVERAL YEARS AGO, A GOOD FOOTBALL BUDDY STOPPED AT MY door. I enthusiastically greeted him. As we talked, I sensed a difference in his personality, and soon his request for financial help led to the tragic story of his battle with drugs and alcohol. He had lost his wife, child, and brilliant career. Initially, I was not only perplexed and frustrated over the foolishness of his choices, but I could not believe how one could give up so much for so little.

Since that experience, I have felt sorrow for my arrogance. I have now witnessed many fine people fall prey to the dreaded disease of addiction. I have seen wonderful families struggle over their children. I have witnessed the brightest and the best leave their home, sacrifice their future, reject their loved ones, and lose their identity. I have heard all too often of suicide, accidental overdose, and drug-caused fatal accidents. It was beyond my reasoning then, but now my compassion has increased as I have become better informed. I also know that addiction touches all our lives and is fast becoming the foremost health problem facing Americans.

Tragically, too many misconceptions are associated with substance abuse. Too many people feel that only the weak and selfish choose the road of addiction, compounding the very sick circumstances that postpone those who need help from receiving it.

I appreciate Phil, a former seminary teacher and religion instructor, for having the courage to write his own story of his journey through addiction. I appreciate his faith in God as he truly walked through the "valley of the shadow of death." I am also humbled by the good people who embraced him, included him, and finally rejoiced with him as he returned to his family and the church that he loves. With patience they instilled in him the *Perfect Brightness of Hope.*

I encourage every parent, teacher, coach, teenager, and superstar to read this book. No one can read it without self-examination. I will never be the same, and I am grateful for that fact.

STEVE YOUNG
NFL HALL OF FAME

$\mathscr{P}$REFACE

$\mathbf{T}$HIS BOOK DESCRIBES SOME OF MY EXPERIENCES AS A MEMBER of The Church of Jesus Christ of Latter-day Saints (LDS). However, the insights and principles taught herein can be applied universally to addiction and to all faiths and religions. For those unfamiliar with the LDS Church, explanations of Church doctrine and history referenced in the book are provided in chapter endnotes. The endnotes are worthy of review, as they provide additional insight.

Numerous excerpts from my personal journals are included in this book. To improve the readability of what were often hastily written entries, I have made grammatical edits. With each entry, I have endeavored to preserve the original content, intent, and feeling.

Quotations from *Matthew Cowley Speaks* are used by permission from Deseret Book Company. Quotations from "Understanding Ourselves and Alcoholism," are reprinted with permission of Al-Anon Family Group Headquarters, Inc. The book *Alcoholics Anonymous* is in the public domain. Where this book is quoted, page numbers are provided for further investigation.

This book is not intended to represent any entity, group, fellowship, or church. The author alone is responsible for its content.

$\mathscr{P}$ROLOGUE

H I. MY NAME IS PHIL. I AM AN ALCOHOLIC AND AN ADDICT— an *LDS* alcoholic and addict. In July 1979, after yet another drinking binge, I wrote a note in the Book of Mormon I had used for the *previous seven years* as a full-time seminary teacher for The Church of Jesus Christ of Latter-day Saints: "July 7, 1979—I am coming Home! I bring experience that may assist in building God's Kingdom on Earth. May I do so with all of Heaven's help." A year later I added, "July 1980 came and went; sadly, little has changed." With the passing of each July, I wrote next to the previous entry the record of another year addicted to alcohol. In July 1984, I gave up on this futile ritual by adding a final remark: "July "81, "82, "83, and "84 have passed and so much has changed—all for the worst."

During my years of active alcoholism, I lost everything of value—family, Church activity, employment, self-respect, and hope. Somewhere along the way, I began reaching out to recovering alcoholics through the fellowship of Alcoholics Anonymous. Persisting in following their advice by working a few simple, although not easy, steps, I began to feel small changes in the way I handled life. Hope began to reappear.

Although this story is primarily about an alcoholic, my drugs of choice and addictions varied along the journey. The phrase "drug of choice" usually refers to something one ingests but can also apply to other compulsive behaviors. Once these behaviors get out of control, they can be described using the term "-holic." I define a "-holic" as anyone who compulsively and repeatedly engages in destructive behaviors—spiritual, physical, or emotional. These include but are not limited to alcoholic, chocoholic, chewaholic, complainaholic, foodaholic, golfaholic, negaholic, pornaholic, sexaholic, spendaholic, smokeaholic, sportsaholic, sodaholic, workaholic, and so on.

We live in an addicted society. Addiction is linked to a multitude of behaviors with varying degrees of compulsion. Alcohol, anger, caffeine, controlling others, criticism, food, gossip, Internet, pornography, pride, shopping, television, tobacco, videos and video games, work, and illegal and prescription drugs—these are just a few of the drugs of choice. Advertisers know that if they can sell products that are addictive, repeated sales are guaranteed.[1]

Stop and think. How many people do you know addicted to one of the following: coffee or cigarettes or food or gossiping or power or pride or soap operas or shopping or sugar or sodas or work or worrying, or something? A completely non-addicted individual is rare. To a lesser or greater extent, all of us go forth daily depending on our drugs of choice.

What is your drug of choice? Are you addicted to a substance or habit that is harming yourself (and others) through compulsive behavior? If you are one of those rare individuals not addicted, than for sure you know someone else who is. This book will help you understand yourself and others. Through understanding comes acceptance and through acceptance (we call it "Surrender to a Higher Power") comes peace. It is a peace that comes when the Lord Jesus Christ, as *The Physician,* touches you. This story testifies that His love does touch freely in the atmosphere of Alcoholics Anonymous and other Twelve-Step programs such as Narcotics Anonymous, Overeaters Anonymous, and the LDS Substance Abuse Recovery Program. This book testifies that all people, addicts included—*when loved and fellowshipped*—can become respected, contributing members of their faith, synagogue or church.

As you open your heart to my story, you will experience vicariously what it is to be an addict. The pain and despair of being trapped in an endless downward spiral will tug at your heartstrings. But I promise, as you read this *entire* story, you will feel the pure love of Christ. Compassion, born of understanding, will increase. You will come to understand that an incredible saving power is released when one simply surrenders all to a caring, loving, and merciful Father in Heaven. You will know why Nephi used "press forward" twice in the following scripture and commented: "This is the way and there is none other way given under heaven for a man to enter in the Kingdom of God" (2 Nephi 31:21).

> Wherefore ye must *press forward* with a steadfastness in Jesus Christ, having a *perfect brightness of hope*, and a love of God *and all men*. Wherefore, if ye shall *press forward* feasting upon the words of Christ and endure to the end, behold, thus saith the Father, ye shall have eternal life. (2 Nephi 31:20; emphasis added).

*N*OTES

1. *Addictive Products.* "Behold, verily, thus saith the Lord unto you: *In consequence of evils and designs which do and will exist in the hearts of conspiring men in the last days,* I have warned you, and forewarned you, by giving unto you this word of wisdom by revelation" (Doctrine and Covenants 89:4; emphasis added).

President Ezra Taft Benson adds this insight:

> The Lord foresaw the situation of today when motives for money would cause men to conspire to entice others to take noxious substances into their bodies. Advertisements which promote beer, wine, liquors, coffee, tobacco, and other harmful substances are examples of what the Lord foresaw. But the most pernicious example of an evil conspiracy in our time is those who induce young people into the use of drugs.

My young brothers and sisters, in all love, we give you warning that Satan and his emissaries will strive to entice you to use harmful substances, because they well know if you partake, your spiritual powers will be inhibited and you will be in their evil power. Stay away from those places or people which would influence you to break the commandments of God. Keep the commandments of God and you will have the wisdom to know and discern that which is evil. ("A Principle With a Promise," *Ensign*, May 1983, 53)

CHAPTER ONE

THE CARROT & THE DONKEY

And what is it that ye shall hope for? Behold I say unto you that ye shall have hope through the Atonement of Christ and the power of his resurrection, to be raised unto life eternal, and this because of your faith in him according to the promise.

—Moroni 7:41

WITH THE WORKDAY OVER, THE SOLDIERS AROUND ME relaxed in the barracks by drinking beer and telling stories. The pungent odors of marijuana, tobacco, and incense filled the air. Seeking sanctuary in the vacant office where I worked during the day, I unlocked the door and stepped inside. Relocking the door, I walked to the farthest corner of the dark, quiet room. Screen windows allowed the heavy, humid Panama air to surround me. The low moan of ocean-bound ships sounded in the distance as they moved along the canal thread and off into the dark jungle night.

Gripping a small serviceman's edition of the Book of Mormon,[1] I hesitated in the dim, bluish-white light that filtered into the room from outside security lamps. Until this moment, my awareness of a Heavenly Father had been tucked away in some remote region of my mind along with the memory of my baptism as an eight-year-old boy into The Church of Jesus Christ of Latter-day Saints. With my Book of Mormon in hand and desire in my heart, I knelt on the cool concrete floor and began my plea to God.

I had grown up in the fifties and sixties in a small town in southern Utah. My grandmother claimed I was fortunate to grow up at all. All who knew of my accident as a toddler agreed it should have brought early termination to my turn on earth. It was springtime. The irrigation canals were bulging with runoff from snow melting in the high mountains that circled our valley home. One afternoon, while we were on an outing, my grandmother and I walked from our home through green alfalfa fields to a bridge that spanned one of the larger canals. My grandmother entertained me by hunting up sticks to cast off the bridge into the swift running water. After tossing a stick, I would run to the other side of the bridge and watch it reappear. Once, when my grandmother had turned away, I hurled a stick with so much exuberance that both the stick and I went into the muddy water. She turned back to see no child on the bridge. A moment later, she saw me float like a cork out from under the bridge. Being a large woman and not at all agile, she screamed for help as she tried to run along the canal bank looking for an opening to fetch me out.

She maintained that what happened next was a miracle, citing two pieces of evidence. First, considering the canal bank was mined with obstacles and the waterway protected with thick willows, it should have been impossible for her to run and catch up with me. Second, when she finally found an opening and waded into the cold canal, she turned upstream, hoping to catch my pudgy little body rolling along *under* the water. Instead, I came bobbing along the surface like a bawling piece of balsa wood. She was right about the miracle. Everyone in town who reviewed the event arrived at the same verdict: "Baby Philip should have drowned!" "You surely have an angel on your shoulder," Mom would later say, referring to an uncanny protection I seemed to have against life-threatening situations.

Growing up, I was the kid-picked-last-for-the-team type, a little overweight and a lot self-conscious. On summer evenings, my cousins and I ran the mile into town to the little theater where the movie of the week played. By the time I arrived, huffing and puffing, my friends would have already been to the market for treats and were seated in the theater. This was typical. I finished last in most childhood activities.

My older brother and sister, on the other hand, excelled academically, socially, and athletically. Although I was a good student, an average athlete, and the guitarist in our school's first rock-and-roll band, my accomplishments seemed insignificant alongside my valedictorian, student-body president, all-state basketball player brother and equally successful cheerleader sister. My brother and sister were always good to me and treated me fairly, but I was convinced my own intellectual and physical skills were no match.

During my freshman year in high school, I fell in puppy love with a pretty, dark-eyed girl, whose short-lived interest in me resulted in my first kiss. It was under an Indian summer moon. Very romantic. Later, at a school dance, I became painfully aware that an older boy, a star on the basketball team, had easily won her affections. My teenage heart was smashed to a pulp. My self-esteem and confidence took a nosedive.

I tried out for and made the basketball team, but I spent most of my time as a benchwarmer. Because I was an excellent three-point shooter, the coach occasionally called on me during practice to represent an opponent's outside attack. The starting five would practice their best defense against my long bombs. Since I seldom played in competitive games, I had little fear of being called on at crunch time. Then suddenly, during a home game when a heated contest was in its final moments, I felt that fear full force. With only seconds left and our team one point behind, the coach called time-out. To my horror, he barked an order for me to enter the game and instructed the other players to get the ball to me for one final, long-range, desperation shot. I had not played five minutes the entire season. Now I was supposed to win the game!

The clock started, and within moments, someone threw me the ball. I fired from thirty feet. The final buzzer rang as the ball swished through the net. The crowd leaped to their feet with a deafening cheer of victory. But the celebration soon turned to a unanimous encore of boos aimed at the referee and, I was sure, at me. Just before releasing the ball, I had shuffled my feet. The violation was caught and the basket disallowed. We lost the game, and I was the scapegoat—from hero to heel in seconds. A lot of me gave up that night. The following year, I tried out for the team to satisfy family tradition and peer expectation. I was relieved when my name did not appear on the final roster.

During my high school years, I often escaped into a world of make-believe. On long school days and at night in bed, I refined my dream. I had a cave high in the mountains. It was stocked with everything I needed. It had electricity, lights, and a kitchen complete with refrigerator to ensure a continuous supply of ice cream. One room housed the most sought-after new invention to arrive in our isolated valley—a television. A creek running through the middle of the cave had a hot spring inlet for swimming. I would imagine playing with my loyal dog in a lush pasture outside the cave entrance. My trusted horse grazed nearby while awaiting a beckoning whistle for an afternoon ride. I conjured this dream in my English class and in church. I summoned the dream in my basement bedroom before drifting off to sleep. My imaginary cave symbolized the melancholy I seemed to have inherited. In my daydream, only my dog and my horse were invited to the secret cave.

I spent many hours by myself hunting rabbits or riding my horse in the foothills around my home. My desire to be alone didn't seem unnatural. It felt comfortable. Later in my teens, sitting alone in my car drinking whiskey was a natural extension of my cave daydream. I found pleasure being by myself, dreaming and feeling the melancholy, especially if I had alcohol. Some of my inclination toward alcohol may have come from the genes of my father.

My mother tried to insulate our family from the effects of my father's binge drinking while still employing every strategy to control it. Mom performed most of the classic behaviors associated with the spouse of an alcoholic—denial, browbeating, assuming more family responsibilities, feeling more guilty, rescuing, bailing out, removing consequences, accepting (and believing) the addict's promises, making idle threats, hiding personal feelings, seldom or never communicating the problem with anyone, and stuffing resentment—all common and often simultaneous actions. Mom expended enormous energy to hide the problem from the public while trying to stop her husband from drinking alcohol. To some extent, our entire family participated in the façade. I remember that Mom and sometimes our entire family would search our ranch for Dad's stash of booze.

Whoever found a bottle would smash it angrily, as if its destruction could stop Dad's drinking.

Our deception included protecting my father's job as *the county sheriff*. For example, once while Dad was drunk, he backed the family car (which also served as the sheriff's car) off a steep embankment and had to abandon it. The next day, a wrecker and several "interested" bystanders showed up to pull the car back onto the road. Our explanation for the sheriff car's predicament was that his seventeen-year-old son—me—was responsible. I went along with the fib. We had to protect Dad.

Our family was at the mercy of alcoholism. We were not dishonest or immoral people. We simply didn't understand the disease and had no idea what to do. Answers existed, but our denial of the problem prevented finding them. When sober, my father was a tender-feeling man. I loved him and never doubted that he loved me. But life would have been much less confusing and destructive had we all been more informed and open about his drinking—had we been aware that each of us was performing a specific role in a play called the *Merry-Go-Round of Denial*.

It is ironic that the few intimate experiences I had with my father occurred on the annual deer hunt while riding horses and drinking together in the mountains above our home. I also had many painful experiences when he had had too much to drink and I had to take care of him. Since Dad seldom showed his emotions, I was always surprised when, after a few drinks, he would loosen up and talk about his feelings and life. It seemed strange to hear him share in this way.

I remember hunting deer one October afternoon when I was nineteen. Sitting on the banks of a sparkling creek high in the mountains, my Dad and I could look down and see the small town in which we lived. In the distance, the square fields of harvested crops appeared like green, yellow, and rust-colored carpet tiles placed neatly on the valley floor. Our horses grazed along the creek bank as we sat in the warmth of the autumn sun, visiting and drinking vodka.

This was an extraordinary experience. The alcohol within us and the nature around us combined to leave their stamp on my mind forever. Dad talked about his love for the valley, for Mom, for me, and for his children. He talked about his frustrations and stresses. I had never heard him share like this. I had not known how deep his feelings were. I sometimes wondered if he even thought about life. Of course, I realized that the vodka had lubricated his vocal cords.

During the last decade of his life, my father achieved success in staying sober. Before his death, he retired with twenty-five years as a successful county sheriff. During his tenure, he was known for his kindness and integrity. His small county jail hardly ever held a criminal, but many a hobo, which we called drifters back then, were fed at the local café and rested the night in the jail's single bed.

Following a lengthy illness, my father passed away in 1996. Of great joy to me was the reassuring fact that my father lay peacefully attired in his white temple clothing,[2] a sign of a worthy, endowed[3] LDS Church member.

Because I was the baby of the family, Mom and I enjoyed a special relationship. Over the years, I was often the only one available to listen to her and give her support when Dad's drinking flared up. Mom and I depended on each other. We enjoyed doing things together. She was game for anything. I remember a sky-blue September Saturday when we completed an eighteen-mile hiking trip to the top of Mount Timpanogos, Utah Valley's twelve-thousand-foot sentinel. This was an extraordinary accomplishment because Mom was sixty-five years old! Etched in my memory is the image of her sliding down the long snow chute that is part of the steep descent on the back of the mountain. With some trepidation, I watched her zip down the glacier toward a small lake below. But I knew she would make it to the bottom safely. We often joked together about whose guardian angel was busiest in preserving our lives. We were always there for each other; something I would come to count on more and more as my addiction progressed. The day following this incredible trip, Mom wrote of her feelings of gratitude and love.

Dear Will Son ["Will" was one of my nicknames]

Just a note to thank you from the bottom of this ole heart for an unforgettable, memorable, beautiful day spent with you yesterday. I loved it all—the beauty of the mountains—visiting with you once more, sharing our inner most thoughts . . . I'm surprised at how good I feel today despite the pain in the front muscles of my legs. It's amazing what a few hours in bed can do to revive the old bones . . .

As I think back on yesterday, I guess I have to give you about ninety percent of the credit for my success in making it to the top. You used super strategy and patience . . . pulling me up the last steep part of the mountain with your hiking staff. I could never have done it without your love, concern, support and physical assistance . . . the scenes of yesterday's experience keep flooding back through my mind in Technicolor. I'll treasure them forever.

Love, Mom

Many nights, while my brother and sister were at school activities, I lay in my basement bed below the kitchen and listened to Mom and Dad arguing, usually over money or alcohol. Before Mom passed away, I was able to tell her of the hellish nights I lay trapped, listening to their verbal battles. She was embarrassed and saddened. I was surprised to learn that she had been unaware of my childhood torment.

I was thirteen when I had my first experience with hard liquor. An associate of my father had parked his truck behind our house. Walking by the passenger-side window, I noticed a small bottle of whiskey exposed in the open glove box. Emanating an almost mystical, magnetic power, the golden liquid sparkled in the sunlight. With little thought of the consequences, I reached through the window, grabbed the bottle, and hid it away in my shirt. I began planning an opportune moment to consume the enticing libation.

In a canyon several miles from my home was an open-air dance hall and small café. Purple Haze, as we called it, was nestled beneath a sheer, purple cliff beside a meandering river. This dance hall provided a romantic setting for youth and adults to gather for dancing on summer evenings. Although I was considered too young to attend, my mother relented due to my persistent pestering. I could go to the dance the coming Saturday, provided that my older brother and sister kept an eye on me. My plan was to smuggle in the bottle, partake of it, and see what happened.

The small container fit nicely inside my cowboy boot as I walked into the dance hall and directly to the men's room. I took a drink. I barely noticed the burning in my throat as the first gulps of whiskey hit my stomach. My face flushed. Suddenly, I felt a wave of relaxation and euphoria. My native melancholy melted away as the alcohol burned deeper into my being. I stepped out into the summer moonlight aglow. My shyness and self-consciousness seemed to disappear. A feeling of well-being, like liquid peace, flowed through my body. The music, the dancers, and the drug combined in a kaleidoscope of emotion beyond anything I had experienced.

The alcohol's effect was swift and overwhelming. A door swung open in my mind leaving a strong craving for more of the drug. I was certain something this pleasurable could never bring unhappiness. Being an active member of my church, whose teachings were against alcohol use, I would feel some guilt, but the result seemed worth it. Alcohol, I thought, was the missing ingredient to raise my self-esteem. It appeared to be a sure remedy for loneliness.

Growing up in an isolated farming community, I seldom heard the word "alcoholic." "Town drunk" and "bum" were the labels used to describe those who spent all day guzzling beer at the local café. Because these labels didn't fit the way I had begun to drink, I was unaware that my alcoholism was serious and progressing. By my seventeenth year, it seemed I had to have alcohol to feel peace of mind or to enjoy any activity. My craving had begun to affect my life in other significant ways. It robbed me of the normal fun I should have been enjoying with other Latter-day Saint youth. A little lying, stealing, and associating with those a bit undesirable were justified to obtain alcohol.

Deer hunting season was the perfect opportunity to further my dependency. With the hard work of the harvest over, the annual hunt was a time for my father, his brothers, and their friends to relax and celebrate. Alcohol was the ritual beverage for these men in every season, but especially the Deer Hunt. The grown-ups were lenient with young boys who had hauled the summer's hay and put up the season's crop of potatoes. Usually, after the uncles had imbibed sufficiently, it was a simple task for young nephews to secure and share a bottle of their whiskey. Additionally, late-night raids on out-of-state hunters' cold-creek liquor stashes provided a consistent source of booze. It was exciting to see how many bottles we could pilfer from the streams and hide away for future use. To us, stealing alcohol didn't seem like a crime. It was more like redistributing the wealth.

I loved the freedom of the hunt. There was alcohol, my horse, the mountains, and little fear of chastisement from the men in camp. My goal every deer season was to have a supply of liquor, then ride off alone to hunt.

One season opener, I crawled from the tent into a foot of newly fallen snow. More snow was blowing down through the canyon. For such an occasion, I had hidden away a full bottle of Loudmouth, as we affectionately called whiskey. The bad weather was not going to mess up my plan for a day of riding and drinking. I would soon be feeling the warmth of the whiskey. The snow added an element of excitement. Ignoring the cold wind, I saddled my high-spirited white mare. Carefully wrapping the whiskey bottle in a flour sack, I tied it behind the saddle, mounted my horse, and forged through the storm toward the ridge top.

Wearing leather gloves, a heavy denim coat, thick leather chaps over my jeans, and my traditional black Stetson, I rounded the first bend, then paused in the saddle for a long drink of Loudmouth. Warmed by its burning, I crossed the ridge top and spotted several deer in an opening below. Dismounting, I let the bridle reins dangle free, took not-too-careful aim at a buck in the group, and fired. My bullet missed the deer. The mare, no doubt annoyed at my stupid plan to coerce her out into the storm, bolted. My precious bottle bounced back and forth against her flank. The mare's unruly antics had placed the day's scheme in jeopardy. If I didn't catch her, I knew the bottle could shake loose and shatter on the ground. I would be left alone to face a cold, *sober* day. Plodding off through the snow, I chased the bottle of whiskey bouncing off the flanks of the white mare like a donkey pursuing the elusive carrot.

Walking in boots and heavy chaps through two feet of snow soon became an ordeal. The whiskey had worn off, and I was longing for more. The mare must have known the game she was playing. On several occasions, I came close enough to almost grasp the reins when, with what I was sure was a mocking sneer, she jumped back and ran off down the hillside.

For hours I followed the dumb animal from one canyon to the next until we both found our way back to camp. When I arrived, she raised her head from a bale of hay and looked at me as if to say, "Well, what took you so long?" I decided against shooting her between the ears when I spotted the flour sack tied securely behind the saddle. The "spirits" had been good to me. I pulled the bottle from the sack and drank deeply. Its warmth made chasing the carrot seem worth it.

I loved to sing and learned to play guitar at an early age. At sixteen, my cousin and I, along with two friends, formed a small rock band and began playing for local dances. During the summers, we performed at the outdoor dance hall where I had first experimented with alcohol. Drinking had become routine. I always used alcohol to enhance my courage to perform. While playing on warm summer evenings, I witnessed many young people open the door to addiction and destruction through alcohol experimentation. But the significance of the harmful paths we were choosing went unnoticed as I sang beneath the mountain cliffs in the soft moonlight.

On several occasions, I drank to unconsciousness and suffered severe hangovers. Alcohol had begun to endanger my life. At seventeen, it made its first serious attempt on my life. It was summer. My friends, a cousin nicknamed Biggy Rat and another buddy we called Itch, and I spent many warm afternoons driving and drinking in the mountains above our home. My nickname was Fats. One evening at dusk, Biggy Rat, Itch, and I stopped at a mountain spring to drink whiskey and chase it with the ice cold water. There, in the mountains we loved, we toasted our friendship. These alcohol rituals seemed to fortify both our friendship and our pledge of loyalty to preserve "our" mountain from the spoils of man. But, true to the addictive pattern we each would experience, alcohol's double face was about to appear. Less than an hour later, Biggy Rat and Itch were engaged in a fistfight as the result of a meaningless argument. Trying to make peace, I wound up in the middle of the scuffle. The battle left us muddy and bloody.

By midnight, the alcohol had almost worn off. We smoothed our ruffled feathers and drove off the mountain—literally! On a steep canyon road, Biggy Rat fell asleep at the wheel, and the truck lunged into the air. When it landed, it rolled and came to a crashing stop, caught on the high side of the canyon by a gnarled pine growing alone in the middle of a wide rock slide. I awakened from my stupor wondering why the ride had suddenly become so rough. Climbing up and out of the window, I took a step to what should have been ground, but instead landed on a bunch of large rocks ten feet below. Fortunately, my posterior hit first, not my head, thus preventing a sudden death. Having observed, or rather heard, my reckless dismount, my companions crawled more cautiously from the truck and dragged me up to the road. We were shaken, cut, and bruised, but bloodier from our earlier fistfight than from the wreck. Incredibly, none of us had been seriously injured.

My tailbone was sore, and I couldn't walk, so Biggy Rat and Itch hiked the ten miles into town to get help. As the eastern sky was growing red with the coming dawn, they returned with the county sheriff—*my father!* The four of us stared in disbelief as the morning light revealed the battered truck lying in the clutches of the old pine a thousand yards above the rocky gorge. My father growled something about God's intervening to cheat Death three more notches on his ledger. Had we not previously eliminated the evidence, he might have said, "Alcohol had been cheated," and we would have been in a lot more trouble.

I graduated from high school with salutatorian honors. One more experience that fell short of my siblings. My parents never pushed me to equal my brother and sister; rather, the opposite. Fearful I would fail and be hurt, their, especially Mom's, encouragements were noticeably subdued, which added to my poor self-image. But, always desiring I be given the same opportunities as the other children, my parents provided for me to attend a small college in Southern Utah.

In these new surroundings, I became shyer than ever, especially around girls. Although I played guitar at the fraternity house and had friends and fans, I was quick to deny praise and attention. To compensate for my timidity, I used alcohol with the belief that the recipe for serenity was simple: Add me to one bottle of booze and anything else. Mix thoroughly.

As my college years passed, I was seldom at peace unless I was drinking. I don't mean to exaggerate. I participated in other activities such as singing and traveling with the choir and competing on the speed typing team, but by the end of my third year, I was carrying a bottle of whiskey in a briefcase to class and spending most of my free time at a nearby tavern. Not yet twenty-one, I had obtained a false ID that allowed me to purchase alcohol freely.

I began my fourth year of college in 1968. Early that year, a pretty girl with long honey-blonde hair took special interest in me. I was beguiled. That November, we married. A baby was on the way. By the end of the school year, my education deferment to the military expired and my draft notice arrived soon thereafter. This foreboding document had one unstated but widely known purpose—to send me to Vietnam! I was to report for Army Basic Training in October at Fort Lewis in Tacoma, Washington.

The bad news had affected me greatly. I increased my daytime alcohol use even more and hid bottles around our apartment to conceal evening drinking. With impending military duty, my expectant wife and I planned that she live with her parents in northern Utah. I now encouraged her to move home early so I could be unhindered in my drinking. She had grown tired of my drinking and irresponsible behavior (I occasionally spent the entire night drinking at the fraternity house) and welcomed the escape. Following her departure, I leaped into a free fall down the alcoholism pipeline. Several summer jobs disintegrated into a continuous drunk that culminated in a weeklong binge as I traveled to Salt Lake City for military induction.

At Basic Training, alcohol was off-limits. Now alcohol-free, my mind cleared, and I began to realize the love that I felt for my new family. During Christmas furlough, I controlled my drinking, enjoying a reunion with my wife and becoming acquainted with our four-month-old daughter, Brooke. Already homesick, my heart ached as I boarded the airplane back to Fort Lewis.

Infantry training had forced my alcoholism into remission. However, Advanced Infantry Training (AIT) provided the opportunity for me to "learn to drink like Army men." Whereas we had forced sobriety in Basic, now we were encouraged to visit the beer halls each evening. I needed no urging. I was restless and unhappy until alcohol was flowing through my veins. I lived each day looking forward to the evening's release from duty so I could drink with my comrades. I had also begun using the popular drug, marijuana, introduced to me by friends as a convenient alternative to alcohol. During AIT, I began to explore the new world of "pot" and looked forward to each opportunity to share a "joint" with friends.

In April 1969, I completed AIT and was anxious about my next assignment. Given the history of our infantry training unit, we were sure bets to become "grunts" in the jungles of Vietnam. But when I opened my orders, I read with great relief: "Report to the 4/20th Mechanized Infantry Battalion, Panama Canal Zone."

I remember a sky-blue September Saturday when we completed an eighteen-mile hiking trip to the top of Mount Timpanogos, Utah Valley's twelve-thousand-foot sentinel. This accomplishment was especially extraordinary since Mom was sixty-five years old! We were always there for each other, something I would come to count on more and more as my addiction progressed.

ⲚOTES

1. *The Book of Mormon.* The title page of the Book of Mormon tells us that the book's main purpose is to convince Jew and Gentile that Jesus is the Christ. To the millions of members of The Church of Jesus Christ of Latter-day Saints worldwide, the Book of Mormon is known as a second witness for Jesus Christ. Bruce R. McConkie, a well-known LDS Church scholar, provides the following definition:

> The Book of Mormon is a volume of sacred scripture which was known anciently and has been revealed anew in modern times. It is . . . an abridged account of God's dealing with the ancient inhabitants of the American continents from about 2247 BC to 421 AD. . . .
>
> During the latter part of the fourth century AD, Mormon, a prophet-general, made a compilation and abridgement of the records of the people of Lehi, a Jew who led a colony of his family and friends from Jerusalem to their American promised land in 600 BC. Mormon's son Moroni added a few words of his own to the record and also abridged, in very brief form, the records of a nation of Jaredites who had migrated to America at the time of the confusion of tongues when the tower of Babel was built. The records of these two great peoples, preserved on the Gold Plates, were translated by Joseph Smith [in the 1820s] and are known as the Book of Mormon. The main part of the work deals with the period from 600 BC to 421 AD during which the Nephite, Lamanite, and Mulekite civilizations flourished.
>
> Moroni, the last prophet to possess the ancient and sacred writings hid them up in the hill Cumorah. Then in modern times, in fulfilment of John's apocalyptic prophecy (Revelation 14: 6–7), Moroni, now resurrected, delivered the plates to Joseph Smith. Miraculously, by means of the Urim and Thummim*, in not to exceed two months' translating time, the Prophet [Joseph Smith] put the ancient record into English. Since then it has been translated and published in scores of other languages." (*Mormon Doctrine* [Salt Lake City: Book-craft, 1966], 98)

* "A Urim and Thummim consists of two special stones called *seer* stones or *interpreters*. The Hebrew words *urim* and *thummim*, both plural, mean *lights* and *perfections* . . . Ordinarily [in ancient times] they are carried in a breastplate over the heart." (Ibid., 818)

The 100 millionth Book of Mormon came off the press at the end of February [2000]. The ancient scripture continues to fulfill its mission "to the convincing of the Jew and Gentile that Jesus is the Christ, the Eternal God, manifesting himself unto all nations" (Book of Mormon title page) . . . Each day some 15,000 copies are printed. The full text is now available in 54 languages, and selections are available in an additional 40 languages. The Prophet Joseph Smith called the Book of Mormon "the most correct of any book on earth, and the keystone of our religion'" (History of the Church, 4:461). ("News of the Church." 2001. *Ensign*, May 2000, 112)

2. *Temple Clothing*. Elder Russell M. Nelson of the Quorum of the Twelve Apostles has taught: "Within the temple, all are dressed in spotless white to remind us that God is to have a pure people. Nationality, language, or position in the Church are of secondary significance. In that democracy of dress, all sit side by side and are considered equal in the eyes of our Maker. Brides and grooms enter the temple to be married for time and all eternity. There brides wear white dresses—long sleeved, modest in design and fabric, and free of elaborate ornamentation. Grooms also dress in white." ("Personal Preparation for Temple Blessings." *Ensign*, May 2001, 32)

3. *Temple Endowments*. In preparation for a man and woman to be sealed together for eternity in a temple marriage, worthy members of the LDS Church go to an LDS temple to make sacred personal covenants to live in harmony with the teachings of the gospel of Jesus Christ. This process is referred to as "becoming endowed," or "taking out one's endowments."

An LDS author, James E. Talmage, describes the endowment in this manner:

> The ordinances of the endowment embody certain obligations on the part of the individual, such as covenant and promise to observe the law of strict virtue and chastity, to be charitable, benevolent, tolerant and pure; to devote both talent and material means to the spread of truth and the uplifting of the [human] race; to maintain devotion to the cause of truth; and to seek in every way to contribute to the

great preparation that the earth may be made ready to receive her King,—the Lord Jesus Christ. With the taking of each covenant and the assuming of each obligation a promised blessing is pronounced, contingent upon the faithful observance of the conditions.

No jot, iota, or tittle of the temple rites is otherwise than uplifting and sanctifying. In every detail the endowment ceremony contributes to covenants of morality of life, consecration of person to high ideals, devotion to truth, patriotism to nation, and allegiance to god. The blessings of the House of the Lord are restricted to no privileged class; every member of the [LDS] Church may have admission to the temple with the right to participate in the ordinances thereof, if he comes duly accredited as of worthy life and conduct. (*The House of the Lord* [Salt Lake City: Deseret Book, 1971], 84)

Elder Russell M. Nelson adds further insight into the endowment:

In the temple we receive an endowment, which is, literally speaking, a gift. In receiving this gift, we should understand its significance and the importance of keeping sacred covenants. Each temple ordinance "is not just a ritual to go through, it is an act of solemn promising."

The temple endowment was given by revelation. Thus, it is best understood by revelation, prayerfully sought with a sincere heart. President Brigham Young said, "Your endowment is, to receive all those ordinances in the house of the Lord, which are necessary for you, after you have departed this life, to enable you to walk back to the presence of the Father, and gain your eternal exaltation (Discourses of Brigham Young, sel. John A. Widtsoe (1941), 416)." ("Personal Preparation for Temple Blessings," *Ensign*, May 2001, 32)

$\mathcal{E}$LECTRIFIED WITH JOY

Wherefore, whoso believeth in God might with surety hope for a better world, yea, even a place at the right hand of God, which hope cometh of faith, maketh an anchor to the souls of men, which would make them sure and steadfast, always abounding in good works, being led to glorify God.

—Ether 12:4

A S I KNELT IN PRAYER, THE SMOOTH CONCRETE FLOOR OF THE office gave off a coolness in contrast to the hot, muggy Panama night. Clutching a small serviceman's copy of the Book of Mormon, I focused my energy heavenward. I don't recall the words I spoke, but I remember the intent. I prayed something like, "Dear God, please help me stop drinking. I have tried to quit on my own but just can't do it. I don't want to live this way any longer. I am unhappy and full of fear. I know I am not worthy of your help, but please, please help me. If you will, I will devote the rest of my life to you."

What happened next challenges my ability to describe. My bosom began to burn with an inward glow. A feeling of peace began to permeate my entire being. I felt as though I were being consumed by spiritual fire. I perceived that something or *someone* was in the room, bearing witness of truth to me. That presence testified to my heart that there was a Heavenly Father whose Son was the same Jesus who had lived on earth, was crucified, and rose in glorious resurrection. I felt as though currents of quickening energy were surging through my body. It was a feeling of peace and joy beyond anything I had known or thought possible. It was as though I was being *electrified with joy!* All fear left me. All desire to drink alcohol left me. All desire to do evil left me! Kneeling there in the quiet room, something penetrated my being to its innermost core. It filled me with an overflowing humility, love, and reverence for the Savior of mankind. I felt as though I were being baptized a second time—but this time—by fire. From that night forward, I have never doubted the divinity and eternal mission of Jesus Christ.[1]

I don't recall how long I knelt in prayer before returning to my little cot in the barracks. The next morning, the same profound feeling of peace still encompassed me. It was as though a spiritual hole—an emptiness in my soul I had always known—had been filled. For years I had tried in vain to stuff the hole with alcohol and drugs. Then, through a simple prayer, my Heavenly Father filled the emptiness with something more powerful than any chemical. My soul overflowed with peace and happiness and a confidence I had never known. I somehow knew my addiction was a spiritual disease, and it was *spiritual medicine that had healed me.*

Saturday, the day following my life-altering experience, was a day off for most servicemen. I opened my Book of Mormon and began reading the ancient American history rich in testimonies and teachings of Jesus Christ. Verse after verse distilled truth upon my soul. Tears fell on nearly every page.

Later that day, I inquired and learned that a branch of Latter-day Saints met in a small church located in the Canal Zone city of Balboa. The next day being Sunday, I took a bus into the city and located the church. Entering the building and locating the chapel, I slipped unnoticed into a back pew. The small chapel was cool and peaceful in contrast to the hot, crowded bus ride. It was the first Sunday of the month, and the meeting was sacrament and fast and testimony meeting. I cried when I partook of the Lord's sacrament. More tears fell as I listened to humble Latter-day Saints share their love for Jesus Christ. Through their sincere and humble testimonies, I felt the warmth and power of truth distilling upon me. I silently repeated to myself again and again, "It's true! It's true! *The Gospel of Jesus Christ is true!*"

Following the meeting, eager to become part of this wonderful group, I took courage and introduced myself to the Air Force captain who served as branch president. Within a few months, this humble man would ordain me to the Melchizedek Priesthood[2] and then continue as a wonderful example of a righteous Latter-day Saint. We became close friends.

During the following week, I consumed my Book of Mormon. I wrote notes in the margins and underlined special verses that touched me. Nearly every verse touched me! My little book was filled with notes, tears, and underlines. I feasted on these scriptures like a starving soul who stumbles upon a banquet hall filled with delicious food. I read of the marvelous rebirth of the prophet Alma and immediately connected with his experience.

> And oh, what joy, and what marvelous light I did behold; yea, my soul was filled with joy as exceeding as was my pain! Yea, I say unto you, my son, that there could be nothing so exquisite and so bitter as were my pains. Yea, and again I say unto you, my son, that on the other hand, there can be nothing so exquisite and sweet, as was my joy. (Alma 36:20–21)

I read on in my precious little book as though I were reliving the ancient American history. With every page I read, the Holy Ghost bore witness that what I read was truth. I knew that everything contained in the pages of the Book of Mormon had happened. Had I been present, I would surely have added my name to those who, after hearing King Benjamin's powerful parting sermon, took upon them the name of Christ.[3]

> And now, it came to pass that when king Benjamin had thus spoken to his people, he sent among them, desiring to know of his people if they believed the words which he had spoken unto them.
>
> And they all cried with one voice, saying: Yea, we believe all the words which thou hast spoken unto us; and also, we know of their surety and truth because of the Spirit of the Lord Omnipotent, which has wrought a mighty change in us, or in our hearts, that we have *no more disposition to do evil, but to do good continually*. (Mosiah 5:1–2; emphasis added)

A mighty change had been wrought in my heart. I too had no more disposition to do evil. I felt the humility and devotion of these ancient Saints. I wanted to be like them.

The first week following my experience, I returned a hundred pounds of small barbell weights I had pilfered from the base gym. I previously had been "borrowing" them, one by one, so I could work out in the barracks. Wanting to make restitution, I made several lopsided trips back to the gym with ten-pound weights hidden in my bag until all had been returned. One might say I was "lifting" my burden of guilt.

Within the week, I finished reading the Book of Mormon. At the end of the little book, I wrote this note:

August, 1970

You are a fortunate young man. You were brought forth in the last days . . . and are living in the days of the fulfillment of this book. It is not too late, possibly, but if you are ever tempted to do any manner of evil again in your short life, remember how close you have come to losing eternal life. Strive with all your heart and strength to keep the Lord's commandments. Love and honor your Father in Heaven. Press forward and endure to the end, and He will indeed reward you with eternal life as he has promised.

The road ahead is going to be an extremely difficult one, but if you hold to the iron rod, or God's love, you will be successful. Phil and Jenny [my wife], obey God's commandments, and you will be the

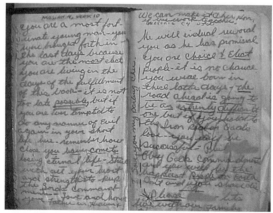

Within the week, I finished reading my Book of Mormon. At the end of the little book, I wrote this note.

happiest people on earth. Don't, and you shall die. Please, Jen, let's live with our family forever.

No longer looking at my life darkly, I did a spiritual and emotional about-face. My confidence increased dramatically. Within weeks, I had moved my wife and year-old daughter to Panama. These were happy days. I enjoyed my little family in a new way. *I could love and be loved.* Our lives revolved around activities with other Church members in the Canal Zone. At work, I was promoted to sergeant and in the Canal Zone Branch, I was called to be Scoutmaster. We were being blessed. The warning that I had written in my Book of Mormon—"If you are ever tempted to do evil . . . the road ahead is going to be an extremely difficult one"—faded into the nether regions of my mind.

The next year passed swiftly. Completing my military obligation, we moved in September 1971 to northern Utah to finish college at Utah State. A baby boy was born the same month, bringing more joy but more responsibility. On a snowy Saturday morning in December, our little family went to the Logan Temple. My wife and I were endowed and sealed together in an eternal marriage.[4] Following the ceremony, our two children, dressed in white, were brought into the special room and then sealed to us by priesthood authority. We were now an *eternal* family.

Completing the final year of college with straight A's, my confidence soared. However, my effort to make up for lost time was having a negative effect on my marriage. Two primary behaviors of an alcoholic—the compulsion to control others and resentment—began to surface. I had been given a spiritual gift, an opportunity to be free from alcohol, but I had not yet earned the gift. I had much to learn, especially this one principle: it is not use of alcohol that defines alcoholism; rather, it is *behavior* that defines alcoholism. It is possible to drink no alcohol and yet behave with the traits of an alcoholic. So it was with me. My resentments and controlling behavior caused occasional marital arguments. Many of these spats originated from differences in how my wife and I disciplined our children. My wife had been raised as an only child and grew up in a small city. Her life had been carefully supervised. My parents, on the other hand, had been far more liberal. For me, a farm boy, riding in the back of an open pickup was common experience. For my wife, such behavior was a threat to her children's lives. Discipline was a constant source of argument. When I set consequences for my children's bad behavior, I could never carry out the punishment. My wife was the opposite. But rather than seeking to understand her point of view, I increased my effort to control her. I didn't see the subtle symptoms of addiction and emerging alcoholism. I chalked it all up as the stresses of college. But classes were nearly over, and I was going to head in a new direction.

My former high school seminary teacher was now teaching at Utah State's LDS Institute of Religion. Our reunion was joyful as I recounted the story of my spiritual rebirth. My attendance at institute allowed us to visit often. One day, he offered me a surprising proposal. Had I ever considered teaching seminary for the LDS Church as a career?[5] Given my desperado background, I had not thought such a thing an option. He explained that my bachelor's degree and teaching certificate, along with training classes and student teaching, would qualify me for consideration. When my mind settled upon this possibility, I felt the strong impression that, in spite of my background, I would become a seminary teacher.

By the end of the school year, I completed seminary training, student taught seminary for a month, and received my bachelor's degree. Although there was strong competition, my interviews and student teaching had received high marks. I was hired to teach at a high school seminary in rural southern Idaho. That summer we moved to a new home on the outskirts of the small Idaho community.

Over the next three years, I would experience the joy of teaching the gospel of Jesus Christ. In my journal, I recorded one of my first experiences as a new seminary teacher.

August, 1972

I am a day late in recording, but because of yesterday's experience, I need to write a few words. As the day ended, I was overcome with the reality that happiness is the direct result of serving our Lord. My soul was filled with joy beyond any I have known, except, of course, during my "born again" experience in Panama. What joy it is to teach young people the gospel of Jesus Christ. There is no doubt that my profession is the coveted one.

I still marvel how, in two short years, I have arrived at this point. The Lord's blessings are so real! What comfort and joy it is to feel the existence daily of the Savior and partake of the peace and rest "He so freely offers me."[6]

Preparing to teach each morning, I knelt in prayer and expressed my gratitude for the special privilege and blessing of being a seminary teacher. I gave all credit to my Heavenly Father for what had happened and what was happening to me. My journals document this gratitude in hundreds of pages of spiritual experiences from teaching seminary.

New Testament was the course of study my first year. During the Easter season, I wrote:

April 4, 1973

Today, April 4, is the celebration of Good Friday in Christian history. Over 1900 years ago, Jesus, King of the Jews, was raised up to his Father and nailed on a rough wooden cross. I've never seen that "Green Hill Far Away."[7] I doubt that it was green. I would think that it would have been a dark hill covered with rocks and small gray bushes.

Jesus was placed on the cross at nine in the morning. While hanging there, he uttered the tortured but courageous words:

"Father, forgive them for they know not what they do."

"Woman, behold thy Son. Son, behold thy mother!"

"I thirst!"

"My God, my God, why hast thou forsaken me?"

"Father, into thy hands I commend my spirit!"

"It is finished!" [See Matthew 27; Luke 23.]

With these words, the sun set on the Savior's day of Perfect Passion. Then, on the first Easter morning, "The Perfect Brightness of Hope"[7] was introduced to the human race. The love of that man! Everything about Him speaks comfort and peace to my soul!

This day does not pass without deep reflection and overflowing gratitude for His precious gift to me—and to all mankind.

The Book of Mormon was the course of study my third year in Idaho. The Church Educational System provided the lessons, but I occasionally used a personal metaphor to modernize the ancient text. On one occasion, I fabricated a story that, unintentionally, became a prophetic warning. The ancient American prophet Mormon had given a remarkable lesson on charity:

> And charity suffereth long and is kind and envieth not, and is not puffed up, seeketh not her own, is not easily provoked, thinketh no evil, and rejoiceth not in iniquity but rejoiceth in the truth, beareth all things, believeth all things, hopeth all things, endureth all things. . . . But charity *is the pure love of Christ*, and it endureth forever; and whoso is found possessed of it at the last day, it shall be well with him. (Moroni 7:45, 47; emphasis added)

As a class, we reviewed Mormon's definition of charity; then I provided this analogy:

> Sunday afternoon in a tavern not far from an LDS chapel sits a drunk. With his head buried in his hands, he mumbles, "I can't live another day like this! Please God, if there is a God, help me! I can't live another day like this!" The bartender, realizing this regular customer has again had too much to drink, escorts him out the door. The sunlight is blinding as he staggers up the street, stumbles, and falls facedown in the gutter. With the stage now set, God answers the poor man's plea by setting in motion a small event. The day before, LDS missionaries who had been proselytizing in the area, had dropped a pamphlet on the ground just inches from where the drunk now lay. A gust of wind blows the pamphlet into the gutter where it then floats on dirty water until it stops against the nose of the bedraggled person. Opening his bloodshot eyes, the drunk begins to scan the words: *"If any of you lack wisdom, let him ask of God, that giveth to all men liberally, and upbraideth not; and it shall be given him"* [James 1:5]. Now sitting on the edge of the gutter, the man continues to read the account of the First Vision[8] given to the young boy, Joseph Smith:
>
> > So it was with me. I had actually seen a light, and in the midst of that light I saw two Personages [God the Father and His Son Jesus Christ], and they did in reality speak to me; and though I was hated and persecuted for saying that I had seen a

vision, yet it was true. For I had seen a vision; I knew it, and I knew that God knew it, and I could not deny it, neither dared I do it! [Joseph Smith—History 2:25].

Hope, barely imperceptible through his pain, begins to stir in the man's bosom. Perhaps there is still a chance, he thinks, as he stands and walks unsteadily toward the chapel he had passed earlier on his way to the bar. His clothes wet, his face red and unshaven, he approaches the church. You, the greeter, see him reaching for the door. Panic invades your mind as you realize that you will be required to welcome this obviously drunken bum into the church. A fragment of text whizzes through your mind, *"and charity is kind..."*

At this point in the lesson, I would stop and ask my students what they were feeling. What would they do? How would they apply Mormon's definition to this test of Good Samaritanism?

But what I never told my students was how close this analogy was to my own life. I could have easily been the drunk approaching the chapel doors. And only in my worst nightmare was it possible that *I might again become that drunk.*

Studying and preparing spiritually to teach seminary created within me a deep love for the scriptures. At every opportunity, I read and pondered them. Occasionally, I drove the five-hour trip alone to southern Utah to visit my parents. On these occasions, I listened to the Book of Mormon on cassette tapes. A journal entry reveals the love I had for the ancient Book of Mormon prophets:

September 12, 1973

I begin this journal entry on a misty-moon, September evening. Trying to earn a little extra money, I spent today cheerfully wandering about the streets of my youth selling excellent—good-for-drying, canning, eating, or just-to-throw-at-husbands, kids, or dogs—Mountain Bartlett pears, $4.50 a bushel. Now back home, I have a few moments to reflect on this special trip.

The sun was setting behind broken clouds and jagged mountain terrain as I drove by a small lake just south of Utah Valley. Traveling down the wide, black freeway, glancing at the sunset provided a special atmosphere for the words of Mormon as he spoke to me through the car speakers.

Beneath pink-streaked clouds, with purple water and dark tree

I never told my students how close this analogy was to my own life. I could have easily been the drunk approaching the chapel doors.

shadows imitating an ocean lagoon, Mormon's words sank deep into my soul. Another testimony of that glorious and peaceful book was born within me. I love Mormon! He lived! He lives again as a resurrected being. His son, Moroni, appeared to the Prophet Joseph Smith and revealed the location of the golden plates upon which was written the ancient American history!

Mormon struggled with the wickedness of hundreds of thousands of God's choicest people and saw their horrible extinction. The book is true, is true![9] I shall always love its stories, teachings and portraits of pure, humble and courageous men. I long for a glimpse into their present lives to tell them, *"I know you! I love you!"*

As I sped along the freeway listening to the ancient testimony, my little Pinto wagon, rich with the smell of ripening pears, was also rich with Mormon's spirit. From the dust of the past, his warm and living voice touched my soul.

Following this trip I received a special message from Mom:

September 11, 1973

Dear Will,

I went to the reception last night. Everyone I saw told me you had been there selling pears and what a handsome, happy, cheerful guy. Seemed like you spread joy all over town as you peddled your wares (or pears).

Again, I am so very proud of you! God bless, keep smiling. You are so very special.

Mom

Although teaching required constant energy, patience and discipline, there was much joy. Seminary was having a good effect upon the youth. I learned about the daily challenges they faced in living the gospel.

Dear Brother Simkins,

I really appreciated the lesson you gave us in class about gaining a testimony. It made me feel better about a lot of things. I had been wondering what was wrong with me; how come I didn't seem to feel and have great witnesses about the truthfulness of the Church. I suddenly realized that I am just like the type of person you described in class. My testimony has come slowly, a little at a time. . . . I have great faith in what I learn from my teachers and Church leaders.

I would like to take this opportunity to tell you that you are a fantastic teacher. I don't know if you realize the real power you hold. Your ability to influence youth will have an effect on many, many lives. Don't ever stop teaching. Don't ever stop singing and playing the guitar either . . .

Thanks again and may God always be with you as He now is.

—A Friend & Student

Over the years, I retained many letters and notes from students. This special "Friend & Student" would never be aware of what her note meant to me when, years later in a time of great despair, I reread her words and my spirit was lifted.

My family's years in Idaho began, for the most part, happily. We enjoyed camping, family home evenings, and picnicking in nearby parks and canyons. My wife and I often took evening walks to a small café to enjoy our favorite dish—Chinese pork noodles. Our stroll would sometimes continue to the library for an hour of quiet reading. My wife usually selected pictorial books about animals or ecology. I read self-help and psychology books.

During this time, I found great joy in playing and being with my children. My journals are invaluable records of this peaceful time.

October 12, 1973

These days will remain as warm in my heart as the autumn sun and as rich as the farewell touch of my little blond boy's lips as I lean down from my bicycle to kiss him good-bye before leaving for school. How my heart aches to be as carefree and clean as this little fellow. How easy to understand that the kingdom of heaven will be home for children—or at least those who possess their traits of purity and humility.

Last night's home evening was special with my children as we talked about Jesus. How sweet and precious were their questions as I thought to myself, *Yes, little daughter, you will be a queen someday, and you my son, a king. All you need to do is remain as pure and innocent as you are this night.*

I'm sure I touched little Sunshine [nickname for my daughter Brooke] as I told her that, because we sometimes choose the wrong, we could never live with our Heavenly Father again. How sad she became before I could make my point and tell her that, because Jesus loved us and had the courage to die to make right our wrongs, we would again live with our Heavenly Father. All we needed to do was feel sorry for our mistakes and then continue to do our very best. It was a tender and glowing moment.

How free the children become with hugs and kisses when I talk of Jesus and when I take time to play with them. On Saturday, I wrestled with Michael [my son] on the lawn and built a reservoir in the sand pile, playing trucks and things with him. In the afternoon, I played school in the playhouse with Brooke and her friend. I was the teacher, Mrs. Peabody. We made up funny names for the students.

It was a typical experience of these beautiful fall days. If only they could last forever.

During our final year in Idaho, increasing conflict between my wife and me escalated my alcoholic tendencies. In addition to routine disagreements over the children, more serious arguments arose over the amount of time that was required of me as a seminary teacher. To succeed as a gospel teacher, I felt I needed to show interest in the students outside of the classroom. Football games, concerts, weekend activities, Sunday firesides, and one-on-one visits were customary. I found it difficult to determine where employment ended and where charitable work began. I often left for school with a heavy heart from contentious words exchanged with my wife.

The growing conflicts affected our physical relationship. The tail end of arguments too often carried into the silent battlefield of our bedroom. We harbored more and more resentments and grew further apart. Our approaches to living the gospel were different. We were just never on the same page, and neither of us sought to understand the other. The situation was serious enough that for a brief time, we met with an LDS marriage counselor. But with little effect.

I was sure I knew what was best for our children and our marriage. When the players in my play wouldn't perform, I became more frustrated. But rather than seeking to understand and change my own behavior, I focused outward, blaming those closest to me and external circumstances. Unable to forget yesterday's anger, I allowed cancerous feelings to deepen into resentment. I pled with my Heavenly Father for help and often fasted for solutions, but I didn't listen for answers. The spiritual hole in my soul began to reopen.

In Panama, the door to my addiction had been shut as a gift from God, but it had not been sealed. Resentment toward my wife began to crack open the door. Conditions were now prime for taking my first step back down the path to addiction. I first began using a mood-altering drug. This concession happened *almost* innocently when I took some cough syrup with codeine for a bad cough. As the drug entered my body, I felt an immediate relief from anxiety sweep over me. My marriage troubles momentarily melted away.

The next day I tried to ignore my conscience. I convinced myself it was a small breach and innocent. But it was one that altered my course. Taking codeine had put me on a slightly inclined but dangerous path. I sensed something was wrong but had no idea how mined this path would be. The warning I had written in my Book of Mormon, "Should you ever do evil again in your short life . . ." began flashing. I didn't notice.

Once again, I found myself trying to fill the spiritual emptiness in my soul with chemicals. Following the cough syrup came narcotic pain pills prescribed for my extracted wisdom teeth. But I knew the ache I was trying to kill came from my heart and not the missing teeth. Christmas holidays brought bigger artillery. I stole strong painkillers from my mother-in-law's medicine cabinet in an effort to escape my emotional distress. Under the influence of these prescription drugs, I was able to mask my heartache, working late into the night on a miniature outdoor scene of gingerbread cake, frosting, and plastic wildlife figures. It was to be a special Christmas present to my wife. By morning, the pills were gone, as was the spirit of the gift. I rationalized that the few stolen pills would never be missed. But I felt sharp barbs of guilt as my addiction path took a steeper descent through this "little" act of stealing.

Returning to teach seminary after the holiday break was difficult. The conflict between body and spirit was growing as I continued to justify occasional concessions to prescription pain medicines. But teaching, along with speaking and singing at firesides and other church and social groups, brought the accolades of my peers, applause from community members, and praise from my students. There seemed to be plenty of good in my life to allow an occasional escape from reality. But I was on a path toward greater isolation and loneliness.

November 9, 1973

Yesterday, I took my two sheepdogs for a run up the canyon. I was looking forward to a long-awaited and much-needed escape into the mountains. I ran along the snow-dusted trail beneath naked trees until my strong legs and pumping lungs carried me to the basin beneath Ski Hill.

Other than my dogs' and my panting, there was only silence. No wind. Nothing but the pines with frosted needles glistening in the shallow morning sun; just my two loyal friends and the freedom of space.

I found a soft spot beneath a large pine and caressed the eager heads of (my dogs) Parley and Charlie (Parley was a border collie and Charlie a large golden collie). After they left to investigate the new surroundings, I knelt and gave thanks to my Heavenly Father from my heart for life, health and strength. Much more felt than will ever be put here in words. Perhaps the feelings of these few moments will never be recalled, or experienced again.

February 6, 1974

I parked the car at the reservoir and ran and walked through snow with Parley and Charlie to my "sacred grove" to pray. I'll remember this quiet, white moment by what I wrote on a scrap of paper—

I've seen the canyon in spring, summer and fall. Now, sitting here in waist deep snow, I see it in deepest winter. An almost warm wind pours down through the canyon meeting no resistance from the naked trees. I love its touch on my face.

There is a splendor in mountain, winter whiteness that the fair weather enthusiast misses. Although nature's multicolored paintings in summer and fall are lovely, there is something hauntingly beautiful about her charcoal sketches in deep winter; a powerful melancholy I can't describe. I guess I'll always be kind of a loner. For now, with my dogs panting softly beside me, I am much with God in quiet whiteness and happy.

I was fooling myself. I was alone and *sometimes* close to God, but I was not happy. Loneliness, resentment, and the influence of a cunning adversary were combining in a deadly attack against the good I was accomplishing as a teacher of the gospel of Jesus Christ. Perfectly poised, I was about to fall into a dark, descending pipeline that would lead to the inescapable reality of one principle: *For the alcoholic, one drink is too many; and then, a thousand not enough!*

I guess I'll always be kind of a loner. For now, with my dogs panting softly beside me, I am much with God in quiet whiteness and happy.

Notes

1. *Holy Ghost.* "When a man has the manifestation from the Holy Ghost, it leaves an indelible impression on his soul, one that is not easily erased. It is spirit speaking to spirit, and it comes with convincing force. A manifestation of an angel, or even the Son of God himself, would impress the eye and mind, and eventually become dimmed, but the impressions of the Holy Ghost sink deeper into the soul and are more difficult to erase." (Joseph Fielding Smith, *Answers to Gospel Questions.* 2 vols. [Salt Lake City: Deseret Book, 1958], 2:151)

"Wherefore I give you to understand, that no man speaking by the Spirit of God calleth Jesus accursed: and that no man can say that Jesus is the Lord, but by the Holy Ghost." (1 Corinthians 12:3)

2. *Melchezidek Priesthood.* Elder Bruce R. McConkie describes the Latter-day Saint concept of priesthood in this manner:

As pertaining to eternity, priesthood is the eternal power and authority of Deity by which all things exist; by which they are created, governed, and controlled; by which the universe and worlds without number have come rolling into existence; by which the great plan of creation, redemption, and exaltation operates throughout immensity. It is the power of God.

"As pertaining to man's existence on this earth, priesthood is the power and authority of God delegated to man on earth to act in all things for the salvation of men. It is the power by which the gospel is preached; by which the ordinances of salvation are performed so that they will be binding on earth and in heaven; by which men are sealed up unto eternal life, being assured of the fullness of the Father's kingdom hereafter; and by which in due course the Lord will govern the nations of the earth and all that pertains to them." (*Mormon Doctrine* [Salt Lake City: Bookcraft, 1966], 594)

3. *King Benjamin's people take upon themselves the name of Christ.*

And it shall come to pass that whosoever doeth this shall be found at the right hand of God, for he shall know the name by which he is called; for he shall be called by the name of Christ. And now it shall come to pass, that whosoever shall not take upon him the name of Christ must be called by some other name; therefore, he findeth himself on the left hand of God. . . .

And it came to pass that there was not one soul, except it were little children, but who had entered into the covenant and had taken upon them the name of Christ. (Book of Mormon, Mosiah 5:9–10; 6:2)

4. *Eternal Marriage*: Latter-day Saints believe that the family relationships of earth may be made lasting and binding beyond the veil of death provided marriages are sealed on earth by the power and authority of the Holy Priesthood—the keys for which were restored to the Prophet Joseph Smith. (See note 64—*Priesthood Authority*.)

James E. Talmage describes Eternal Marriage in this manner:

Latter-day Saints . . . recognize the full legal validity and moral obligation of any marriage entered into under the secular law; but civil marriages and indeed all marriages made without the binding authority of the Holy Priesthood, they regard as contracts for this life only, and therefore lacking the higher and superior elements of a complete and perpetual union . . . The Latter-day Saints affirm that perfect marriage provides for the *eternal* relation of the sexes. With this people, marriage is not merely a contract for time, effective only as long as the parties shall live on earth, but a solemn covenant of union which shall endure beyond the grave. In the complete ceremony of marriage, as ordained by the [LDS] Church and as administered only within the temple halls, the man and the woman are placed under covenant of mutual fidelity, not until death do them part, but for *time and for all eternity*. (*The House of the Lord* [Salt Lake City: Deseret Book, 1971], 86; emphasis added)

5. *LDS Seminary Program*. The LDS Church Educational System employs a number of full-time religious instructors to teach in high schools, colleges, and universities throughout the United States, Canada, and internationally. These positions are highly competitive and carefully screened. Those individuals hired, receiving annual salaries, devote all of their time to teaching the gospel of Jesus Christ.

6. *Hymn—I Stand All Amazed*. "I stand all amazed at the love Jesus offers me, Confused at the graced that so fully he proffers me. I tremble to know that for me he was crucified, that for me, a sinner, he suffered, he bled and died. Oh it is wonderful that he should care for me enough to die for me! Oh, it is wonderful, wonderful to me!" (*Hymns of The Church of Jesus Christ of Latter-day Saints*, 1985, no. 193)

7. *Hymn—There Is a Green Hill Far Away.* "There is a green hill far away, Without a city wall, Where the dear Lord was crucified, Who died to save us all . . . Oh, dearly, dearly has he loved! And we must love him too, and trust in his redeeming blood, and try his works to do." (*Hymns of The Church of Jesus Christ of Latter-day Saints*, 1985, no. 194)

8. *Perfect Brightness of Hope.* "Wherefore, ye must press forward with a steadfastness in Christ, having a perfect brightness of hope, and a love of God and of all men. Wherefore, if ye shall press forward, feasting upon the word of Christ, and endure to the end, behold, thus saith the Father: Ye shall have eternal life." (Book of Mormon, 2 Nephi 31:20.)

9. *First Vision of Joseph Smith.* In the Spring of 1820, at the age of fourteen, Joseph Smith entered a quiet grove of trees in upstate New York to seek his Heavenly Father's counsel. During this time of great religious revival, Joseph was confused as to which church he should join when he came across the following passage of scripture in the Bible: "If any of you lack wisdom, let him ask of God, that giveth to all men liberally, and upbraideth not; and it shall be given him" [James 1:5].

Joseph describes the effect of reading this scripture:

Never did any passage of Scripture come with more power to the heart of man than this did at this time to mine. It seemed to enter with great force into every feeling of my heart. . . at length I came to the conclusion that I must either remain in darkness and confusion, or else I must do as James directs, that is, ask of God."

Joseph describes his experience in the grove:

After I had retired to the place where I had previously designed to go, having looked around me, and finding myself alone, I kneeled down and began to offer up the desires of my heart to God. I had scarcely done so, when immediately I was seized upon by some power which entirely overcame me, and had such an astonishing influence over me as to bind my tongue so that I could not speak. Thick darkness gathered around me, and it seemed to me for a time as if I were doomed to sudden destruction. But, exerting all my powers to call upon God to deliver me out of the power of this enemy which had seized upon me, and at the very moment when I was ready to sink into despair and abandon myself to destruction—not to an imaginary ruin, but to the power of some actual being from the unseen world, who had such marvelous power as I had never before felt in any being—just at this moment of great alarm, I saw a pillar of light exactly over my head, above the brightness of the sun, which descended gradually until it fell upon me.

It no sooner appeared than I found myself delivered from the enemy which held me bound. When the light rested upon me I saw two personages, whose brightness and glory defy all description, standing above me in the air. One of them spake unto me, calling me by name, and said—pointing to the other—"This is my beloved son, hear him."

My object in going to inquire of the Lord was to know which of all the sects was right, that I might know which to join. No sooner, therefore, did I get possession of myself, so as to be able to speak, that I asked the personages who stood above me in the light, which of all the sects was right—and which I should join. I was answered that I must join none of them, for they were all wrong, and the personage who addressed me said that all their creeds were an abomination in His sight: that those professors were all corrupt; that "they draw near to me with their lips, but their hearts are far from me; they teach for doctrines the commandments of men: having a form of godliness, but they deny the power thereof." He again forbade me to join with any of them: and many others things did he say unto me which I cannot write at this time. When I came to myself again, I found myself lying on my back, looking up into heaven.

Joseph later testified of this unexpected and supernatural experience:

It caused me serious reflection then, and often has since, how very strange it was that an obscure boy, of a little over fourteen years of age, and one, too, who was doomed to the necessity of obtaining a scanty maintenance by his daily labor, should be thought a character of sufficient importance to attract the attention of the great ones of the most popular sects of the day, and in a manner to create in them a spirit of the most bitter persecution and reviling. But strange or not, so it was, and it was often the cause of great sorrow to myself. However, it was nevertheless a fact that I had beheld a vision. I have thought since, that I felt much like Paul, when he made his defense before King Agrippa, and related the account of the vision he had when he saw a light, and heard a voice; but still there were but few who believed him; some said he was dishonest, others said he was mad; and he was ridiculed and reviled. But all this did not destroy the reality of his vision. He had seen a vision, he knew he had, and all the persecution under heaven could not make it otherwise; and though they should persecute him until death, yet he knew, and would know to the last breath, that he had both seen a light, and heard a voice speaking unto him, and all the world could not make him think or believe otherwise. So it was with me. I had actually seen a light, and in the midst of that light I saw two personages [God the Father and His Son Jesus Christ], and they did in reality speak to me; And though I was hated and persecuted for saying that I had seen a vision, yet it was true; and while they were persecuting me, reviling me, and speaking all manner of evil against me falsely for so saying, I was led to say in my heart, Why persecute me for telling the truth? I have actually seen a vision, and who am I that I can withstand God, or why does the world think to make me deny what I have actually seen? For I had seen a vision; I knew it, and I knew that God knew it, and I could not deny it, neither dared I do it, at least I knew that by so doing I would offend god, and come under condemnation. (*History of the Church* 1:4–8)

On June 27, 1844, at the age of 39, Joseph Smith was killed by a Missouri mob. Having never denied his testimony of The First Vision, he gave his life as the final sacrifice for that which he believed in.

10. *How to know truth.* "And when ye shall receive these things, I would exhort you that ye would ask God, the Eternal Father, in the name of Christ, if these things are not true; and if ye shall ask with a sincere heart, with real intent, having faith in Christ, he will manifest the truth of it unto you, by the power of the Holy Ghost. And by the power of the Holy Ghost ye may know the truth of all things." (Book of Mormon, Moroni 10:4–5)

$\mathscr{S}$TEAK &
COOKING SHERRY

And behold, others he flattereth away, and telleth them there is no hell; and he saith unto them: I am no devil, for there is none—and thus he whispereth in their ears, until he grasps them with his awful chains, from whence there is no deliverance.

—2 Nephi 28:22

RECEIVING A SABBATICAL FROM TEACHING TO PURSUE A MASter's degree at BYU brought my three precious years of teaching in Idaho to a close. We moved into a new, but modest, home in Provo. Directly across the street from our home was a fruit orchard and a willow-lined canal. Over the next three years, the orchard provided for cross-country skiing practice, and the canal was a fun place to play with my children on hot summer afternoons. My wife and I would enjoy our fireplace on winter evenings. I had renewed hope that a break from the pressures of teaching seminary combined with new skills from my family life education course of study would eliminate conflict and breathe new life into our marriage.

Arriving a few months before school began, I found work with a chain-link fence company. Digging postholes all day was hot, exhausting work. After three years of mostly mental effort in a classroom, I welcomed the hard physical labor. I liked my fellow workers. Initially, they were skeptical of this squeaky-clean seminary teacher. But, over time, my genial attitude and willingness to work won them over. Although I didn't hang out with them much after work, we became good friends. Their beer drinking ritual performed right at 5:00 p.m. was a far different celebration than the good-natured fun we seminary teachers often shared at the end of a long teaching day.

Part of me enjoyed watching these hardworking fellows celebrate at the end of a hard day's labor. Their refreshment was always the golden brew touted by advertisers as the official drink of the blue-collar worker. I secretly envied their carefree attitude. Throughout the summer, I had an aggravating feeling of wanting to join in their end of day revelry. It was annoying that the notion even entered my mind. After all, I was a Latter-day Saint, a BYU student, and a seminary teacher on leave. I tried to ignore these thoughts and hoped my friendship and good example was having a positive effect upon my new peers.

July 15, 1974

> I type out this note of record with aching, sore hands as a result of my new job building chain-link fence. It doesn't pay much, but it is work—and I do mean work!
>
> It is interesting to watch the men I work with keep their not totally foreign to me habit of observing "beer-thirty" as each work day ends. I don't criticize or look down on them. I wish I could convince them of the futility of using alcohol as a source of happiness. The bright face of my clean, sweet little boy greeting me at the end of the day is far greater reward than the cold beer the boys toss down. Oh yes, far more. How grateful I am to have been granted this insight.

Watching my coworkers drink beer had a powerful effect on me. In my mind, I went through the motions of drinking with them. I was naïve to the truism that every action is preceded by a thought; or in the case of the alcoholic's action—every drink is preceded by a think!

My moments of joy, including feeling the influence of the Spirit, had been decreasing proportionately to my occasional indiscretions to prescription drugs.

July 17, 1974

Sitting on the porch, I played my guitar and sang John Denver songs deep into the warm summer night and then came down into my makeshift basement office to write these few lines. My empty journal doesn't indicate all that is happening. To keep a personal record one must feel good about one's life. I believe President Spencer W. Kimball said that.

Having stayed up as late as 2:00 a.m. several nights this week, I have been violating much of what I thought I believed in. No early morning runs, just heavy nights—heavy with codeine pills borrowed from my wife's private dispensary. I have been losing the battle without much fight each night this week. I wake with spirit aching and make promises to myself only to repeat the same behavior again.

I tucked my precious daughter in bed earlier tonight (or would it be last night?) and talked of Jesus for several minutes. We talked of His forgiveness; His love for us and our hope to live with Him again. My heart burned with love for her when she said, "I can feel Jesus when I'm in Primary. It makes me warm and happy all over." The humble testimony of a little child sweeps over this proud, Babylonian world like stardust on the soot-covered stacks of Geneva [Steel]. All this I am desecrating with my weak will.

I guess watching those I work with affects me more than I admit. An older man named Bob, trying to turn a buck for booze, works by my side. The sweet smell of alcohol pours from his sweating body as he beats the ground with a pick while quoting scriptures about the ills of man and speaking of his love for Jesus Christ. He has made me think more about the meaning of "Love thy neighbor" [John 15:12]. Jesus ate with the sinners and publicans. "The whole have not need of the physician, but the sick" [Matthew 9:12]. Let me understand the devil's power—drugs, men fallen and caught—love them, help them!

So, must I be tried in the Refiner's fire? Yet I am so weak. Am I burning up? *My Father, please help me!*

Many alcoholics are also perfectionists who focus relentlessly and unrealistically on their own (and others') imperfections. My personal failures resulted in extraordinary guilt, maybe more than was warranted by my shortcomings. As a seminary teacher, I feared seeking official counsel would bring scrutiny. I couldn't risk this. I judged and convicted myself over and over. Guilt oozed from my journal entries.

August 16, 1974

More and more I search for escape. These few journal lines become my only confessional, a place to lay down my weighty burden for a few moments, to express what lies beneath all this hypocrisy, and sin, and heartache. Yet, I don't even know what this is all for.

Tonight, my heart aches as if bitten in the chest by a snake whose deadly venom spreads throughout my body. The pain is real and I can't find an antidote. I say to myself *that maybe a drink would help* or another pill to dull the bitter pain; but I am helpless. Under the Lord's omniscience, I hide nothing.

So, in this complicated turmoil, I reel from study books to knees to service. I try to understand why my wife is so angry. I pray and I try. We concentrate on the bitter and allow the daily wound to go unhealed. I have nearly forgotten what it is like to hold someone I love—to touch and be touched back. For my wife, nothing to offer or to receive—neither a touch nor a kiss. No words spoken, but many thought: competition, control, criticism, resentment and frustration. These empty words don't console, they just condemn me.

My BYU courses began with many activities and new responsibilities. I had been granted a teaching stipend that required me to instruct several undergraduate courses per semester. Graduate courses required learning a new language fraught with complex ideas and expressed in fancy words. Teaching college students was challenging. The drugs I had flirted with during the summer retreated into winter shadows—a short respite.

Writing graduate essays, correcting student papers, and preparing for and giving final exams placed great demands upon my time and energy. As the months drew on, I began using a different, more subtle drug—caffeine.[1] Although not as powerful as narcotic pain pills, it still affected my mind, body, and spirit. I began depending more and more on my new drug of choice.

April 19, 1975

It is with a rather numb body that, at this 1:00 a.m. hour, I peck out a few words of record for the past week. It is finals week, and I find myself in the usual mess of attempting to show evidence of learning while seeking the same from my students.

My body is saturated with caffeine and weary from stress. From a stupor, I view the world passing by and continue in my self-deception. My soul is truly weary and tired. My nerves feel ragged and overloaded as if electricity is shooting through them in every bizarre, unordered direction.

I had used caffeine earlier in my life but had abstained from it for several years. Now, last-minute cramming required extra energy. Cola drinks provided me the pep I needed to maintain the late-night grinds. I soon discovered that caffeine tablets were a faster and more convenient method for getting the drug into my system. I enjoyed this quick form of energy and gave little thought to its addictive effect. It seemed to help me accomplish things that I thought I couldn't get done otherwise. But there was a trade-off. Caffeine was dulling me spiritually. It increased my overall feelings of anxiety and numbed my sensitivity to be thoughtful toward my family. The more caffeine I ingested, the less patience I had with my children and even less desire to listen to my wife. Everything seemed annoying. The more I used the drug, the less I felt like praying or studying the scriptures. Somehow, depending upon this "energy booster" removed my feeling that I needed to depend on my Father in Heaven. My caffeine habit was beginning to excavate spiritual material from the deepening hole inside me.

Although my personal discipline was weakening, I was having marvelous experiences at BYU. Seeking a master's degree in family life education, I had been teaching undergraduate courses in marriage and family relationships and child development. At the end of my second year at BYU, because of my on-leave status as a seminary teacher, I was assigned to teach in the Religion Department. I was provided a small office in the basement of the historic Joseph Smith Building. Teaching religion at BYU! What an honor! Although I didn't feel worthy, I was deeply grateful.

Learning the material and preparing to teach in this new role inspired me. In spite of my shortcomings, the Spirit's influence was still present in the classroom as I taught courses in Gospel Principles and Practice and the Book of Mormon. I was enthusiastic for teaching and had a special love for my students. I felt their love for me.

June 12, 1976

Dear Brother Simkins,

I just wanted to let you know how grateful I am for having you as a teacher. I thank my Heavenly Father daily for you and for your preparation of the Book of Mormon classes and most of all for your testimony. You have strengthened mine so much and I am so grateful. You have made me realize how to relate the Book of Mormon to everyday experiences and to live a better life.

I also want you to know that you have influenced and guided my friend Dorothy to the point that she wants to be baptized when she gets home. I have noticed a remarkable change in her. She has a beautiful spirit and I am so happy for her. [Dorothy was later baptized.]

It is also important to me that you know that I know Jesus is the Christ and that the Book of Mormon is the word of God. I am so grateful for my testimony. It is my most precious possession.

Thank you for everything!

Marnie

Teaching religion provided me spiritual highs, but there were an equal number of lows as a result of ongoing marital conflict. For three years, I had studied the principles for a healthy marriage. My hope for a better relationship had not materialized. I had learned valuable principles, but was not internalizing ways to change my own behavior. I was gaining knowledge but not wisdom. If anything, our relationship had worsened in spite of my "superior knowledge." Now that I was a "marital expert," I increased my attempts to teach (control) my wife. This was met with resistance and disdain. On occasion, I medicated my increasing frustration with prescription drugs.

In preparing to teach religion classes, I came across warnings from Church presidents and other members of the Council of the Twelve[2] that, all too often and with painful accuracy, described my own condition.

Journal Entry—1976

Quote From Brigham Young

For a man to undertake to live [as] a Saint and walk in darkness is one of the hardest tasks that he can undertake. You cannot imagine a position that will sink a person more deeply in perplexity and trouble than to try to be a Saint without living, as a Saint should, without enjoying the spirit of his religion.[3]

I wanted to be a saint, but I also wanted to escape reality through drugs. During this time, I wrote: "A monstrous battle rages within me between two foes—my natural-man[4] body—ignorant of God—bent on its own pleasure, and my spirit—born of Heavenly Parents—fighting to save me. This struggle is leaving me a scarred and torn battlefield."

During this period, I kept a personal tradition that resulted in some of my spiritual victories. At the end of each summer, I went backpacking alone into the mountains to meditate, pray, and prepare for another school year. These trips were special pilgrimages and always free from drug use.

August 13, 1976

I write by candlelight from my sleeping bag while Parley [my dog] lies curled up on my coat outside the tent flap.

A warm canyon breeze rustles the aspens causing their leaves to shimmer silver in the moonlight. The evening campfire has reduced to a soft flicker. The soft sound of the creek nearby filters through my ears to touch yet one more sense.

The richness of this moment adds a final capstone to a pure and precious three days spent hiking over 75 miles in the mountains above my childhood home. In purposeful fast, I have abstained for the last 24 hours from food and water, which has greatly heightened these feelings.

All of this has touched my soul with great effect. I am filled with peace and joy and the incredible awareness of God's presence and His creations. Since that night in Panama, I have never doubted. Tonight, I am left to wonder why I should be granted these experiences; this intense sense of well-being that God lives and loves me. Surely I have not earned the right to this feeling.

Tomorrow, I have been invited to speak in sacrament meeting in the ward where I grew up. I plan to continue my fast until then, praying that I will have the Holy Ghost's influence to speak with the "tongue of an angel."[5]

Tonight my body, my being, my soul is filled with God's presence, His marvelous work and wonder, His Light! Tonight I know He lives! He loves! *He forgives!*

The following day's spiritual experience ranked as one of the most profound that I had known since the Panama night when my life's pendulum swung back toward God. Having been invited to speak at my parents' sacrament meeting (the ward of my youth), I used self-made charts and maps to lead the congregation through ten centuries of Book of Mormon history. As a result of fasting, prayer, and my three-day purging trek, spiritual power seemed to flow through me and out into the congregation as though it were quickening light. My prayer to be able to testify by the Spirit had been granted.

I was grateful for a special side benefit, that of honoring my parents. They were proud of me. Their tears were not uncommon in the congregation as I ended my talk by playing my guitar and singing, "A Poor Wayfaring Man of Grief."[6]

In the months immediately following this spiritual experience, it felt as though Satan approved overtime for special devils to work on me. I'm sure he dispatched a brigade with the orders: "Tempt Phil with his weakness for liquor."

Until this point, I had avoided drinking alcohol. It is revealing to review my circumstances. Along with the use of caffeine, I was occasionally using prescription pain pills. I had even smoked marijuana once. This use happened during a visit to my parents.

My father, as county sheriff, had seized a large crop of illegally grown pot and was holding it in a metal shed behind his house until it could be properly destroyed. I obtained the key to the shed and secretly removed a small supply of the plant.

Incredibly, even with the marijuana, I never considered these substances in the same seriousness-of-sin category as liquor. I had abstained from using alcohol, not because I thought I was an alcoholic and could not handle the first drink. Rather, it was because I was fearful of breaking the Word of Wisdom, which specifically counsels Church members against using "tea, coffee, *liquor*, and tobacco."[7] I reasoned that I could not answer the temple recommend[8] questions truthfully if I were using any of *these* substances.

But I was not making any voluntary appointments to be interviewed for temple worthiness. I knew I wasn't worthy.

Late in the summer of 1976, I gave in. I did not consume hard liquor, but rather cooking sherry purchased from the supermarket. I rationalized that entering a state liquor store would be a greater sin than going into a grocery store. Along with the sherry, I bought several steaks to disguise my intent. If someone recognized me, they would never suspect such an innocent purchase. My behavior was not unlike other *legal* addicts who readily buy prescription drugs to feed their craving but who would never think of meeting a drug pusher for a bag of dope. But the truth is, alcohol is alcohol, whether purchased as cooking sherry or in whiskey bottles; and drugs are drugs, whether purchased in plastic prescription bottles or hastily wrapped plastic bags. *What* we use doesn't matter. *Why* we use does.

On a hot Friday afternoon in September, after sprinkling a little sherry on the barbecuing steaks, I stepped into the hot, stuffy darkness of my carport closet with the sherry bottle in hand and pulled the door shut. Stuffing thoughts of the consequences, I guzzled the nasty, warm, salty liquid. The alcohol entered my blood and flowed to my brain bringing an immediate release of tension and anxiety— a cheap, counterfeit answer to dull my emotional pain. After the deed was done, there were more than a few stabs of barbed guilt. The chilling memory of a scripture went through me like a lightning bolt and comprehension thundered down through my soul: *"And yea and behold, Satan doth subtly drag them down to hell."*[9]

Years later, I searched my journals for the impact of that "first drink" but found only disguised references to my increasing use of alcohol.

January 7, 1977

We went ice skating on New Year's Eve afternoon. I will not soon forget glimpsing my children here and there amongst the crowd and skating arm in arm with my wife. However, I couldn't seem to get into the New Year's Eve spirit, so later I tried artificially. I'm afraid the old year went out not in good fashion, as I once again imbibed a little heavily in the wine meant for steaks.

My heart is heavy. Why must I submit to such . . . but I hurt. I didn't take the sacrament Sunday, fast Sunday. I fasted, going without food or water my normal 24 hours. I cried during the last ten minutes of the meeting, probably just melancholy mingled with regret.

Walking from church, my little Sunshine asked me why I was crying. I couldn't talk. I just squeezed her hand tightly.

In a journal entry, written after a trip to Wyoming to scout out my next potential seminary-teaching assignment, I wrote with deepening awareness that the path I was on was becoming a dangerous tightrope.

June 1977

We spent the night in a cozy, cabin-like motel in a small town deep in the mountains of Colorado. It had rained. I remember how rich the damp night air, mingled with pine and fireplace smoke, smelled. What prompted me, my desire, I don't know. Maybe no romance in such a romantic setting. My wife was asleep early in the evening.

Lonely and restless, I walked the quiet wet streets of the little town for over an hour. Not far from the motel, I stopped at a late-closing grocery store to buy a snack. Instead, losing the spirit-body battle, I purchased a bottle of wine. Used to Utah's stringent liquor laws, it was unusual *and tempting* to see wine in a grocery store. I knew no one, except He Who Counts, would know of my Word of Wisdom infraction.

I fought the desire that night and didn't drink the wine. I thought I had won a major battle. Stupid me. Not throwing away the full bottle should have been a tip-off.

We parked the next day at a rest area beside the Green River. The bottle of wine was in the camper refrigerator—*waiting*. I barely fought. The old familiar warmth filled me as I secretly drank the wine. Sitting in a lawn chair on the grassy bank, I watched swirls of water like melting chocolate, appear and disappear, as the muddy river moved by.

I don't know why I record this. I just feel I must for its significance in my life, be it for good or evil. If nothing more, perhaps someday someone will read my journals and learn firsthand of the folly of tempting personal destruction by choosing to walk a tightrope. It is funny I should even write this way, as though I can't—or won't—stop.

The BYU-graduate-student era ended. I had finished all coursework but still lacked a thesis paper to complete my degree. Three years of around-the-clock school had been enough. Believing that I would return to BYU the next summer and finish my thesis, I accepted a new seminary teaching position in Wyoming.

With deep melancholy, I packed up my basement office in the Joseph Smith Building. It was difficult saying good-bye to university life and the young people who had touched my life. I felt as though I was leaving the best part of

On a hot Friday afternoon in September, after sprinkling a little sherry on the barbecuing steaks, I stepped into the hot, stuffy darkness of my carport closet, sherry bottle in hand, and pulled the door shut. Stuffing thoughts of the consequences, I guzzled the nasty, warm, salty liquid.

me behind, and perhaps I was. I had played guitar and sung and loved and borne my testimony to the most wonderful young people on earth. I had known a degree of peace and joy well beyond the normal.

Despite the emotional pain of my deteriorating marriage and my growing addiction, I regrouped around this new opportunity. For now, I was flying high, high enough to soar over the eastern Rockies to the windy prairies of Wyoming—where I would come down.

𝒩OTES

1. *Caffeine*. Decades before America seemed to adopt caffeine as its standard energy drink, LDS Church scholar John A. Widtsoe observed:

The people of the United States appear today to be in the clutches of dangerous, habit-forming drugs. There never was a time when liquor, tobacco, and habit-forming drinks were in such demand. It is coming to be that from offices to shops the workers must have their daily "lifts," which means the stimulating effect of caffeine and similar drugs. *The caffeine or theobromine slave soon moves by natural transition to tobacco, then to liquor, and on to the weakened will for life's righteous toil and duty.* Those who have had experience in this field have seen many a young life ruined by the caffeine habit . . . Intelligent, devoted Latter-day Saints will refrain from using anything which injures the body, and is therefore, contrary to the spirit of the Word of Wisdom. The attempt to justify the use of beverages, found harmful by modern investigation, because they are neither tea nor coffee, is quibbling. *The Church, founded on truth and the practices derived from truth, expects every member to use his intelligence by learning truth and using it in his life.* Certainly, in this day, we should stand firmly against any encroachment upon our health. (*Gospel Interpretations*, 176–81; emphasis added)

2. *Church Organization.* The Church of Jesus Christ of Latter-day Saints is organized in the same manner as Christ's original church. A prophet and president of the Church along with two counselors make up the First Presidency, which presides over the Church. This group stands at the head of a special quorum ordained as apostles in the Melchizedek Priesthood. These men, referred to as General Authorities, are set apart as special witness to Jesus Christ and are called the Quorum of the Twelve Apostles of Jesus Christ.

The Quorum of the Twelve Apostles are "given all of the keys of the kingdom of God on earth. This apostleship carries the responsibility of proclaiming the gospel in all the world and also of administering the affairs of the Church. Christ "chose twelve, whom also he named apostles' (Luke 6:13), and upon their shoulders the burdens of the kingdom rested after he ascended to his Father" (*Mormon Doctrine* [Salt Lake City: Bookcraft, 1966], 47).

For administrative and ecclesiastical purposes, the Church is divided into geographical areas called *stakes*. Stakes are presided over by a General Authority called by the First Presidency. Each stake is organized as to carry on the full program of the Church. A *stake president* and two counselors preside in the affairs of the stake. A stake consists of several *wards*. Each ward is presided over by a *bishop* and two counselors.

The stake presidency and ward bishoprics contribute much time in these positions but receive no monetary compensation.

A bishop deals primarily with temporal concerns as the presiding high priest in his ward; however he presides over all ward affairs and members. A bishop is a common judge in Israel [Doctrine and Covenants 107:74]. . . .

A bishop must be blameless, as the steward of God; not self-willed, not soon angry, not given to wine, no striker, not given to filthy lucre; But a lover of hospitality, a lover of good men, sober, just, holy, temperate; Holding fast the faithful word as he hath been taught, that he may be able by sound doctrine both to exhort and to convince the gainsayers" [Titus 1:7–9; 1 Timothy 3:1–7]. (Ibid. 89–90)

3. Brigham Young, *Journal of Discourses*, September 1, 1859 (Church of Jesus Christ of Latter-day Saints), 7:238.

4. *Natural Man.*

For the natural man is an enemy to God, and has been from the fall of Adam, and will be, forever and ever, unless he yields to the enticings of the Holy Spirit, and putteth off the natural man and becometh a saint through the Atonement of Christ the Lord, and becometh as a child, submissive, meek, humble, patient, full of love, willing to submit to all things which the Lord seeth fit to inflict upon him, even as a child doth submit to his father. (Book of Mormon, Mosiah 3:19)

5. *Speaking with the tongue of an angel.*

Wherefore, my beloved brethren, I know that if ye shall follow the Son, with full purpose of heart, acting no hypocrisy and no deception before God, but with real intent, repenting of your sins, witnessing unto the Father that ye are willing to take upon you the name of Christ, by baptism—yea, by following your Lord and your Savior down into the water, according to his word, behold, then shall ye receive the Holy Ghost; yea, then cometh the baptism of fire and of the Holy Ghost; and then can ye *speak with the tongue of angels*, and shout praises unto the Holy One of Israel. (Book of Mormon, 2 Nephi 31:13)

6. *Hymn—A Poor Wayfaring Man of Grief.* "Then in a moment unto my view, the stranger started from disguise. The token in His hand I knew. The Savior stood before my eyes. He spake and my poor name he

named, "Of Me, thou hast not been ashamed. These deeds shall thy memorial be. Fear not, thou did'st them unto me." (*Hymns of The Church of Jesus Christ of Latter-day Saints*, 1985, no. 29)

7. *Word of Wisdom.*

> A revelation given to Joseph Smith, February 27, 1833, containing a part of the revealed counsel in the field of health. Because it begins, "A Word of Wisdom, for the benefit of . . . the church," [it] is now commonly known as the Word of Wisdom. As a revealed law of health dealing particularly with dietary matters, it contains both positive and negative instructions. Its affirmative provision gives directions for the use of meat and grain by both man and animals; its prohibitions direct man to refrain from the use of certain specified harmful things. . . .
>
> Three types of things are prohibited to man by the Word of Wisdom—tobacco, strong drinks, and hot drinks. By strong drinks is meant alcoholic beverages; hot drinks, according to the Prophet's [Joseph Smith] own statement, mean tea and coffee. Accordingly the negative side of the Word of Wisdom is a command to abstain from tea, coffee, tobacco, and liquor. . . .
>
> Abstinence from these four things has been accepted by the Church as a measuring rod to determine in part the personal worthiness of church members. When decisions are made relative to the granting of temple recommends or approving brethren for church positions or ordinations, inquiry is made relative to these four items. (Bruce R. McConkie, *Mormon Doctrine* [Salt Lake City: Bookcraft, 1966], 845)

These excerpts from the Doctrine and Covenants provide the essence of the Word of Wisdom:

> Given for a principle with promise, adapted to the capacity of the weak and the weakest of all saints, who are or can be called saints. . . . In consequence of evils and designs which do and will exist in the hearts of conspiring men in the last days, I have warned you, and forewarn you, by giving unto you this word of wisdom by revelation— That inasmuch as any man drinketh wine or strong drink among you, behold it is not good, neither meet in the sight of your Father, only in assembling yourselves together to offer up your sacraments before him. And again, tobacco is not for the body, neither for the belly, and is not good for man. (Doctrine and Covenants 89:3–5, 8)

8. *Temple Recommends.*

It is the practice of the Church to issue certificates, commonly called *recommends* . . . to certify to their [Church members] worthiness to receive certain ordinances or blessings. . . . When a worthy Church member desires to participate in the sacred ordinances of the temples, he is given a recommend certifying as to his worthiness to gain the desired blessings. . . .

It appears from 2 Corinthians 3:1 that the practice prevailed among the primitive saints of introducing faithful members of the Church from one group of saints to another by means of epistles of commendation or letters of commendation. That is, the saints were commended, introduced, or *recommended* to the various local churches by these written certifications. These would correspond to "recommends" in modern times. (*Mormon Doctrine* [Salt Lake City: Bookcraft, 1966], 620; 230–31

Elder Russell M. Nelson of the Council of Twelve Apostles adds this insight:

Our Redeemer requires that His temples be protected from desecration. No unclean thing may enter His hallowed house. Yet anyone is welcome who prepares well. Each person applying for a recommend will be interviewed by a judge in Israel—the bishop—and by a stake president. They hold keys of priesthood authority and the responsibility to help us know when our preparation and timing are appropriate to enter the temple. Their interviews will assess several vital issues. They will ask if we obey the law of tithing, if we keep the Word of Wisdom, and if we sustain the authorities of the Church. They will ask if we are honest, if we are morally clean, and if we honor the power of procreation as a sacred trust from our Creator.

Such requirements are not difficult to understand. Because the temple is the house of the Lord, standards for admission are set by Him. One enters as His guest. To hold a temple recommend is a priceless privilege and a tangible sign of obedience to God and His prophets. ("Personal Preparation for Temple Blessings," *Ensign*, May 2001, 32)

9. *Devil.* "And thus we see the end of him who perverteth the ways of the Lord; and thus we see that the devil will not support his children at the last day, but doth speedily drag them down to hell." (Book of Mormon, Alma 30:60)

$\mathcal{R}$OCKY MOUNTAIN HIGH

Wherefore, men are free according to the flesh; and all things are given them which are expedient unto man. And they are free to choose liberty and eternal life, through the great Mediator of all men, or to choose captivity and death, according to the captivity and power of the devil; for he seeketh that all men might be miserable like unto himself.

—2 Nephi 2:27

THE WYOMING LEGISLATURE HAD APPROVED A BILL ALLOW-ing high school students to leave campus for religious education. My assignment was to replace early morning seminary with daytime seminary in two high schools in one of the larger cities in Wyoming. Pondering this assignment, I felt deep feelings of unworthiness. I would again be teaching high school students regularly. I needed to be in tune with the Spirit to succeed.

Before leaving Utah, I made an appointment with my ward bishop to confess my intermittent use of alcohol. As a condition of employment, seminary teachers must have a current temple recommend (see chapter 3, note 8). Strict obedience to the Word of Wisdom is a requirement to qualify for the recommend. Realizing that my job could be at risk, I awaited the interview with anxiety. During our visit, I explained to the bishop that I had, from time to time, been drinking alcohol. He listened until I had finished my confession, then reminded me of the good I had accomplished in the ward. He counseled me to begin keeping all the commandments and to pray for strength to fully live the Word of Wisdom. I felt his love and genuine concern. With sincere intent, I promised that I would never drink alcohol again. I was sure that by exerting all my will-power, I would keep my commitment. We *both* believed me. I was greatly relieved to receive my bishop's blessing to continue teaching seminary. I could now approach my new assignment in Wyoming with lightened conscience and greater enthusiasm.

Preparing to leave for Wyoming produced feelings of melancholy mingled with excitement.

July 6, 1977

We said good-bye to our home in Provo—farewell to our canal and orchard playground across the street, BYU, Mt. Timpanogos, Bridal Veil Falls, skiing trips, water games at Utah Lake, ice skating, my deeply loved little office in the Joseph Smith Building—regret and questions as to why I didn't finish my degree.

Before leaving for Wyoming, we stayed several days in Tooele with Faye [my mother-in-law]. I spent one day trying to load our station wagon and dog trailer with all that was left after the moving van pulled away. Drugged on caffeine as usual, I was detached from my work but not my melancholy. My heart ached as I glanced up, from time-to-time, at Settlement Canyon, where I had spent many hours running with my dogs, playing with the children, and praying in my sacred grove.

To avoid the July heat, we left for Wyoming at dusk—constant travel along the dark black freeway—the children sleeping deeply in beds made in the back of the car—Charlie and Parley tucked in their little trailer being whisked along through the night to a strange new land.

Early morning found us parked beside a tree-lined river flowing swiftly over smooth, black stones. After family prayer in knee-high grass, we drove up a winding canyon and out onto the high plains.

We lived fifteen months in this high-plains city while I labored to establish released-time seminary. The countryside appealed to me. on the high prairie grass waving in the wind like a strange green ocean had a relaxing, hypnotic effect. As each month presented its full moon, the striking color, size, and unusual brightness of the orb rising above the rolling hills were profoundly beautiful. With each full moon came an intense loneliness that seemed to energize me with another month's worth of melancholy. This Wyoming land spoke to me like the friend I needed—but it spoke to the darker side of my soul.

The daily routine was exhausting. After teaching classes at seven and 8:00 a.m. in the stake center, I loaded projectors, screens, tape recorders, and often my dog Parley, and drove across town to a Church member's home to teach a third class. Then, again loading everything up, I traveled back across the city to another member's home for the last class of the day. I repeated this process Monday through Friday in addition to teaching an institute class on Thursday evenings. I also spoke frequently at firesides and sacrament meetings, which sometimes involved traveling hundreds of miles.

These demands would have been challenging to the most spiritually fit seminary teacher who enjoyed healthy family support. But I was spiritually out of shape and expended a great deal of energy trying to balance my family's needs with my church and work duties.

The loneliness of the windswept land encouraged a generous sprinkling of liquor stores to dispense medication for its inhabitants. The easy access to alcohol, combined with my tedious daily routine and increasing marital tension, pushed the promise to my bishop not to drink past the breaking point. One late night, I stopped at a remote liquor store's drive-up window. My purchase was accompanied by terrific guilt and terrifying questions. *What was I doing? Where was my willpower? What would happen if I were recognized?*

As I drank the alcohol, I knew I had double-crossed my bishop, my Heavenly Father, and myself. Promises, prayers, good intentions and tons of willpower had little effect on controlling my craving. I felt powerless; or the *alcohol's* power felt greater than *my* power. But once the drug was in my body, I didn't care.

To the outside world, I appeared successful. I had established the new seminary program. But inwardly, with more late-night Pony Express stops at drive-in liquor stores, I was becoming a wreck, a pendulum of extremes, swinging from resolve and repentance to concession and guilt.

October 3, 1977

I begin this year's journal while wife and children sleep next to the warmth of cheery-red coals burning in our Woodsman stove that, I am proud to say, I installed successfully (We hope!) in the basement of our new home on the prairie.

I could write a book about spiritual (and physical) challenges, the agony of learning (or not learning) lessons over and over, of trying, winning, failing. But there's no time for books or even a short story, just a few lines about scattered pieces of time.

These past few years, my life seems to fit an object lesson I once taught in Idaho from the seminary curriculum. It was based on a sermon by President Spencer W. Kimball titled "Hidden Wedges."

The lesson was taught with four blocks of wood—three square and a fourth in the shape of a wedge. Written across two of the square blocks were the words "My" and "Self." These two blocks were held together, side by side, with an elastic band. The third square block was labeled "Big Sin," and it was placed on top of My and Self. The wedge-shaped block was labeled "Little Sin."

If you tried to force the Big Sin block between the two rubber-banded My and Self blocks, it could not be done. But if you placed the point of the Little Sin wedge in between the crack where the My and Self blocks met, then placed the Big Sin block on top of the Little Sin wedge, the wedge split apart the My and Self blocks. Now, Big Sin could follow and split apart the My and Self blocks. This lesson illustrated that small sins act as wedges to force the soul apart allowing more serous sin to follow.

At first, my Little Sins were drinking cola drinks and depending upon the caffeine for energy. This resulted in agitated nerves, deadened spirit, and neglecting to pray and study the scriptures. The caffeine opened the way for Big Sin; a reoccurrence of old indulgences [alcohol], which ended almost in a tragic way.

I got a hold on myself and went on the "magic elixir" lemon juice cleansing fast for several days. I prayed long and hard. The darkness in my bosom began to be replaced with the old familiar feelings of peace, love, and a knowledge that I was being forgiven. The gap in My-Self closed.

Once again, I am amazed at the love of my Heavenly Father and His forgiveness. I have known and felt His presence these last few days.

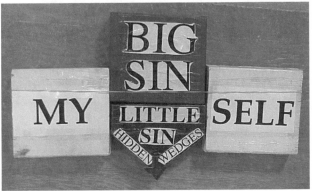

This lesson illustrated that small sins act like wedges to force the soul apart, allowing serious sin to enter.

I believed the answer to my growing addiction lay in my willpower and the redoubling of my efforts to swear off alcohol. However, my repenting to God and promises to myself were short-lived. Within weeks, another stop at a liquor store window added momentum to my headlong slide into full-blown alcoholism.

My wife was aware of my drinking, but I don't believe she realized how serious the problem was becoming. If she did know, she didn't appear too concerned. There were even a few times when we went out to eat at remote dinner clubs that she shared a bottle of wine with me. Drinking alcohol suspended the conflict between us and lessened her resistance to romance. I didn't discourage these episodes. However, my feelings of guilt and hypocrisy drove me further down the road to addiction. Still, I experienced a few spiritual victories when, exerting all of my willpower, I was able to slow my descent.

October 30, 1977

This weekend, I enjoyed an experience more spiritually moving than anything in the past few years. The setting was a retreat for LDS youth at the YMCA of the Rockies above Estes Park, Colorado.

The weekend began as I arose early Saturday to go jogging. Wearing flimsy protection against the cold, I ran in a snowflake-filled mountain morning up a steep road until I found a place of solitude. The snow, falling softly in the morning stillness, filtered down through the tall, dark-green pines like diamond dust. Kneeling on a cushion of needles beneath a century-old tree, I welcomed the day in prayer.

During the morning, President S. Dilworth Young addressed our group of young adults from the Wyoming and Colorado areas.

Later in the afternoon, I drove up a narrow dirt road toward the mountain peaks. Reaching the end of the road, I took my guitar in case and began climbing. Wearing my heavy, wool-lined, John Denver-style, imitation leather coat, I struggled up the steep slopes of a small peak that stood out far beneath the 14,000-foot mountain peaks of the Continental Divide. Lugging the guitar, I crawled the last hundred yards to just below the summit, where I perched on a rock jutting outward. This vantage point gave me a circular view of the pine-filled valley below and mountains above. The sun's golden rays showered over the snow-covered peaks to the west. The wind whipped briskly about me. The beauty of the towering mountains above, with sun-tinged, snow-dust streamers blowing over their peaks like strange nightcaps struggling to stay on, filled my being.

With the last feeble warmth of the sun on my back, I took out my guitar and sang, "Sunshine on My Shoulders" and "I Guess I'd Rather Be in Colorado" plus a few other John Denver ballads. It was a sacred feeling singing my hero's songs in such a Rocky Mountain high.

After warming my cold-numbed fingers in my coat, I climbed down into a sheltered spot between the cliffs and knelt in prayer. My surroundings had filled me with awe and gratitude mingled with a strange and lonely sadness. Tears fell freely until I could no longer speak. I confessed my weaknesses and again begged my Father's forgiveness. With all my heart, I sought to feel some answer. I asked to feel the peace of the Spirit once again . . . if only I could be forgiven.

In the evening, as part of the fireside program, I spoke to, and with my guitar sang to and with the young people. How precious it was to feel again the confidence of the Spirit. My earlier prayer had been answered. I felt much love for the young people, and peace, and joy in the feeling that I was being forgiven.

In my state of mind, I felt that I was the worst of sinners, but I was exaggerating. It is true that I was breaking the Word of Wisdom, but no other sin at this point. I tended to magnify my weakness because of the guilt I felt by being a drinker and a seminary teacher. I was sure that if I admitted my problem in order to obtain help, I would be terminated from the work I loved. I chose to remain silent.

My disease worsened with each episode of drinking. More late-night stops for liquor led to a growing fear that a student or parent might recognize me. My guilt increased, becoming a constant burning ache inside me. Yet, despite my use of liquor and the resulting feelings of guilt, I still felt that the Holy Ghost was helping me in my classes. I gave all credit for this blessing to excellent seminary curriculum and to the fact that, regardless of the condition of my students' teacher, the youth deserved to feel the presence of the Spirit. A journal entry records my affection for the students and my own children and that the marital breach was widening.

October 31, 1977

Through the basement window, I see a sliver of moon hanging above the dark prairie horizon. A fire flickers through the small window in the stove. The children and wife sleep deeply. I sit at my typewriter brooding over feelings of gospel warmth, excitement, weariness, and human coldness.

Fifty seminary students filled our home this night for a Halloween party. They danced, laughed, yelled, and played. Then, after cleaning the house, they left, leaving me more in love with them and more disheartened in my weakness.

My wife stayed hermitted away in the bedroom while my two children, awed at the antics of the teenagers, wandered about. I will remember them. Michael [my son] sat in a corner of the kitchen with a baseball hat smashed down over his long blond hair. Glazed, past bedtime eyes could barely see from under his hair and hat. He asked me if he could carve a pumpkin, but, being too busy with the students to supervise, I denied him. Later, I found him with a screwdriver in hand and pumpkin in which he had poked out something that resembled eyes, mouth, nose, and even a tooth he proudly pointed out.

Does he know how my heart glows with love when I hold him? I hope he doesn't sense the ache that is there also. Oh my son, I love you! And daughter fair, golden hair in pigtails, you also I love. And wife? You would say I know nothing of love. But how I love, and ache, and pray, and search for answers. Twist the tale and the knight lays slain with empty fingers before the Holy Grail.

The end of this journal entry documents that the conflict continued in my marriage. Rather than joining with me in my successes, my wife retreated. The more attention I received, the more withdrawn she became. I wanted her to share in the honor that came from our position, but I didn't know how to do it. It may be that I was so caught up in *my* career that she felt neglected and insignificant. Perhaps her apparent lack of concern regarding my drinking came because it was at least one indication that I was human and vulnerable.

As the year progressed, my love for the students grew. It was as honest as my testimony was sincere. Although I was failing personal tests, feedback from students documented that I, and the seminary program, was having a good effect upon them.

November, 1977

Dear Brother Simkins,

I would like to express my gratitude, love, and deep respect for you. I hope you'll accept this letter as speaking for all of your students and not just myself because I'm sure everyone else feels the same.

We can feel your Christlike love, not only for each of us, but for the Lord. It is a great blessing to be of such a loving, spiritual nature as you are. We greatly appreciate the gifts you share.

Brother, it seems to take so much to get you discouraged. I want you to know that, as long as you are teaching us the way you do, you should never be discouraged. Even at those times when you think we are not learning the exact dates, towns, or people's names, or when we're looking bored, there is no cause to be discouraged. Many valuable lessons are being taught us at those times. We are very much aware that you don't lose your patience with us; that you believe in all you teach; that you love these Saints we learn of.

You are a blessed man in the most valuable areas possible and a great example to all the young men and women.

Bless you!

A Sincere Student

Painfully aware of my hypocrisy, notes such as this one super-charged my guilt. No matter how sincere the compliments, they were impossible to accept.

The weeks of autumn passed slowly. It seemed like an entire school year passed between September and Christmas. The prairie winds, the tedious teaching rounds, and the coldness between my wife and me were depressing and exhausting. I turned more and more often to the immediate relief of whiskey.

Most of the year passed with my making few journal entries. A brief note I wrote at a spring conference for seminary teachers reveals my spirit-versus-body battle was escalating. On that occasion, I had been asked to sing and share my testimony for one of the meetings. I knew, but others could not have suspected, why my tears fell so easily and why I spoke of other's strengths while belittling my own. Had they been mind readers, the unimaginable fact would have been revealed—an active alcoholic was addressing them. Following the meeting, a fellow seminary teacher put his arm around me and said, "Brother Phil, you are an easy man to love!" I smiled and thanked him, but living with constant self-loathing, I cringed, rejecting his heartfelt compliment.

April 20, 1978

Months have passed since writing in my journal, or what's left of it. I write this note at a seminary teacher's conference at Aspen Lodge above Estes Park, Colorado.

Elder Jeffery Holland, Commissioner of Church Education, has just addressed us. He taught about the relationship between the spirit, body and original intelligence. Incredible knowledge! His description hits home. I wonder if others have experienced, as I have, the spirit-body battles he describes?

Sitting here, all of Longs Peak is revealed through the large window next to me. I now feel a reverence for this scene. Very early this morning, I ran and climbed to her snow-covered summit. It was further and harder than I thought it would be. I barely made it back in time for the first meeting.

Now, I view the thousands of dark pines blanketing her side. Firm and dignified in their tall, dusky-green thickness, they hardly sway in the stiff breeze. But I can't feel their beauty when such a cold wind howls through my soul.

The school year ended with my barely having enough emotional energy to get through the day. I could no longer keep up my Brother Jekyll and Mr. Hyde façade. Using the excuse that I needed to return to BYU to complete my degree, I requested a year's leave of absence. I wanted to believe that I would graduate, get control of my life, and return to teaching seminary. But the truth was, my addiction wasn't going to go away because I wanted it to. It was just the opposite. My use of alcohol was leading me to other addictions. The use of alcohol, drugs, and some behaviors have the effect of enhancing one's base physical appetites while numbing one's conscience. I began committing other typical "sins" of an active addict: occasionally viewing pornographic material and watching R-rated movies; lying to cover my actions. These sins were easier to commit now that alcohol had broken down my resistance. In addition, I felt sorry for myself. I rationalized that I had an affectionless marriage. Wasn't I due these concessions? These not-so-little wedges were slowly splitting apart "My" and "Self," making way for the "Big Sin" to rend me in two. I took the next predictable, but gargantuan, step downward into immorality.

It was late summer in Wyoming when I confessed to my bishop. Although he lived across the street from us, he had no suspicion of my alcoholism. We, my wife and I, had hid it well. Confessing just a drinking problem would have been simple. After all, I had confessed this once before to my former bishop. But immorality! The days that led up to my visit with him were filled with intense guilt and remorse. I was learning the proverbial hard way, that injuries to the spirit are as traumatic as injuries to the physical body. Seared spiritual flesh is intensely painful.[1] My flesh was smoking. I was badly in need of the Savior as the Physician!

When I met with my bishop, I confessed *everything*. I informed him that I would be taking leave from the seminary program. He listened carefully. My circumstances were terribly serious. However, as a counselor by profession in Wyoming Social Services, my story was not atypical—although he had not expected such a story from "the seminary teacher across the street." He spoke to me with an understanding beyond my comprehension. He knew how long the road to recovery was going to be. At that time, I had no clue. For reasons that he did not explain, he chose not to initiate a Church court. Perhaps the Spirit prompted him otherwise. Perhaps it was because my immorality was not in the letter of the law, adultery. I will never know. But whatever his reason, it did not invalidate the verity that *consequences follow choices.* Although I was grateful to escape formal Church discipline, my choices would eventually convict me.

Several weeks following my visit with the bishop, I confessed my infidelity to my wife. Choosing an afternoon when the children were at school, I bolstered my courage with alcohol and sat down with her. There had been so much conflict and so little communication between us. I thought there were no feelings of love left. I even hoped that she might be aware of my wandering affections and would just not care. But, as I was soon to discover, she did care and she had no suspicion of what I was about to tell her.

Speaking in a general way, I spoke of breaking my marriage vow of fidelity and began to seek her forgiveness. But suddenly, I realized how poorly I had judged her love. I would have welcomed her hitting me or screaming. But there was no anger. Instead, with uncontrolled tears, she crumpled to the floor in a heap. Despite the alcohol in my body, I felt the full weight of my actions. The magnitude of my sin pressed down on me as a heavy blackness. I fell to my knees beside her. She clung to me and sobbed. There was nothing I could do. No words could *ever* undo the pain my selfish act had caused.

Continuing to counsel with my bishop, he soon realized, though I was clueless, that I was an alcoholic. His rather strange (to me) advice was that I should go to the experts—Alcoholics Anonymous.

Because alcoholism thrived in this windy Wyoming city, so did AA. Groups met nightly in a building constructed of lodge pole pines. I recall the setting vividly because of the powerful impression my first visit left on me. There was one large meeting room furnished with worn but comfortable sofas and chairs arranged in a large circle. End tables and footstools were placed so as to hold numerous ash-trays and coffee cups that would be used during the evening.

September 12, 1978

My bishop made the suggestion. "I want you to attend an AA meeting." I agreed immediately, thinking, *I'll gladly do anything you ask. For sure, an AA meeting can't hurt!*

It wasn't easy finding the building. It was as if it was disguised in a brown paper bag. Sitting in my car, I drank whiskey from a paper cup and watched several people enter the building. Waiting until the last minute, I finally went in.

There were two dozen or so people of various ages seated around the room, chatting cheerfully, smoking, and sipping coffee from mugs they refilled often from a large urn. As a newcomer, I was greeted warmly by everyone. Although the room was buzzing with conversation, I didn't hear anyone talking about alcohol or drinking. I don't think anyone, except myself, had been drinking.

Sitting in a large sofa, I waited anxiously for the whiskey to kick in. A man at the front of the room tapped the table with a wooden gavel and said, "Hi folks, my name's Bob. I'm an alcoholic. I'd like to welcome you to our meeting tonight."

Everyone, except myself, responded in unison, "Hi, Bob!" He said something like, "Let us pause in a moment of silence for the alcoholic who still suffers." (I wondered if he meant me!)

Next, Bob called on a young lady who also greeted the group with her first name. All responded, "Hi, Marge." These people were well rehearsed.

Marge read a passage from a book she called "The Big Book." [The name AA members affectionately use to refer to their basic text—*Alcoholics Anonymous*.] After she read, Bob spoke with a deep confident voice about what using alcohol had cost him and how he had stopped. He talked about twelve steps, or rather, "*The Twelve Steps*," like they were the Ten Commandments or something.

I understood very little of what he said, but I knew one thing for sure—there was Peace with a capital "P" in the room. It was like a fast and testimony meeting, but more from the gut, honest and straightforward and mingled with a little profanity.

I was sure Bob was not saying what he thought others wanted to hear. He was telling it like it was for himself. When he finished, another person introduced herself and received the same unison greeting.

I don't remember much of what was said, but most everyone talked about how alcohol had nearly destroyed them and how they had stopped. Most of them mentioned that God, or a Higher Power, had granted them a new life. I began to realize the room was full of miracles.

They were aware they had a first-time visitor. My smell, if not my speech, was a sure giveaway. They mentioned "our visitor" a number of times, but no one preached or spoke directly to me. They spoke about themselves and their experience. Definitely real people. The principles they spoke about sounded like they came right out of the Bible.

This was a new experience for me. In spite of the thick tobacco smoke, slurping coffee, and occasional good-hearted profanity, the Spirit of the Lord was in abundance. Maybe not religious, these men and women *were spiritual*. I hadn't known what to expect—but I hadn't expected this.

Going around the room, each person spoke in turn. Some gave their first name, received the greeting, and then said, "I guess I'll listen tonight." Eventually it came my turn. I should have just given my name and shut up, but instead I launched off into some whiskey-driven seminary sermon about being moved by the Spirit in the room. As I think back, I'm sure most of their smiles were not prompted by my dumb attempts to make jokes as they had, but rather, at me.

When the meeting ended, we all stood in a circle, joined hands, and repeated in unison, The Lord's Prayer. *Everyone knew it better than I.*

Before I could escape, several people introduced themselves, asked if I wanted their phone number, and invited me back.

I was deeply affected by my introduction to AA. Just as I was sure that the gospel of Jesus Christ was true, I was sure that these people knew the principles they embraced were true. Having lived in an LDS culture all my life, I was surprised to encounter good people who used coffee and tobacco and still exuded spirituality. I was sure they were expounding true principles. It was obvious they were having success in their lives by living in harmony with these principles. Before leaving Wyoming, I attended a dozen more meetings—enough to *barely begin* my education in recovery.

As the summer of "78 ended, evidence of my escalating alcoholism was mounting. After only a year of teaching in Wyoming, I requested another sabbatical from the seminary program. I used the excuse that I needed to return to BYU and complete my degree. But the truth was, I knew I was not worthy to continue. I had made several insane drunken trips back and forth to Utah. I had committed a serious moral transgression. I had quit partaking of the sacrament. My temple recommend had expired and could not be renewed. I had broken my wife's heart. My children (now ages eight and ten) were confused as to why we were selling our home and moving. I was sure they sensed something terrible had happened, but my wife and I didn't try to explain. I was up to my neck in quicksand, but I still couldn't accept the obvious—*I was powerless over alcohol, and my life was unmanageable* (Step One of AA's Twelve Steps of Recovery).

The year ended with much heartache. As a final sadness to our Wyoming era, our beloved dog and my best pal, Parley, died suddenly from an unnamed illness. We buried him in a pet cemetery on the windy prairie. Late in October, we loaded a U-Haul truck with everything we owned, along with one lonely collie, two rabbits, our two older kids, and a new *one-month-old baby boy*. We retreated to Utah.

*N*OTES

1. *Spiritual Pain.* Elder Boyd K. Packer has observed:

   All of us sometime, and some of us much of the time, suffer remorse of conscience from things we did wrong or things left undone. That feeling of guilt is to the spirit what pain is to the physical body. But guilt can be harder to bear than physical pain. Physical pain is nature's warning system that signals something needs to be changed or cleansed or treated, perhaps even removed by surgery. Guilt, the pain of our conscience, cannot be healed the same way. (*"The Touch of the Master's Hand," Ensign*, May 2001, 22)

As a final sadness to our Wyoming era, our beloved dog Parley died suddenly from an unnamed illness. We buried him in a pet cemetery on the prairie.

$\mathscr{D}$ADDY, HAVE YOU STOPPED DRINKING YET?

And if ye have no hope ye must needs be in despair; and despair cometh because of iniquity.

—Moroni 10:22

ARRIVING BACK IN UTAH VALLEY LATE AUTUMN 1978, WE RENTED a home close to BYU. My graduate program had remained open and thus no entrance interview was required to continue my schooling. I tried to convince myself that my recent confession to my bishop, another rededication to stay sober, and a return to BYU classes would herald a new beginning. Standing on this shaky platform, I applied for another teaching assistantship. Having left BYU in good standing, I was granted entrance. Naïve to the enormity of my transgressions and the power of alcohol, I sincerely believed that I would complete my degree and return to teaching seminary.

Alcohol had weakened my resolve in other areas of my life. I had hoped the income from my stipend would support my family until I graduated. To help bridge the financial gap, I took part-time work at a grocery store. We still came up short. The down-payment money we had set aside for a new home was soon exhausted for rent and food. I stopped paying tithing.[1] In prior years, even in tight times, we had always had enough money to meet our needs. Now, I forfeited the Lord's blessings that come through paying tithes and offerings.[2] We were on our own. The financial problems grew worse, and stress stoked the fire of my addiction. As fear replaced faith, my will power was a puny weapon against the power of alcohol. Within a month, I was drinking again.

My memories of our time spent at this home are as dismal as the dark basement coal room I had converted into a study. It was here that I hermitted away to read, write, pray, and drink. On several occasions, my daughter (and still my pal) caught me drinking alcohol. Being emotionally mature for her age, she was also my confidant. Although I did not understand the disease myself, I attempted to explain my drinking problem and tried to reassure her with promises. She revealed her concerns in little messages that she left on my desk. I kept these in my journal.

January 16, 1979

She drew faces on the following note providing a multiple-choice answer. I chose the *sort-of* option writing the comment, "Still trying hard! I love you!"

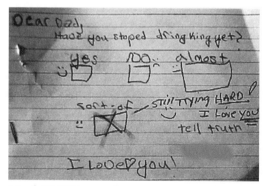

March 17, 1979

In the early years of my addiction, robust health and self-resolve gave me a false sense of control. But I had crossed that inevitable line that separates weakness from full-blown disease. In retrospect, I believe I crossed this line the day I drank the cooking sherry. Now, I couldn't stop drinking—not for my wife, my parents, my career, my church, or my children—*Not for anything!*

A few month's later, my daughter left this note in the little type-writer I used to make my journal entries:

```
dear dad,

it seems you don, t love me to much  ;
  i was dumb to think you would sstop drinking.
```

May 23, 1979

My life early in alcoholism was like riding a giant roller coaster. I encountered a few short-lived highs followed by sudden plummeting dives to long sections of lower track. I tended to write at the peaks when I thought I had stopped drinking for good.

February 16, 1979

I won't write much about the long silence since my last recording. Needless to say, I feel like I've been to hell and am now returning.

On Tuesday, after teaching my morning class at BYU, I drove up Hobble Creek Canyon and found a secluded spot to pray. I don't believe, up to this point, I have ever felt more despair. Tritely put— rock bottom. Words can't describe the agony of the battered spirit, the sickened body, the hopelessness of continued concessions to the appetites—to have once again used alcohol to numb the black burning within me.

I prayed with all my heart but was sure relief would not come so quickly. Often during the last year, I have knelt and sought for help only to lose the battle. This time it was different.

Earlier in the morning, I had attempted to teach sixty college students with little physical or spiritual energy. My mouth was so dry that I could barely speak. My fingers trembled, and the paper I was reading from shook. My bosom was filled with blackness and fear. I thought of bolting for the door to escape the sixty pairs of accusing eyes. My mind raced at the consequences. This would be the end. I wouldn't be able to explain my actions *one more time*. Then I thought *I just have to do this*. I proceeded to teach the most horrible lesson of my life—but I taught it!

Heartsick and aching in every cell from alcohol abuse, I had to get away from the piercing gaze of my students. Following class, I left the building and walked quickly down the long steps of BYU to my car. I had to find a place of retreat to lick my wounds and pray for relief from this madness.

After my prayer in the canyon, I returned to teach my afternoon class, determined to make the change back to what I once was. With aching body, mind, and spirit, I stood again in front of another large class. But this time, with a new hope that I could end this hell for good. I made it through class and then through the rest of the day with no alcohol. The next day was difficult. I hurt badly but it was a little better.

Today, I can think clearly enough to make some observations— where I have been—and to have some confidence about where I am going. I feel the old familiar energy. I speak with my Heavenly Father often and feel that He is hearing and helping. I want to save my feelings about my love for the Savior until I feel closer to Him.

I never got around to feeling closer to, or writing about, the Savior. I didn't stay sober. The months blurred by while I went through the motions of teaching and attending classes. By the end of winter semester, I had made no progress toward completing my master's thesis. With no energy left, I resigned my career as a graduate student, college instructor, and seminary teacher. I had received an offer to teach seminary the coming year at a high school in northern Utah. I had even visited the seminary and met with the principal. But I knew, before making this trip, I could not continue living a double life. I had just wanted one more visit inside a seminary classroom. I had hoped to feel the sweet spirit of a brother seminary teacher one last time. But I knew as I visited with the seminary principal that I was no longer a "brother." Returning home, I mailed my letter of resignation.

Late that spring, I experienced my first formal treatment facility for alcoholism. I became aware of this facility through the media. It promised a quick fix for the mess my life had become. I was convinced this treatment would be *the* answer. I felt I had to go through with it at all cost. *Cost* was about all it was. No longer employed, I had no insurance to cover the cost. My parents, also hoping this would be the answer, borrowed and paid the required ten-thousand-dollar fee.

This program's approach to alcoholism focused on the physical rather than the spiritual or emotional roots of the problem. The goal of treatment was to make the alcoholic so violently ill through drinking alcohol that he would never touch another drop.

May 4, 1979

I now prepare for the first of *five* treatments. I feel I am ready. I have spent a great deal of time thinking and praying about what has happened. I anticipate the coming experiences as kind of penance. Maybe, if I take some of the suffering, it will lessen that which I must place upon the Savior.

I am fortunate to be young and still have my health and family. Most of those I meet here have ruined health, failing minds, and shattered lives. There is much sadness in their faces. Alcoholism destroys all that is good.

(Later that day) I finally feel well enough to write about Treatment One. As I write, the stinking yellow bile still seeps up through my throat and nose and into the metal pan beside me.

I waited anxiously for my turn. When it came, I entered the treatment room decorated to appear as a modern drinking lounge. Kaye, the nurse, reviewed the process once again. First, you get the drug that closes off the pyloric valve so alcohol won't enter the small intestines and be absorbed; then the drug to keep your blood pressure down; and finally the Emitine to make you puke your guts out.

The small chatter stopped for a moment while Kaye stuck the needle in my rump. Next, she handed me a shot glass filled with water and Emitine. More chatter while we waited for the nausea to begin. Whiskey, gin, vodka, beer and exotic liquors all around. Still we waited. My mouth began to salivate. I spit into the large metal bowl placed strategically in front of me.

Then it began. First the vodka mixed with more Emitine; then the straight Jim Beam Whiskey. I barely got it swallowed before it came back up. More whiskey, puke. Now a little vodka, more puke. Perhaps you'd care for a lot of scotch? More puke. Runny nose, aching throat, tears and puke, plus the smell and sight of alcohol everywhere.

Dear Father, what did I do to end up here? More puke. *It must be close to the end.* The nurse handed me salt water to drink, which, when I threw it back up, would wash out the last of the alcohol (as if there was any left). Next came the tongue depressor. "Push it back," she said, "and gag yourself. Get it all out so I don't have to put the tube down your throat and pump your stomach."

No problem here lady. I poked until the back of my mouth ached. "You got it all up?" she asked mercilessly. *Yeah, lady, there's nothing left of me to throw up.*

(Back in my room.) *It's finally over. That's the last time I need to throw up. No, one more time, worse, can't breathe. No nurse around. I'm going to die with my head in this dang bowl!*

May 5, 1979

I mentioned at dinner to the other inmates how our surroundings resembled a prison—only our own personal madness made up the bars. Few people understand how desperately we want our sanity back. How many people would voluntarily accept torture like this? Yet when we leave here, unless God walks with us, *we will drink again.*

May 12, 1979

I will never forget these two weeks, the sharing, laughing, tears, ache, and common hope. I love these people. Their suffering has made them compassionate. They truly care about others.

But it's funny (not really) how even here I have followed my old cycles. First, sickness from severe alcohol abuse; then, feelings of guilt and melancholy followed by an acute awakening of love for my family; next, desperate homesickness for my old life as a seminary teacher, mingled with consistent and sincere prayer; and then, within a week, diminished spiritual feelings, increased caffeine use, shorter prayers, no prayers, confusion, depression, ups and downs.

After leaving the treatment facility, I obtained employment selling recreational properties. With good interpersonal skills, I quickly succeeded in making money. I purchased a flashy sports car and was on the road much of the time, showing properties throughout the state. With time by myself, a little money, and much unresolved guilt, I resumed my descent into alcohol purgatory. At first, I was able to drink and work. To a degree, alcohol seemed to increase my tenacity as a salesperson. But as the summer turned to fall and then winter, I made less money and drank more. I had to sell my sports car, but that would be the least of my worries.

As a result of the choices I was making while drinking, a serious, life-altering event occurred: the day of judgment I had postponed. Shortly after Christmas 1979, two men from the stake high council delivered to me a personal notification. The official document requested that I attend a formal church court to investigate alleged immoral behavior. I sat before twelve high priests and spared them the difficult task of questioning by quickly admitting to the charges. The week after my excommunication[3] from The Church of Jesus Christ of Latter-day Saints, I wrote:

January 16, 1980

I wish I could write this day of joys spent with my family. Only pain fills my heart. As I read from yesterday's journals and remember, I ache to be clean and pure again and enjoy my family as I once did. Oh, how I love them.

What little joy I now have comes when I am with them. My sweet Josh [my youngest son] teetering around on just-learned-to-walk legs with smiling eyes and a voice of curious wonder. Josh and Sunshine, and Mike [my oldest son] are my only glimmers of light in a gloomy world.

I was excommunicated the day after Christmas. Opening the small temple suitcase given me by Grandpa Haycock, I placed all of my temple garments[4] inside next to my white temple clothes and closed the lid.

Will I ever have the privilege of wearing them again? How ignorant we are of what we have until we lose it! Trite maybe, but oh, so true. How precious was my membership and priesthood. Will I ever be a member again? Will I ever hold the Priesthood? How far I have fallen!

I try to pray but just feel empty. If it really is darkest just before the dawn, with the sun just setting, it seems such a long way until morning.

My writing doesn't make me feel any better. I know I won't sleep when I lie down. It's supposed to rain tomorrow.

To the extent that I had been spiritually electrified with joy in Panama, I was now being electrocuted with guilt. The consistent torment of the memories of teaching seminary, activity in the gospel, and playing contentedly with my children replaced any feelings of happiness. Years earlier, I had shown my seminary class a film of a terribly handicapped man who had overcome much adversity. Deeply impressed by the courage of this little fellow, his thick spectacles, and shriveled body, I had recorded some of his inspiring statements in my journal. I still retain the image of his raising his head from his Bible study and uttering, "Adversity has ever been considered the state in which a man most easily becomes acquainted with himself." This statement had remained with me over the years like a prophecy. I was becoming better acquainted with myself than I wanted. But, in my case, I knew I had brought on my own adversity.

I knew God forgave *others*. But I was sure my sins were extraordinary. I seriously doubted that I could be forgiven. I even questioned whether I had committed the unpardonable sin, *denying the sun at noonday*, or in other words forsaking Jesus Christ after having received a special testimony of his divinity.[5]

Years earlier I had written on a blank page in my Book of Mormon a piercing quote from Brigham Young. At the time I recorded it, it was intended as a reminder. Now it had become a condemnation:

> Many think that the devil has rule and power over both body and spirit. Now, I want to tell you that he does not hold any power over man, only so far as the body overcomes the spirit that is in man, through yielding to the spirit of evil . . . *if the spirit yields to the body, the devil then has power to overcome both the body and the spirit of that man.*
>
> When you are full of evil passion, and wish to yield to it, then stop and let the spirit, which God has put into your tabernacles, take the lead. If you do that, I will promise that you will overcome all evil, and obtain eternal lives. *But many, very many, let the spirit yield to the body, and are overcome and destroyed.*[6]

President Young's words *overcome* and *destroyed* stood out like a flashing-red neon sign. They burned into my soul like a branding iron. I felt every bit as branded as Hester in the *Scarlet Letter*. I couldn't understand how my life could once have been filled with deity's light only to fall to humiliation, , and hopelessness.

March 15, 1980

I find my life impossible to figure out. I keep thinking, Dear Father, *why did you touch me that Panama night? I had done nothing to prove worthy. Just a simple, feeble plea for help.*

But You touched me with Your Spirit and filled me with fire, peace, and joy. You turned my world upside down—for this?—to end in the insanity of alcohol addiction and blessings lost? Have You forgotten me? Do I still have any destiny in Your plans? Dear Father, do You still care?

But the heavens remain silent and my heart continues to ache under the dull pain of yesterday's sin. I see my sweet children and say in my mind, Oh, please God, spare them the test. Guide them away *from Satan's snares so cunningly conceived and set.*

I kissed my sweet son Mike's sleeping face this night. Tears fell from my eyes onto his cheeks and ran off onto the blanket pulled up beneath his chin. How I love him.

Through all this pain, I still know my Redeemer, and His Father, live. I love Them—but They are silent! [7]

The year following my excommunication was a pitiful scene. Living in my own disgrace, I would gather all of my willpower to try to stay sober, attend church, and earn the right to be forgiven. Still working at, but having no success in, my sales occupation, my bishop helped me obtain employment as a laborer at a local manufacturing plant. Memories of better times depressed me terribly. Stuck in the cycle of addiction, my guilt, fear, and the day-to-day problems of just living built up inside me until I drank again. My wife attempted to deal with the insanity of my alcoholism alone but wearied under the burden. She was reaching a decision of her own about our future.

My drinking binges drove me back to AA. Friends there preached the philosophy of "let go and let God." I still stubbornly held to my philosophy that people who drank alcohol were weak-willed and evil. If all that was wrong with me was a weak will, then I reasoned that more will power was the answer. It was still too soon to comprehend the key paradox of the disease—*in admitting defeat lies the answer to winning.* Eluding me was the fact that *spiritual power*, the only medicine that can combat a *spiritual disease*, is set in motion by *surrender to God*. Like the person who can't see the forest for the trees, I saw my life as a lot of unrelated drinking incidents. If I could just control these events, life would get better.

May 5, 1980

Sitting here in disbelief, I wonder how I can write one more time about what *I allowed* to happen. I had been feeling a little better, believing that something good was going to happen. After two weeks of hard fought-for sobriety, I became discouraged over a sale I had been working on. I became so despondent that I didn't even try to close the deal. I just knew the couple wouldn't buy. Then I committed a gross error—I bought a beer—just one and that would be all. I wonder *how I could possibly have been so blind as to believe "only one beer" after the scores of times I have experienced the destructive outcome?*

The one beer led to nearly a week of insane drinking that ended when I drove my old truck off the freeway into the median lane. I hardly remember it. I guess only God kept me from dying, or far worse, bringing harm to someone else.

In a recent prayer, I asked my Father not to give up on me. I told Him I felt my soul was like a character I saw in a movie called *Rocky.* Rocky was an underdog boxer who, fighting for the world championship, was being brutally beaten and battered. Every time a powerful blow knocked him down, he would struggle to his feet and fight back, blow after blow, match after match, until he won the championship.

In my prayer, I shared with my Heavenly Father that I saw myself a little like Rocky—only the championship was winning back my life. Every time my spirit has been battered, beaten, and knocked down by the use of alcohol, I have struggled to stand, only to be knocked down again. Getting back up, another deadly blow is delivered. I prayed that someday, somehow, my spirit would stand victorious over my body.

I keep thinking, *Why, why, why, Father? Why did You touch me and lift me so high in Panama only to let me crash down like this? All I want is to get well! Why can't I?*

I recently spoke with my children about my drinking problem. With one simple phrase my darling son Mike swept all the garbage away. With teary eyes he said, "I heard you praying in your room, Dad. I prayed for you!"

I was accepting no responsibility. I actually blamed my Father in Heaven for "letting me crash down," as if he'd had anything to do with it. Because I hung on so tenaciously to *my will*, my precious *willpower*, I could not admit that alcohol had defeated me. As time passed, I was learning more about the disease, but at a turtle's pace.

June 15, 1980

I spent Father's Day initiating "sobering-up-rites" at the ARC [Alcohol Recovery Center] that included long, horrid hours which developed into another sleepless night, pacing, wandering and wondering, nearly without hope this go-around.

The next day, I called my wife to see if she would come and get me. She agreed. While waiting, I talked with the director of the ARC. He counseled me to stay for a few weeks of rehabilitation. I promptly declined. He was a funny looking little man with big ears and a short crew cut. But what he said wasn't funny: "Phil, you're not ready to stop drinking, are you? You must to be willing to *crawl on your stomach through cut glass* to recover from alcoholism. You have to want it that bad!"

I thought, *but I do want to quit. I will crawl on my belly through anything to stay sober forever!*

My mind was still foggy from being submerged in alcohol for a week, so I don't remember everything he told me. But I know it affected me.

To make it absolutely clear, this truth I now state to myself: *If I take one drink of alcohol into my body, the cycle will start all over again! It only will end in great physical pain and spiritual, emotional horror, just as it has this time. I cannot have just one drink. I don't want one drink. I don't want to live this way any longer.*

I left the ARC that Monday and was drunk within a week. Attending more AA meetings, I learned short parable-like stories that illustrated the insanity of alcoholism. A good example was the Parable of the Jaywalker.

There was a man named Pete Powerless who had acquired the habit of jaywalking. The first time Pete yielded to the urge to jaywalk, he cut across a busy street and, struck by a car, suffered a broken arm. The next week, his arm in a cast but unable to fight his compulsion, Pete again ventured into a busy intersection and was struck by a van.

His leg was broken in several places. Weeks later, his arm and leg in casts and hobbling on crutches, he challenged a busy thoroughfare and was run over by a bus. A concussion, another broken arm, another broken leg, and some crushed ribs, put him in the hospital for a lengthy stay. The doctors strongly counseled Mr. Powerless against jaywalking and warned him that death was imminent if he didn't stop. Upon his release, he was able to control his habit for over six months. But in a moment of weakness, Pete challenged a fast moving freeway. A semi-truck was his demise. [8]

This parable would appear as a ridiculous situation. No one would continue to jaywalk after experiencing such painful consequences. Or would they? I would have traded any night of the physical and mental horror of coming off alcohol for something as simple as a broken arm or leg. I was being run down repeatedly by the Alcoholism Express but continued to jaywalk.

July 27, 1980 (Sunday. Written after a week of heavy binge drinking.)

My heart aches with a deep, dull constant pain. My body feels as if every nerve has been rasped to the bleeding point. In spite of this, I need to record the feelings of the past several days. Perhaps someday, someone experiencing this hell will read my accounts and be helped—or at least *warned*.

Friday night, having determined to dry out again, I lay on the couch awaiting the horror of the coming hours. Anticipating the real, or imagined—I don't know anymore—demons that I knew would come as the alcohol wore off, I lay two mild, almost worthless, sleeping pills beside me to take when the pain got really bad. I was determined to just suffer it out. Maybe my mind would be so seared with the utter truth of this hell, and the possibility of it lasting forever, that I would never turn back to alcohol or any other concession to the Evil One.

After lying on the couch for an hour or so, I began to feel the evil demons gathering about me. Every time I opened my eyes, they seemed to appear in dark, vapor-like forms more hideous and grotesque than is imaginable. [This] progressed like this until my eyes, shut or open, I could still see them.

For hours the agony continued. Towards morning, I took the two pills and dozed a little, yet still felt awake. I began having a nightmare, or dream, or vision. I couldn't tell if it was real or conjured.

I found myself knocking at the door of a large structure. The man who welcomed me I knew to be Satan, or represented him. The building was tall, elegant, and beautiful from the outside, like the great and spacious building in Lehi's dream.[9]

Upon entering, I found the rooms were ransacked. There was broken glass and spilled wine everywhere. The house was full of people engaging in a riotous party. They wore very little clothing, with the men having long hair, beards, and strong, tanned bodies. The women were sensual, proud, and beautiful. When they saw me, they began jeering, laughing, and pointing at me.

I turned to run but they grabbed me, encircled me, and threw me around. I fought with all my strength but couldn't get away. Finally, they flung me to the floor on top of a large broken wine bottle. I felt the sharp pain and saw the blood gush from my stomach. Struggling to my feet, I ran towards a large window. Diving through, I broke out the glass and crashed down onto the pavement below. *Crawling through the broken glass on my stomach*, I was able to get up and run towards my old truck parked a short distance away. The people ran to catch me but I was able to reach the truck, pull myself into the seat, and drive away just before they caught up. In the rearview mirror, I could still see them laughing and pointing at me.

I woke, or came to reality, pleading, *Oh God, please don't let me die! Please don't let me suffer this torment and anguish forever! Please don't let anyone suffer like this.* For some reason, I appealed in this prayer, not only for myself, but also for every suffering alcoholic and drug addict. [Note: It was the morning following this dream, a Sunday, while walking for hours through neighborhoods filled with families going to church, that I conceived of writing a book about my experiences as a Latter-day Saint alcoholic.]

As desperately as I pled, that night would not be the last time I would be haunted by demonic apparitions or have agonizing nightmares. It was only beginning.

Another era of life was coming to an end. My wife, unwilling to suffer along any longer, filed for divorce. I read from my daughter's journal, "Daddy is drinking again. It's pitiful!" Only I knew how pitiful. By the end of the summer, my divorce was final.

The day before I was to leave home for the last time, I sat, in a stupor, in my little dingy basement office. As I stared at the cement walls, my eyes rested on each of the special posters I had collected over the years teaching seminary and at BYU. Each image seemed to taunt me. The scripture poster from Paul: "This one thing I do, forgetting those things which are behind, and reaching forth unto those things which are before, I pressed toward the mark." My Winston Churchill banner: "Never Give Up, Never, Never, Give Up!" My weight-lifting poster: "No Gain Without Pain." My Grand Canyon poster: "You see things as they are and ask "why?" But I dream things that never were and ask why not." And my sun-rising-over-the-mountains poster: "Tell the rising sun that Earth with all her many voices praises God!"

Removing each poster from the wall, with disgust I crushed them into the garbage can. Then my eyes rested on my favorite poster, the Ballet Lady. I read again the once inspiring words written under her dancing feet: "If you can imagine it, you can achieve it! If you can dream it, you can become it!" My heart softened. Removing her from the wall, I rolled her up and stuck her into a mailing tube. I seriously doubted I would ever free the dancing lady from her cardboard tomb.

Alcoholism destroys all that is good, but it wreaks the greatest havoc on the family. My marriage was over, my career was halted, and my wife's and children's hearts were broken. That summer's false promises, running drunks, and immorality had extracted from my family its last vestige of hope. I was spiritually, emotionally, morally, and financially bankrupt. My spirit was being drug along by my body like some lifeless rodeo dummy tied to a raging bull—a bull that had ransacked everything in its path.

Along with the Ballet Lady, I crammed what I could into a large backpack. Then, fighting back tears, I hugged my children good-bye and drove away on the only thing I owned—a small Honda motorcycle.

Notes

1. *Tithing.*

   One tenth of the interest or increase of each member of the [LDS] Church is payable [by commandment] as tithing into the tithing funds of the Church each year . . . for the carrying out of the purposes he [The Lord] had in view: for the gathering of the poor, for the spreading of the gospel to the nations of the earth, for the maintenance of those who were required to give their constant attention, day in and day out, to the work of the Lord [such as seminary teachers], and for whom it was necessary to make some provision. Without this law these things could not be done, neither could temples be built and maintained, nor the poor fed and clothed. Therefore the law of tithing is necessary for the church, so much so that the Lord has laid great stress upon it. . . .

Payment of an honest tithing is essential to the attainment of those great blessings which the Lord has in store for his faithful saints. (Bruce R. McConkie, *Mormon Doctrine* [Salt Lake City: Bookcraft, 1966], 796–97)

2. *Tithes bring the Lord's blessings.* "Bring ye all the tithes into the storehouse, that there may be meat in mine house, and prove me now herewith, saith the Lord of hosts, if I will not open you the windows of heaven, and pour you out a blessing, that there shall not be room enough to receive it" (Malachi 3:10).

3. *Church Courts* and *Excommunication.* In the LDS Church, temple endowed members commit to live a highly moral life. Breaking this moral code is serious enough grounds for a member to face a church court. Where there is sufficient cause, a bishop's court is usually called to examine evidence. After review of the circumstances by the bishop and his two counselors, if the offense deals with immorality and a Melchizidek Priesthood holder, the case is referred to the Stake High Council court. These courts are made up of twelve men proven worthy to officiate as common judges in Israel. The court is presided over by the stake president and his two counselors.

Results from a Church court can range, depending upon the seriousness of the moral infraction, from a person's being disfellowshipped and losing some membership privileges, to being excommunicated from the Church and losing all membership privileges.

Bruce R. McConkie adds, "the highest punishment which the Church can impose upon its members is excommunication. This consists in cutting the person off from the Church so that he is no longer a member . . . (1 Timothy 1:20; Matthew 18:15–19; 1 Corinthians 4, 5:1–5) By baptism, entrance can again be gained into the Church of our Lord, and following testing and faithfulness all their former blessings may be restored." (*Mormon Doctrine* [Salt Lake City: Bookcraft, 1966], 258–59)

4. *Temple Garments.* The temple garment is a special piece of clothing worn under outer garments that is placed upon worthy church members in the temple as part of the temple ordinances. The garment is worn on a daily basis to serve as a personal reminder of covenants made and to encourage modesty. When a member of the Church is excommunicated, the privilege of wearing the garment is taken away.

Elder Russell M. Nelson explains that "wearing the temple garment has deep symbolic significance. It represents a continuing commitment. Just as the Savior exemplified the need to endure to the end, we wear the garment faithfully as part of the enduring armor of God. Thus we demonstrate our faith in Him and in His eternal covenants with us." ("Personal Preparation for Temple Blessings," *Ensign*, May 2001, 32)

5. *Denying the Holy Spirit.*

> Thus saith the Lord concerning all those *who know my power, and have been made partakers thereof,* and suffered themselves through the power of the devil to be overcome, *and to deny the truth and defy my power*—They are they who are the sons of perdition, of whom I say that it had been better for them never to have been born; for they are vessels of wrath, doomed to suffer the wrath of God, with the devil and his angels in eternity; concerning whom I have said there is no forgiveness in this world nor in the world to come—Having denied the Holy Spirit after having received it, and having denied the Only Begotten Son of the Father, having crucified him unto themselves and put him to an open shame. (Doctrine and Covenants 76:28–35; emphasis added)

6. Brigham Young. *Journal of Discourses of Brigham Young* 2:255, emphasis added).

7. *Repentance Takes Time.* Elder Neal A. Maxwell provides insight into the process of repentance:

> There can be no real repentance without personal suffering and the passage of sufficient time for the needed cleansing and turning. This is much more than merely waiting until feelings of remorse subside. Misery, like adversity, can have its special uses. No wonder chastening is often needed until the turning is really under way . . . In

the anguishing process of repentance, we may sometimes feel God has deserted us. The reality is that our behavior has isolated us from Him. Thus, while we are turning away from evil but have not yet turned fully to God, we are especially vulnerable. Yet we must not give up, but, instead, reach out to God's awaiting arm of mercy, which is outstretched "all the day long" (Jacob 5:47). ("Repentance," *Ensign*, November 1991, 30)

8. Original story found in *Alcoholics Anonymous* (Alcoholics Anonymous World Services Inc., 1976), 37–38.

9. *The great and spacious building.*

And the multitude of the earth was gathered together; and I beheld that they were in a large and spacious building, like unto the building which my father saw. And the angel of the Lord spake unto me again, saying: Behold the world and the wisdom thereof; yea, behold the house of Israel hath gathered together to fight against the twelve apostles of the Lamb; And it came to pass that I saw and bear record, that the great and spacious building was the pride of the world; and it fell, and the fall thereof was exceedingly great. And the angel of the Lord spake unto me again, saying: Thus shall be the destruction of all nations, kindreds, tongues, and people, that shall fight against the twelve apostles of the Lamb. (Book of Mormon, 1 Nephi 11:35–36.)

$\mathcal{T}$HE THORNBIRD

That at that time ye were without Christ, being aliens from the commonwealth of Israel, and strangers from the covenants of promise, having no hope, and without God in the world.

—Ephesians 2:12

August 26, 1981 (One year following my divorce.)

In welcome contrast to the muggy evenings of the last few days, a cool breeze rustles the old cottonwood trees in front of my little house. Earlier today, I placed canvas over the top of an old rusted swing I found along the roadside, and, although not much to look at, it is functional. I placed it in front of the little house I now live in. I have named it the "Mule Home" because the landlord raises mules that bray outside my window. I spent some time this evening sitting in the swing, playing my guitar, and singing to the mules; my attempt to get even. Kind of like one jackass singing to another, I guess.

It has taken longer than usual following this last binge to stop hurting physically. Tonight, thoughts of happier times fill me with deep sadness. It is heavy to bear. I don't know what to do. I can't stop thinking about things—days of joy teaching seminary—my children. I was happy then because I was at peace with myself. Those days are gone.

After spending the day cleaning the house and yard, I pitched my tent on the front lawn. Resting in the swing and reflecting, the little pup tent reminds me of yesterdays. My heart aches because no children played in it today. There are no children. The tent flap just rustles back and forth in the wind. I thought about sleeping in it tonight . . . kind of like when I was a kid and slept in the big bed we placed outside each summer. Just one more painful thought.

Sunday was Sunshine's *thirteenth* birthday. *How did she get so old so fast?* Although I was anxious and miserable with only my second day off alcohol, we [my ex-wife had invited me] had a picnic up the canyon to celebrate her birthday. While at Tinny Flats, Mike remembered having played "soldiers" there a few years earlier. I remembered it, too. It was a wonderfully warm, summer day. We ran repeatedly into the cool creek to avoid the enemy. Such rich joy in contrast to the awful sadness I have come to know as life.

My kids kiss me and say they love me. I know they do, but their eyes reveal their pain and bewilderment of what has happened. My kisses back say the same thing. *Oh, what did happen?* I have prayed, and cried, and tried, and wanted to be close to God and to have my old life back, but with no success.

My desire to live is feeble. Chances for a sober, happy life seem remote. It feels like this is just the way things were planned out for me a long time ago; I don't know. My alcoholism keeps picking up momentum like a giant snowball plunging down a steep, endless canyon. Nothing seems to turn it aside. I don't want to drink, but I don't know how much longer I can stay in my body the way I feel tonight.

During these years, I had few friends and worked one job after another. Living in the guilt of yesterday and the fear of tomorrow stopped me from living the "one day at time" AA taught about; and, with its despair and fear, today didn't seem to be any better of a choice. As my alcoholism worsened, there were times when I wished I had *never* existed.[1] These were not suicidal thoughts. Even in the darkest hours, I never considered taking my own life. Years earlier, I had attended a devotional featuring a distinguished philosophy teacher at BYU. I remembered his saying, "Suicide is just a change of scenery." I knew he was correct. I was sure that checking out of the mortal realm and into the spirit world would not be an escape from pain.

I once read an account of a person's experience in the spirit world after he had died. This man suffered severe pneumonia in a war hospital and had been pronounced dead. After several minutes, his spirit reentered his body. But during the interval, he had visited a realm of spirits. He saw a young man desperately pleading with a mortal, middle-aged woman, begging her forgiveness, telling her that he was sorry—but in vain. She could not hear him. The man had committed suicide. He hadn't realized the pain that taking his own life would bring to his mother. As a spirit, his sorrow was immense.[2] From personal experience and from my own studies about the spirit world,[3] I believed this account was true. I was sure that if I were to take my own life, I, along with my pain and troubles, would only be conveyed to a different scene in the *same* play.

I made a more serious attempt at AA. The Old-Timers (as I refer to those with lengthy and successful sobriety in AA) often advised: "Go to thirty meetings in thirty days. Then, if you don't like what we have to offer you, we will gladly refund your misery!" Attending more AA meetings, I wrote in my journal that I had gone through the first step of AA, "*admitting that I was powerless over alcohol and that my life was unmanageable.*" But I would need more time and experience before I understood the meaning of *being powerless* over alcohol and admitting defeat. I would need to learn that one doesn't go *through* AA, as though it is a treatment program to complete; rather, when the principles begin to work, AA *goes through us.* It creates a lifestyle change!

October 26, 1981

I have been sober an *entire month* and continue going *through* AA. I have attended *twenty-seven meetings in thirty days!* AA has kept me sober. I often share in meetings, feeling relaxed, helpful, and a little hopeful. There *is* a Power that permeates all in attendance. I feel God's presence there. I know there is no hope for recovery without God, the Group, and AA's Twelve Steps.

I have taken Step One, "Admitted I was powerless over alcohol, and that my life is unmanageable," and Step Two, "I came to believe that a Power greater than myself could restore me to sanity." I attempt to live Step Three daily: "Turning my will and my life over to the care of God, as I understand Him." I know I need to take the Fourth Step soon: "Make a searching and fearless moral inventory of myself."

For now, the most important keys are living one day at a time while surrendering my will, pride, resentment and selfishness over to God and continuing to go to AA (See Appendix I, Part 3). As they say in [AA] group, *"It works if I work it!"*

My birthday just passed. It would be marvelous if, on my next birthday, I could celebrate my first year sober in AA. One simple day at a time and with the help of God, I know it is possible!

Had I continued going to AA, I might have achieved that elusive "first-year-of-sobriety." Instead, violating the Old-Timers' advice that *one must be willing to go to any lengths to get sober,* I tired of the daily AA meeting routine and, with a false sense that I had *achieved* sobriety, I stopped attending altogether. A modern-day Apostle of the Lord describes this self-sabotage in a passage I had read but given little attention to *before* my active alcoholism. Years later, I came across the passage again. This time, I realized the author described my condition perfectly.

> We are promised deliverance, but the Lord will not kidnap us. The ground rules about free agency insure that we will not be held hostage against our will. Countless times, however, some mortals have insisted on breaking away from His saving grasp in order that they might swim back to the sinking ship![4]

I felt as though I were that captive passenger on an ill-fated ocean liner. Each time I gathered the willpower to swim to land, I would weaken and dog paddle back to the hapless vessel—a bottle of booze.

November 5, 1981

It is around 1:00 a.m. and I am about half drunk. I stopped going to AA meetings some time ago. Then Saturday night, I ignored all I have been learning in AA, and, in total defiance of logic, bought a pint of whiskey and started the whole, horrible cycle over again.

The Old-Timers say that AA is a simple program for complicated people. I feel that way, complicated, I mean. I'm sure I began drinking because I ignored the keys: I stopped praying, surrendering to a Higher Power, going to meetings, and doing the simple things that keep my disease in remission.

I hope to go back to work tomorrow if Dan [my boss] will let me, but I don't know how I can go through this effort one more time.

I went with Dennis [a friend in AA] to an AA meeting in Mona last week. We had dinner with Lynn and Jannette, and I played with their children, singing and playing like a horse for them to ride. I wonder why? I love my own children. How I miss them. I want to have them back. It hurts so badly. I just don't understand why I have to drink.

This morning, I dreamed I was teaching an elders quorum class. Several members got up and left, disgusted I guess, because an alcoholic was instructing them. But with those who remained, I was able to share a few things I had been learning in AA. I taught the Serenity Prayer,[5] especially about letting go of things we cannot control or change—past events, future events, other people's behavior, and external circumstances (like the weather).

I taught about having the courage to ask God's help and then work on the only thing we can change—our own behavior in the present moment. (Although I haven't had much luck doing this except for a little learning and a few baby steps.) In the dream, following class, several Elders approached me and said that what I was teaching was an answer to their prayers regarding problems in their marriage and at work.

But it was only a dream. I'm a billion miles away from controlling my own behavior let alone teaching any gospel class. Why can't I be free of alcohol so I can share the knowledge that God has given me? I wonder why I'm even writing, or to whom? Oh well.

During periods of sobriety, I sometimes accompanied my ex-wife and our children on outings to visit her mother. We were still attempting to make things work but having little success. Every moment spent with my children caused divided emotions—one part of me feeling gratitude to be with them, another side of me aching with the memories of happier times.

November 15, 1981

On Saturday afternoon, we took the kids to see Grandma in Tooele. I played football with Mike, Josh, and Sunshine in the large piles of autumn leaves we had raked. On his turn, Josh would run, diving and giggling, into the crunchy golden mounds. It was a melancholy time.

I kept looking up at the mountain canyons remembering the hikes, jogging trips, and special prayers I had enjoyed therein. But the memories only served as a painful reminder of a happier time when I knew joy in my family and when I was a seminary teacher.

No matter what happens, I will always love my Heavenly Father and my brother Jesus. I remember how close I felt to them while running in the canyons. I felt so alive. I would run for miles and then, reaching my special sacred grove, would kneel and give thanks for the rich blessings in my life.

Such a sad lonely feeling now—remembering, wishing, but knowing how long and hard the path is to regain even a little of what I have known. Too weak and too far to go to even try.

The relationship with my parents was being tested to its limits. I had once held the status of being the *only* seminary teacher our small town produced. My parents had been very proud. Now, my active alcoholism and excommunication was a source of embarrassment and pain. Not knowing how to reverse this situation and feeling a great personal shame, I often overreacted to anything that I interpreted as their judging me. Our behaviors were confusing to one another and there was much misunderstanding. Our condition was typical to alcoholism—the eventual disintegration of *all* relationships.

I attempted to teach my parents about alcoholism. From my personal experience, I knew that other's judging and giving unsolicited *advice* was like pouring gasoline onto a wildfire. I tried to teach my parents about the paradox of alcoholism: that to the alcoholic, the common-sense advice—"Why don't you just stop drinking?"—is like saying, "Why don't you just stop having cancer or diabetes? It is the opposite of what is needed. What *is* needed is an understanding of alcoholism as a *disease; and that it is a family disease.* True understanding turns gasoline to water. The fire can be put out.

Mom was not aware that she was also a victim to the disease. She was being affected emotionally and spiritually from her failed attempts to control the alcoholics in her life. I had learned in treatment that family members who don't educate themselves to the disease come to resent and even hate the addict. They believe that in order to stay in the relationship, they must blindly accept the unhappiness that results from his/her drinking. They become lost to their own choices and unable to detach from the emotions of the other. This condition is unnatural. It gradually destroys feelings of affection. The alcoholic reciprocates with withdrawal, resentment, and anger until the relationship is irreversibly damaged.

Mom willingly read the AA literature, but the most important help she needed would come from attending Al-Anon[6] meetings—the Twelve Step group for spouses of alcoholics (see Appendix I, part 3). Due to the remote area where Mom lived, there was no Al-Anon Group meeting within fifty miles. With no one who could understand her situation, Mom was alone and uninformed in trying to cope with the sick people in her life. Neither she or I were immune to the cumulative effects of chronic alcoholism. The disease ate away at the once-strong bonds of our relationship.

January 12, 1982 (Journal—letter from Mom)

Dearest Son,

Call it Monday blues, January blues, first of the New Year hang-ups, whatever, but either way or all the way, I seem to have "em. I'm trying and fighting. Seems like most of all, I can't shake the feeling that you and I are no longer the good friends we used to be. That fact I cannot live with, or ever accept.

I just need to tell you once again, at the beginning of another year, that I do love you with all of my heart, as much as it is humanly possible to love. I always will—forever.

You pointed out to me that things are better than they were a year ago, and yes, I am ever so thankful for that. I do wish you a happy and successful New Year.

I ask you to bear with me and try to understand. Please don't shut me out of your life, ever, OK? I am proud of you. I do admire you in so many ways. I do have faith in you and always will. I know you are trying hard to make your life better. Please let me help you in any possible way I can. I will try harder to keep my feelings to myself, also my advice and suggestions. I don't mean to judge you, or anyone else, as I hope no one will judge me. I still say, until one has walked in another's moccasins, judge not!

May this always be your home and the valley you love. May you always feel welcome and know that your Dad and I love you and want you to return whenever you can.

Loving you forever,
Mom

While I did very little to reciprocate, Mom offered a sincere effort to understand and not judge me. She read the literature and tried to view alcoholism as a disease rather than a sin. Although I gave her plenty of reason, she never resented me. Her attitude made *all* the difference. Her powerful love and accepting attitude saved our relationship from deteriorating beyond the point of repair.

In the spring of 1982, I was working ten-hour days at a manual-labor job, going to AA, and trying to stay sober. The Old-Timers used the acronym *H.A.L.T.* as a "red light" to remind the alcoholic of four conditions dangerous to a fragile sobriety. "If you don't want to fall off the wagon, don't let yourself get too *Hungry, Angry, Lonely, or Tired.*" At the tail end of two months' sobriety, I was running red lights on all four conditions.

March 31, 1982

It is very late. I have no idea why I am writing. Oh, there are a few special moments like when the old fellow from the rest home came into the gas station where I was buying a soda begging for a "silver quarter or a George Washington dollar." I gave him a paper buck. His eyes rewarded me richly for the small deed. I felt love towards him. I knew we weren't that much different.

The merry-go-round continues moving up and down but going nowhere. I lasted a few days past *two months* sober and then took that first dang drink again. I didn't think I would ever get off the stuff. Without calling in, I missed a week of work. I walked in the cold rain, lay in bed, and drank beer in a futile attempt to stop the pain.

That Friday, a few weeks ago, I crawled out of bed and went out into the rain to buy another day's supply of alcohol. In the 7-11 store, I struggled in front of the beer cooler. I just couldn't go another day drunk. I uttered a little prayer followed by the Serenity Prayer and then bought orange juice instead of beer. It was a strange feeling. Even in my stupid drunkenness, I know God helped me at that moment.

All that day, I walked the back roads in the on-again-off-again rain, trying to divert my mind from the pain. While walking, a tiny highlight occurred, which resulted in the new companion now curled up beside me.

As I walked past the sewage treatment plant, which also serves as a drop-off point for homeless animals, a black-and-white kitten ran out on the road and began following me. She was soaking wet and looked as lost and miserable as I. Picking her up, I stuffed her inside my wool-lined Levi coat, where she promptly began purring.

After walking several miles, the rain stopped and the sun came out. I removed the kitten from my coat and, setting her down on the road, said, "OK, if you want to live with me, you'll have to prove it." I began walking. With white-tipped tail sticking in the air, she took up the pace and trotted along behind me like she had just found her mother.

Well, "Tippy" as I call her, hasn't found her lost mother, but she has found a lost drunk, and a friend, and a home—well, sort of a home. It's good to have some company.

[Note: Tippy kept me company in a most gentle and affectionate manner *for the next 18 years!*]

Another bit of good news—I got my job back. Dan said this was my last chance. If I missed work again, he would be unable to keep me employed. I went to AA tonight. It helped. It always helps!

Sober or drunk, I often shared my testimony of the gospel and tried to encourage others. Although most of my personal encouragement came from my friends at AA, occasionally other people outside the fellowship made a special effort in my behalf. On one such instance, a letter arrived from the wife of a work associate, Shauna. She had given birth to a little girl with brain damage. This

Well, Tippy, as I call her, hasn't found her lost mother, but she has found a lost drunk, and a friend, and a home—well, sort of a home.

unexpected condition had caused her and her husband serious soul searching. Before the child's birth, I had shared with them some of my experiences in dealing with life's challenges. Shauna wrote me a note on gold and silver stationery, embossed with a picture of an LDS temple:

July 15, 1982

Dear Phil,

As I sit here at the kitchen table, looking out the window at the soft rain falling on the green mountains, my thoughts center around my Heavenly Father and those family members and friends who have been a special part of my life. I take much for granted and don't stop to realize just how blessed I am. I see friends and family members struggling with difficult problems and can't help but feel a deep love and respect for their enduring patience and understanding.

This love and respect burns inside of me for you, Phil, for you truly are an example to me. Your constant efforts, your smile, and your experiences that you've shared with Andy and me, have strengthened me and lifted me when no one else seemed to. As an outsider looking in, it would seem as though I barely know you, yet, deep inside, you are one of my dearest friends. Your spirit has touched me.

As I lay in the hospital last week wondering and asking the question *Why, why did our little Amberlee have to suffer?* my thoughts drifted back to words I have heard many times, "Our Heavenly Father will never give us more than we can bear." Those comforting words seemed to soothe my spirit and help me realize that everything will always be as our Heavenly Father planned. Even though we are called to have different problems, our Heavenly Father promises us that He will be our constant companion through everything.

I just wanted you to feel how grateful I am for your example, love, and the concern you have shown for Andy and I. I know many others feel the same as we do as you have touched the lives of all of us.

We Love You,

Shauna and Andy

Self-loathing prevented me from accepting this young mother's sincere compliments and encouragement. Few could have understood the sense of hopelessness that dominated my life during this time. My every attempt at sobriety met with failure. Intense physical, emotional, and spiritual pain occurred after every drinking spree—which were frequent. Simultaneous with this pain, I would make futile attempts at self-analysis that would be followed by ever weakening efforts at *making* my life right. Sometimes I wondered if it wouldn't have been easier to just stay drunk all the time.

The AA Old-Timers described my binge drinking as "field testing." In other words, experimenting with, but not internalizing, the principles of AA. Their oft-repeated slogan was: "A belly full of booze and a head full of AA doesn't mix."

Stated another way, the more one learns about alcoholism in AA, the harder it is to continue drinking. Either sobriety or death from alcoholism will eventually occur, but it is the alcoholic's choice. A choice for sustained sobriety is *totally dependent* on complete and honest surrender to a higher power followed by fierce commitment—not toying, not straddling the fence between "Thy will" and "my will"—not half measures. (See Appendix I, Part 1.)

Each of my field tests, which inevitably ended up as binges, painfully underscored the truth that taught in AA—that I was powerless. And each drinking episode made me more determined to live by the Twelve Steps.

I had come to realize that one doesn't take Step One (*I admitted I was powerless over alcohol—that my life is unmanageable*), Step Two (*Came to believe that a power greater than myself could restore me to sanity*), and Step Three (*Made a decision to turn my will and my life over to God, as I understand Him*), and then move on. Rather, I was coming to understand that these steps must be taken, or admitted, *each day, every day.* In prayer, I began "turning my life over to God" as a daily routine. Then it came time to tackle Step Four—*Make a fearless and searching moral inventory of myself*—and Step Five—*Admit to God, to myself, and to another human being the exact nature of my wrongs.*

During the hot days of August 1982, I completed Step Four as I typed out twenty-one pages of moral inventory. I detailed everything that caused me shame and guilt. I was now ready to take Step Five.

It had never occurred to me that I might take this step with a fellow such as Steve H. At first acquaintance, I was convinced that this man was more insane than everyone in AA combined! His long, curly hair fell a foot past his shoulders, and his thick beard hid much of his face. A "motorcycle man," he was regularly attired in black pants, boots, leather jacket, and chains. Steve was a Vietnam veteran. Some said he was a war hero. He had experienced things few could comprehend.

At one AA meeting I attended with Steve, a prankster threw a large rock at the outside of the wooden building where our group was meeting. The impact resulted in a sound like a loud gunshot. Everyone was startled, but Steve instinctively leaped from his seat, sending his chair and books flying, and dived under a table. After he realized what had happened, he emerged, but he didn't stop shaking for several minutes. I am sure all of us were wondering what ghastly war image this incident had conjured up for him.

For over a year in AA meetings, I listened to Steve share his experience, wisdom, and hope in recovery. Compared to his struggles, mine seemed insignificant. He described the higher power he believed in as something inside him that gave him direction, peace, and purpose.[7] The serenity that he displayed in his life testified that his philosophy for recovery was working.

August 4, 1982

At the end of my last binge, I was driving into town on the Orange Steed [nickname for my small motorcycle] to spend my last few bucks on another case of beer. Sick and tired of being sick and tired, I uttered a little prayer and turned back to the Mule Home to begin the sober-up vigil.

Walking dozens of miles over the next several days to get through the physical pain, I spent two days fasting and writing a moral inventory as part of the Fourth Step: "Make a fearless and searching moral inventory of myself." Upon completion, I felt a little closer to my Father in Heaven.

I wondered whom I might take the Fifth Step with—"Admitting to God, myself, and another human being, the *exact nature* of my wrongs." In kind of a spiritual answer, I decided to ask Steve H., a straight shooting, bearded, and long-haired Vietnam vet who views

Mormons as mostly hypocrites. His parents are active Latter-day Saints, but his negative attitude toward Mormons is based on the way he feels he has been treated by them. In spite of my "Mormonness," we have become good friends. Still, it is interesting that I should choose *him*.

Steve arrived early Sunday morning. We sat in my old swing sipping coffee and watching the sun come up. After visiting, I read to him my 21 pages of moral inventory. He talked warmly, but directly, giving me advice that only one who has learned through experience can. He told me to go to church and hold my head up—that there would be no one there any better than I.[8] His understanding and unconditional love touched some part of me I hadn't felt in years.

We talked AA for a while, and then he got on his big black motorcycle and drove away in a cloud of dust, leaving me with a *who-was-that-masked-man?* feeling.

I got ready and went to church. It was fast and testimony meeting. As a result of my long fast and burden-lifting visit with Steve, as I sang the words of the closing hymn, ""O bless me now my Savior, I come to thee,"[9] my tears flowed freely.

After several years of continuous sobriety, Steve passed away from complications of tuberculosis. Before his death, he seemed to have found a peace that few obtain. His occupation had been that of a US postal carrier. At his passing, a friend in AA placed a small note in each mailbox along Steve's route. It read:

> In memory of Steve H., our friend and mailman. We have much evidence of God's existence in the strength that many have received from Steve's acts of faith and his venture of belief. We will miss him.

Seven days later at three in the morning, I wrote in my journal:

The insanity continues. Having been in a semi-surrender-to-God state, and having enjoyed a little serenity, I let down and let my self-will take over. I kicked God out and got back in the driver's seat then immediately went out of control. I just can't seem to completely *let go and let God*.

I have been off alcohol for about fifty-five hours now and have not slept. My liver is swollen, my eyes burn like hot coals, and my head throbs. My heart smolders in emotional and spiritual pain and I ache deep inside my soul. I am a hopeless drunk. I cannot get free of this madness.

Because I was behind on my rent at the Mule Home, I moved to a cheap motel in south Provo. In mid-December, I chalked up one more predictable consequence for alcoholics. I had been working sporadically with the fence company that had once employed me. Now it was winter, and there was little work. This particular week, the fence company had managed a few jobs between snowstorms, and I had received a small paycheck. It was my first money in over a month, and it was the week before Christmas. I went shopping for presents for my children. Driving an old Rambler donated to me by a compassionate friend, I was returning to the motel. A policeman's chilling blue and red lights began flashing through my back window. I was drunk on cheap wine and couldn't walk a straight line. The officer handcuffed and hauled me off to jail. Several weeks later, I was fined, lost my driver's license for a year, and assigned a parole officer.

In one of her many letters of encouragement sent during this period, Mom included a quote from the book *The Thornbirds*. As I read the passage, I knew what she was trying to tell me: *My dear son, I am finally beginning to understand.*

> The bird with the thorn in its breast, it follows an immutable law; it is driven by it knows not what to impale itself, and dies singing. At the very instant the thorn enters, there is no awareness in it of the dying to come; it simply sings and sings until there is no life left to utter another note. But we, when we put the thorn in our breast, we know. We understand. And still we do it. *Still we do it.*[10]

NOTES

1. *Wishing to not exist.* The Book of Mormon prophet Alma shares his experience in wishing to "become extinct" in this way:

> But I was racked with eternal torment, for my soul was harrowed up to the greatest degree and racked with all my sins. Yea, I did remember all my sins and iniquities, for which I was tormented with the pains of hell; yea, I saw that I had rebelled against my God, and that

I had not kept his holy commandments. Yea, and I had murdered many of his children, or rather led them away unto destruction; yea, and in fine so great had been my iniquities, that the very thought of coming into the presence of my God did rack my soul with inexpressible horror. Oh, thought I, *that I could be banished and become extinct both soul and body*, that I might not be brought to stand in the presence of my God, to be judged of my deeds. (Book of Mormon, Alma 36:12–15; emphasis added)

2. George G. Ritchie, *Return From Tomorrow* (Grand Rapids, MI: Fleming H. Revell Company, 1978), 58–59.

3. *Spirit World.* LDS Church President Joseph F. Smith received a vision in which he learned specific details regarding the spirit world or that realm where the spirits of men and women reside between death and the resurrection: The Doctrine and Covenants records this vision:

On the third of October, in the year nineteen hundred and eighteen, I sat in my room pondering over the scriptures; I opened the Bible and read the third and fourth chapters of the first epistle of Peter, and as I read I was greatly impressed, more than I had ever been before, with the following passages: "For Christ also hath once suffered for sins, the just for the unjust, that he might bring us to God, being put to death in the flesh, but quickened by the Spirit; By which also he went and preached unto the spirits in prison." [1 Peter 3:18–19] "For for this cause was the gospel preached also to them that are dead, that they might be judged according to men in the flesh, but live according to God in the spirit." [1 Peter 4:6] . . .

As I pondered over these things which are written, the eyes of my understanding were opened, and the Spirit of the Lord rested upon me, and I saw the hosts of the dead, both small and great. And there were gathered together in one place an innumerable company of the spirits of the just, who had been faithful in the testimony of Jesus while they lived in mortality; They were assembled awaiting the advent of the Son of God into the spirit world, to declare their redemption from the bands of death; . . .

I beheld that the faithful elders of this dispensation, when they depart from mortal life, continue their labors in the preaching of the gospel of repentance and redemption, through the sacrifice of the Only Begotten Son of God, among those who are in darkness and under the bondage of sin in the great world of the spirits of the dead. . . .

Thus was the vision of the redemption of the dead revealed to me, and I bear record, and I know that this record is true, through the blessing of our Lord and Savior, Jesus Christ, even so. Amen. (Doctrine and Covenants 138:1, 6–12, 16, 57, 60)

The Book of Mormon prophet Alma wrote about the spirit world in this manner:

There is a space between death and the resurrection of the body, and a state of the soul in happiness or in misery until the time which is appointed of God that the dead shall come forth, and be reunited, both soul and body, and be brought to stand before God, and be judged according to their works. (Alma 40:21)

4. Neal A. Maxwell, *We Will Prove Them Herewith*. Salt Lake City: Deseret Book, 1982, 42.

5. *Prayer for Serenity* (extended version):

God, grant me the serenity to accept the things I cannot change, the courage to change the things I can, and the wisdom to know the difference.

Living one day at a time, enjoying one moment at a time, accepting hardship as a pathway to peace, taking, as Jesus did, this sinful world as it is, not as I would have it.

Trusting that You will make all things right if I surrender to Your will; So that I may be reasonably happy in this life and supremely happy with You forever in the next. Amen. (Reinhold Niebuhr. Original source unavailable)

6. *Al-Anon.* Al-Anon, the sister companion to AA, provides group meetings, literature, and support for families of alcoholics and addicts. In their Preamble to the Twelve Steps, they describe themselves this way:

The Al-Anon Family Groups are a fellowship of relatives and friends of alcoholics who share their experience, strength and hope in order to solve their common problems. We believe alcoholism is a family illness and that changed attitudes can aid recovery . . . Al-Anon has but one purpose: to help families of alcoholics. We do this by practicing the Twelve Steps, by welcoming and giving comfort to families of alcoholics, and by giving understanding and encouragement to the alcoholic. (From Al-Anon pamphlet, *Freedom From Despair*, 1964,

Al-Anon Family Group Headquarters)

7. *AA concept of God.* In the book *Alcoholics Anonymous,* we read:

> Much to our relief, we discovered we did not need to consider
> another's conception of God. Our own conception, however inad-
> equate, was sufficient to make the approach and to effect a contact
> with Him. As soon as we admitted the possible existence of a Cre-
> ative Intelligence, a Spirit of the Universe underlying the totality of
> things, we began to possess a new sense of power and direction, pro-
> vided we took other simple steps. We found that God does not make
> too hard terms with those who seek Him. To us, the Realm of Spirit
> is broad, roomy, all inclusive; never exclusive or forbidding to those
> who earnestly seek. It is open, we believe, to all men. (Alcoholics
> Anonymous World Services, Inc., 1976. 46)

8. *The Good Man.* Apostle Matthew Cowley once remarked, "The good
man—no matter how bad he is, how low he has sunk—is the man who
starts coming up. The bad man is the man who, no matter how high he
has reached in his goodness and morality, begins to come down." (Henry
A. Smith, *Matthew Cowley: Man of Faith,* Salt Lake City: Bookcraft,
1954, 147)

9. *Hymn—I Need Thee Every Hour.* "I need thee every hour, Most gra-
cious Lord; No tender voice like thine can peace afford. I need thee, O
I need thee, Every hour I need thee! O bless me now my Savior; I come
to thee!" (*Hymns of The Church of Jesus Christ of Latter-day Saints,* 1985,
no. 98)

10. Colleen McCullough. *The Thornbirds,* New York: Harper & Row,
1977, 530, emphasis added.

$\mathcal{T}$INY DANCER

Was it not the hope which you had, in consequence of your belief in the existence of unseen things, which stimulated you to action and exertion in order to obtain them?

—Joseph Smith, *Lectures on Faith*, 1:11

February 12, 1983

A few weeks ago, I ran into Merlene [a woman I had worked for several years earlier]. She mentioned she had opened a new health club, so I asked, half-jokingly, if she was hiring. I think she sensed my query was more in earnest than I had let on. Her generous heart couldn't refuse. The next day, I began working as an exercise trainer and handyman.

My reason in writing tonight isn't to describe another meaningless job, but rather to record that a bit of light has appeared into what has otherwise been a long and dismal winter. Last week at the health club, I met someone special. I was in the weight room when the rhythm of a tap dance routine echoed throughout the gym. Tracing the sound, I discovered it was coming from the aerobics area. Moments earlier, a large group had panted their way through another laborious routine and had vanished as fast as they had appeared. The room was now empty—almost. As I peered in, a petite and pretty girl was tap dancing in the middle of the hardwood floor. Because of her delicate skill and beauty, I felt as if I was watching a tiny dancer atop a music box.

I would not have normally approached a complete stranger

but I felt impressed to meet this lady. Taking courage, I introduced myself and complimented her on her dancing. Her cheeks flushed with embarrassment as she realized she had been observed. Her dark brown eyes sparkled with a soft light. Having just displayed so much talent, her shyness surprised me. She introduced herself as Vickie Lee. Looking into her eyes, I had an almost haunting feeling that I had known her from somewhere before.

My relationship with my ex-wife had ended permanently. I hadn't been seeking any relationship since my divorce, but Vickie Lee and I were at ease from the beginning. Her strong character and zest for life, together with a gentle and affectionate nature, appealed to what remained of my spiritual being.

Vickie's first marriage, in her late teens, had lasted ten years before ending in divorce. From that point on, she had supported her four children alone. On our first date I learned that, several years earlier, she had been a counselor at the alcohol recovery center where I occasionally surfaced to get sober. I had even been present in one of her group sessions, but we had never formally met. As our conversations continued, I recalled that I had also seen her in some closed meetings of AA. (Only confessed alcoholics are permitted in closed meetings.)

As we spent more time together, I learned that she was a Latter-day Saint but had never been to the temple. She commented that she held on to the dream of being married there someday. I knew I would not be a viable candidate for temple marriage anytime soon, but our LDS and Twelve Step backgrounds meant we shared a common philosophy.

For reasons I couldn't grasp, Vickie was willing to add me to her

As I peered in, a petite and pretty girl was tap dancing in the middle of the hardwood floor. Because of her delicate skill and beauty, I felt as if I was watching a tiny dancer atop a music box.

already heavy burden. Early that spring, she moved me from the motel, half-drunk, sick, and months behind on rent, into a home she had recently leased. I wondered why Vickie would have the least bit of interest in me. She has since explained that, shortly after our meeting, she heard a voice speak to her heart yet audible as if someone were addressing her face-to-face. The words she heard left no doubt: "This man is the one, and his book too." (I had shared with her my idea of writing a book about my experiences as a Latter-day Saint alcoholic.)

Vickie understood alcoholism intimately, as an alcoholic, as the wife of an alcoholic from her previous marriage, and as a counselor. Most important, she understood alcoholism from the hours she had listened to the Old-Timers in AA and Al-Anon.

Vickie had some unique attributes that allowed our relationship to grow in spite of my alcoholism. She never criticized me. She never made me feel guilty. She never told me I couldn't drink, but she also never lessened the consequences when I did. She never poured out my alcohol. She never yelled at me. She never came to my rescue. All of her actions and words faithfully affirmed that *she believed* I was going to get well. I wanted to believe her.

With Vickie in my life, I tried even harder to remain sober. Instead of getting drunk *at* someone, I wanted to stay sober *for* someone. But I couldn't! I attended numerous treatment centers, staying at some for weeks and others for shorter periods. Fearing the pain of alcohol withdrawal, I often sought replacement drugs to ease off alcohol.

May 9, 1983

Except for Vickie Lee, little has changed in my life. It is supposed to be a spring afternoon but there is a cold breeze. Looking south, my gaze flows with the north wind over the new green of the valley, up the snow-covered ridges of Mt. Nebo to end on its marshmallow smooth summit. It makes me shiver clear through.

I am again sick from alcohol, getting drunk only four days after my release from Payson Hospital. Afraid of the withdrawal pain, I went to Payson's detox unit hoping to get some Valium.

I don't want to die or be sick. I just can't stand the pain of living sober surrounded by thoughts of what might have been, has been, and is.

Vickie and I occasionally attended our LDS ward but with some difficulty. We never found the welcome mat. Most members knew we shared the same address but not the same last name. This fact placed us in a class by ourselves. We did not appear, and justly so, to be a couple with the potential of putting our shoulders to the ward's wheel.

A year passed when a new bishop in our ward stopped to visit. I was sitting on the front porch wearing cut-off Levis and smoking a cigarette, a habit I had picked up while going to coffee shops following AA meetings. Sipping coffee without a cigarette was like eating cake with no icing. I had smoked as a teenager and in the Army, so this was not a new experience. Several months after my first puff, I realized my casual tampering with tobacco had led me back to the miserable habit. I was addicted.

When Bishop Bruce introduced himself, I anticipated the same cool treatment I had come to expect from our neighborhood. But his casual manner and sincere warmth caught me off guard. His questions seemed only to get to know me better. He wanted to understand my past and present circumstances. As we conversed, I found it easier to tell him about myself. This was the first time in years I had felt understood by anyone outside of AA. In fact, "Mormal Normans" (Normal Mormons), the term used in local AA groups to describe the behavior of the prevalent culture, never seemed to listen at all. Mostly, they judged us based upon our use of coffee and tobacco. Most alcoholics already use tobacco and coffee as stimulants to kick-start their day. When they are trying to get free of alcohol, the craving for something, usually tobacco and coffee, is stronger than ever. To some degree, these two drugs serve as temporary crutches for the *recovering* addict. This fact is often overlooked, or unknown, by the Mormal Norman, who tends to view *all* use of tobacco and coffee as a barometer for low moral character. (See Appendix I, Part 4.)

Bishop Bruce was not a Mormal Norman. He told me that years earlier, as a construction worker, he had both smoked and drank beer. This fact explained why he was able to approach me without condescension or judgment. He didn't have any of these feelings! The bishop wasted no time in urging Vickie and me to return to Church activity. He challenged me to set a goal for Church membership.

The first step was pretty obvious as he advised, "You two need to get married!" There had been circumstances we were using to justify postponing our marriage. The bishop made it clear that we needed to resolve the issues and get on with it.

With the bishop's challenge and support, Vickie and I set a goal to be married in the autumn of 1984. The date arrived. The night our bishop married us, I felt a special spiritual "tingle;" and a longing for something I once knew. Arrayed in a white dress embellished with blue, yellow, and white flowers, Vickie was lovely. Our parents and friends came to join in the celebration. Everyone seemed to be looking to the future and encouraging us toward a better life. Vickie and I tried not to look back. We both felt that our Heavenly Father was more concerned about the direction we were headed than where we had been. (Note: It is common behavior for alcoholics and addicts to ignore the present. Rather, they live in the *guilt* of yesterday and in the *fear* of tomorrow. This focus leaves them powerless to affect their lives for good in *the Now*.)

Shortly after our marriage, another man came into our lives to provide needed encouragement and course correction. Bob, a Mexican-American, had recently moved from California into a home across the street. I knew he had often observed me smoking, and more than once wind had blown beer cans from my yard into his. In spite of this, and notwithstanding the fact that I usually ignored him, Bob always waved and yelled out a friendly greeting.

One day while I was working in the front yard, Bob crossed the street and introduced himself. Within minutes, he was relating his story. As a young man, he had lived a rowdy life. Then he was introduced to The Church of Jesus Christ of Latter-day Saints through missionaries and the Book of Mormon. He and his family were baptized. His eyes filled with tears as he related overcoming his addiction to drugs and alcohol. Then, he bore his testimony of the gospel of Jesus Christ. As a result of his warmth and openness, I felt an immediate bond of brotherhood. When Bob finished, I told him my story. But there were no tears with my telling and no happy ending. Bob understood.

Within a few weeks, my new friend had arranged a meeting with the elders quorum president, Brother Herbert, who, coincidentally, had also had a previous problem with the Word of Wisdom. With a similar nonjudgmental attitude as the bishop's and Bob's, President Herbert ignored my history and current condition and simply bore his testimony of the peace I would find by returning to Church activity. At the conclusion of our visit, he assigned home teachers[1] to visit Vickie and me.

Our first home teachers lasted only a few months. Before the year was over, I had alienated two more sets. My behavior toward the unsuspecting elders was demanding. Nearly all of those assigned to visit us followed the standard home teaching protocol of procrastinating the appointment until the last weekend of the month. When they did, I would tell them, more or less rudely depending upon my level of beer consumption, that I was not interested in helping them get their 100-percent-home-teaching mark for the month. In spite of my behavior, a set of good men kept doing their duty. Occasionally, I allowed them to visit. When they did, their humility and example had a special influence on me. I felt that I was taking tiny but sure steps forward.

March 9, 1985

I have worked nine months at the company where Vickie works. Performing numerous menial tasks at first, I have since worked up to project manager. I have repaid five thousand dollars on back child support and have helped Vickie with the bills for a change. Nearly everything I earn goes toward back child support and alimony, but at least I'm working steadily.

After a long day, I continue drinking in the evenings. For the most part, I feel crummy and run down, but things have been improving a little. I have even thought that maybe someday I could be rebaptized.

Last Sunday, Vic and I attended all of our church meetings. I have been exercising a little. I am slowly reaching that point the [AA] Old-Timers talk about of being "sick and tired of being sick and tired." I am sure something is changing for the better.

I don't have time to get into my children, their circumstances, my feelings, and so on. For now, I will just say I love them more than my own life. I ache for them. I am lonely and empty without them.

That summer, the bishop challenged me to be baptized.

July 7, 1985

I have spent the last hour reading through a few of the hundreds of pages of my old journals. Although it hurts to remember, I value this record of past experiences and feelings. I'm unsure if renewing the memories inspires or depresses me. Both, I guess.

I have been trying hard to stop drinking and smoking with little result. Following a business trip to Orlando, I failed to return to work for a week. No excuse. I was fired. Alcohol again.

I have worked full-time for the National Guard for the last month. The work should last until September then I have no idea what I'll do. I began jogging a little in the evening only to have it end in alcohol abuse.

I have been able to see my children occasionally of late.

I cling to little faith that I can overcome the addictions, and even less hope, *praying* occasionally. The bishop gave me a challenge to be baptized on August 31st. I don't see that miracle ever happening. I still love all that is good.

For every real effort I mounted, a real adversary had a counterattack. With cunning, he used discouragement, guilt, self-pity, and fear to derail my attempts to improve my condition. I hung on to a dim recollection of the feelings of the Spirit. I doubt there was ever a more lost and wandering sheep.

September 7, 1985

It's a cool, cloudy, fall evening—matches my mood. It has already snowed on Mt. Timp, and winter is not far away. Two months have passed without writing. I do so now only to distract from how I really feel. Not working. I'd say it's funny how life changes, if it was funny. Not much fun here.

I still work for the National Guard, at least until the end of September. Then what, I don't know. I have been alcohol sick and missed some work. I drink to numb the unbearable sadness; then drink to kill the pain created by the alcohol.

I prayed today for the first time in a month. But it just seems so hopeless. Vickie continues to encourage me. She is such a special lady. I appreciate her understanding and love her deeply. I just can't seem to do anything with myself.

Two of my children's birthdays just passed. I didn't get to see them. I feel farther from them than ever, but my love doesn't change.

I don't know how much longer I can keep this up. All I see is a cold, long, winter ahead. The IRS and Recovery Services [child support] hound me weekly. I will soon have no job. I am still a hopeless alcoholic.

Vickie is my friend. I love her but there are too many memories and too much pain to balance things out. *If only, if only . . . I could still teach seminary someday.* One thing is for sure, if I ever do, I'll be super-qualified to testify regarding Brother Alma's observation that "wickedness never was happiness."[2]

Although I failed to make my August baptismal date, the bishop continued to take a special interest in me. I tried to attend church more and harass the home teachers less. One of our home teachers was a seminary teacher. We became friends to the extent that an alcoholic excommunicant can be a friend to a pure and faithful man. Our relationship produced within me a longing for righteousness. Impressed by the light radiating from his face, he reminded me of someone I once knew—*me.* Whenever I was around him, memories of teaching seminary would flood my mind. Each recollection was a strange mixture of gratitude for having had the experiences and pain that I would most likely never have again. Interestingly, this pain was a growing pain in that these feelings increased my desire to someday be a righteous man.

My home teachers, aware that I had a love for music, encouraged me to join the ward choir. The bishop gave his permission and I began to attend. My first visit at practice was a new experience for the choir members. Like a fire-breathing dragon, I blew my whiskey and tobacco breath out over those seated around me. The occasional dagger-like glances from a few let me know I was inappropriately invading their space. I knew I was guilty. I didn't want to offend anyone. It was simply who I was at this time.

The only person in the choir who gave me more than a casual greeting was the *other excommunicant* in the group—the choir director. He had been rebaptized years earlier and had a sincere, happy demeanor. He was kind to me. His unmistakable concern for my welfare touched a part of me I had thought was past feeling.[3] The spirit of the hymns stirred a place in my soul that had been lifeless.

More than once, tears filled my eyes and I choked on the words. I felt the Spirit in my bosom; yet I ached with remorse at the same time.

These small stirrings had great effect on me. I was the hungry soul described by Elder Boyd K. Packer in one of his many sermons encouraging Latter-day Saints to fellowship less-active members of the Church.

> Undernourished children must be carefully fed; so it is with the spiritually underfed. Some are so weakened by mischief and sin that to begin with they reject the rich food we offer. They must be fed carefully and gently. Some are so near spiritual death that they must be spoon-fed on the broth of fellowship or nourished carefully on activities and programs.[4]

This little ward choir fed my soul chicken soup. The choir director provided fellowship for my starving spirit. Although their reasons may have been ones of desperation needing help for the struggling choir, I was grateful that they allowed my gentle feeding. Maybe it was a fair trade-off. I stunk, but I didn't sing half-bad. Dining on small portions of spiritual food at each choir practice began to nourish my weakened spirit.

November 11, 1985

> I have been practicing with the ward choir for several months. Yesterday, I sang with them in sacrament meeting—the first time I have participated in a Church meeting in *six years*. I debated outside the church whether to go in with Vickie, or just skip it. Choosing to go, I thought to myself that I wouldn't sing if the choir was called upon.
>
> When the announcement came for choir members to gather on the stand, Vic gave me a nudge and I stood up. Walking up the aisle with what felt like a zillion eyes burning holes in the back of my head, I took a seat in the choir.
>
> I'm glad I made the effort. How I enjoyed singing the beautiful hymns. Others saw, or smelled, me with unappreciative glances—at least from my guilty perception—but it was special and worth the nonverbal scolding.
>
> Yesterday may be as close as I ever get to any real church participation. Someone may find out that I am not a member and get me kicked out of the choir. Thank goodness for a bishop that understands, as the Savior taught, that "the Physician is for the sick." I

remember him once saying in a sacrament meeting something like, *I wish you could turn to some of your neighbors and not mind the smell of tobacco smoke on them. Then I would know that everyone feels welcome in our midst.*

I miss my children, especially on winter evenings like tonight. I remember playing with them in the snowy orchard on Grandview Hill, pulling them on the sleigh, building snow forts and snowmen, laughing, and being their friend. This is what makes it so hard. But I must keep hoping and believing that life will get better—if I just keep trying.

My fear of being unemployed turned out to be wasted energy. Late in the autumn, I interviewed and was hired in a full-time position with the Army National Guard. I would be providing administrative support for the Troop Medical Clinic at Camp Williams. My new boss was a bishop, and my working associates were active Latter-day Saints.

I hid my alcoholism for several months. Following Christmas, my evening drinking escalated into a major binge. I missed a week's work. With no excuse for my absence, I summoned all the courage I could to return to the clinic. My boss was prepared with an ultimatum. He informed me that the Army doesn't fire its drunks on the first strike. To remain employed, I would have to complete the VA Hospital's thirty-day alcohol rehabilitation program.

January 30, 1986 (VA Hospital in Salt Lake City)

On Sunday, I spent one more night of torture trying to get free of alcohol for the mandatory twenty-four hour period in order to be admitted into the VA hospital's alcohol rehab program. My new job is safe for the moment. I am hopeful about this program.

I stopped smoking *twenty days ago*. I have a feeling that I am at the beginning of a new way of life. I may be wrong, but pray I am not. I am hoping for rebaptism and activity in the Church. I pray God will help me use my experiences for good. For now, I feel a little peace and some confidence. I miss Vic and the kids.

The director of the VA's alcoholism program was a medical doctor, a recovering alcoholic, and an active member of the LDS Church. Dr. McFarland was the right person to encourage my growing hope.

We walked and talked together often. Understanding my guilt, he referred me to relevant scriptures, such as this one:

> Remember the worth of souls is great in the sight of God, for behold the Lord your Redeemer suffered death in the flesh; wherefore he suffered the pain of all men, that all men might repent and come unto him . . . And how great is his joy in the soul that repenteth. (Doctrine and Covenants 18:10, 13)

I had taught the process of repentance to others but could *not* apply it to myself. There were times I even wondered if I were beyond the Atonement's power. Dr. McFarland testified to me of simple facts that were encouraging and challenging.

"God places great worth on each of his children," he said. "God forgives *all* of His children *when* they repent."

Professionals, AA Old-Timers, and personal experience had correctly convinced me that alcoholism was a disease. My question to the doctor was, "How do I repent of a disease?"

Dr. McFarland taught me that I had already paid the price of my immorality through excommunication. He counseled me to stop giving so much attention to my alcoholism and get on to Church activity. With renewed faith in the healing power of repentance, I became truly hopeful.

After completing the VA program, I managed three months without coffee, tobacco, or alcohol, my longest period of sobriety in six years. I began paying tithing and, with new confidence in myself to remain sober, I felt worthy to approach my bishop for rebaptism.

Four years had passed since that Sunday morning when I read my moral inventory to Steve H. and took AA's Fifth Step—*Admitted to God, to myself, and another human being the exact nature of my wrongs.* During my stay at the VA, I realized I had not completed the actions for the next steps. Before meeting with my bishop, I wanted to make sure I had completed Steps Six through Nine as part of the repentance process.

I made a serious effort to work on Step Six—*Were entirely ready to have God remove all my defects of character.* I reviewed and added to the moral inventory I had written in Step Four. Then I began Step Seven with sincere prayer—*Humbly ask God to remove my shortcomings.* I knew this step could only be officially complete with the washing away of my "shortcomings" through rebaptism.

The Eighth Step is—*Make a list of all persons I have harmed, and become willing to make amends to them all;* and the Ninth Step— *Make direct amends to such people, wherever possible, except when to do so would injure them or others."* These two steps require significant courage to complete, and thus separate those persons willing to go to any lengths to achieve sobriety from those who are not. It takes great fortitude to complete these steps honestly. Persons who do complete them are more likely to achieve lengthy sobriety. Those who do not, eventually let the guilt of unresolved issues drive them back to their addictions. I was determined to travel this difficult stretch of the recovery path. I summoned all my courage.

I needed to make amends with only a few key people. My family members for sure. There were some others. One was especially difficult, the owner of the grocery store where I had worked after moving from Wyoming. After several months, I had quit this job in order to attend BYU. Years later and fully addicted to alcohol, I still shopped at the same store. I often used food stamps for payment. It was always embarrassing to encounter someone I knew. When I had no food, no money, no stamps, and no alcohol, I *still* made shopping trips to this store. With the knowledge I had acquired from my previous employment, I knew when security was most lax. It was then that I would wait for the opportune moment and fill my large basket with food, beer, and other things. Then, when I thought no one was watching, I would exit the store.

My last attempt at pulling off this caper ended suddenly when, as I was hurriedly pushing a basket of stolen items through the parking lot, a hand grasped my shoulder. When I turned, my heart sank. I was looking into the face of a store employee who had, years earlier, been my working associate. I will never forget the young man's sad expression or the grave words he spoke. "Phil, please don't do this to yourself!"

For reasons I didn't deserve, he still held some respect for me. He did not call the police, but the humiliation of jail would not have hurt worse than his next biting words. Speaking with authority, he said: "Just leave here now! And don't ever come back!"

Wishing I could cease to exist, I hung my head and walked from the parking lot. In that instant, my smoldering guilt burst into flame and torched in a tiny poof of spiritual smoke what was left of my self-esteem.

Now years later, having made a list of people I had harmed and wanted—needed—to make amends to, I made an appointment to visit the store manager at his home. I planned to apologize and offer restitution. With trepidation, I rang the doorbell. The man I knew well opened the door and invited me in. After I had confessed my shameful acts, sought his forgiveness, and offered to make things right, I was shocked at his response.

"Phil," he said, "your presence here today and the words you have spoken are restitution enough. I don't know why you did the things you did. You must have been pretty desperate."

I was unprepared for his kindness. I told him I was preparing for rebaptism and that my visiting him was an important step toward that goal. He seemed to understand. As I was departing, he commented that my coming had meant a great deal to him. He wished me godspeed.

February 17, 1986 (Journal Record—Letter to Bishop)

Dear Bishop,

I would like to express the feelings of my heart, which might be considered in the matter of my rebaptism. First, I did go through a period of anger and bitterness following my excommunication, but it was not directed at the Church. Rather, my anger was directed at me. I couldn't accept that so much bad had happened. My life has been one of extremes, from burning with joy as I taught the gospel, to the burning of blackness that comes from transgressing the laws of God. I have come to totally accept the judgment of the Church High Council Court and realize the blessing this has been in my life.

The years following my excommunication have been ones of pain and darkness. I have lived in remembrance of my testimony. I have had little peace. I have believed I would never control my alcoholism. I know that my use of alcohol led directly to actions that resulted in my excommunication. I felt hopeless and in total despair. I have tried in every way I know to stop drinking. I have never stopped praying in my heart and on my knees that I would somehow get help. For years, the heavens have seemed closed and dark.

I have attended many meetings of Alcoholics Anonymous. I have felt a spiritual power there and learned much about my disease. My hope is that someday I might use my experience to bring insight to other Church members who have drug and alcohol problems.

My wife and I hope that someday we might be able to enter the temple together and know the joy of having an eternal marriage. I live in gratitude for all my Heavenly Father has given me. I am especially grateful for experiences that have taught me a little about life. I desire deeply to be numbered among the Saints again, to join my testimony and work with theirs.

Sincerely,

Brother Phil Simkins

A month later, I received a letter from the stake where I was excommunicated. The document informed me that the high council required my presence as they reviewed my petition for rebaptism. As I entered the high council room on an evening in March 1986, the experience I had was exactly opposite of that on December 26, 1980. Five years earlier, I had appeared before stern men sitting in judgment. This night, this same council radiated a "welcome home" love and a respect for my sincere repentance. They asked questions about my worthiness. How long had I been living the Word of Wisdom? Since my release from the VA Hospital. Was I paying a full tithing? Yes. Was I keeping the commandments required for rebaptism? Yes.

I was able to answer their inquiries honestly and from my heart. Following their decision to recommend my rebaptism, each hugged me warmly. These were men whom I barely knew. Still they cared and expressed joy that I was coming home.

During that evening, I experienced the saving power that comes through Church disciplinary action. During my years of excommunication, some people told me that the Church had no right to take away my membership or enter into my personal life. I wanted to believe them but I knew that Church discipline was based upon correct principle of *choice and consequence*. That night, the Holy Ghost witnessed the truth of this to me. According to these judges in Israel, I had satisfied the requirements for rebaptism. My repentance qualified me for Church membership.

When the day of my baptism came and as I was dressing in my white baptismal clothes, my bishop came to offer some wise counsel. I recorded his words in my journal.

> Phil, although I am baptizing you tonight, remember this doesn't mean that you must live perfectly from here on. None of us do. You may even have a slip with alcohol in the future. Don't let that set you back. Keep coming to your Church meetings, forgive yourself, *be your own best friend,* and continue forward.

Although I appreciated his counsel, it seemed out of context in view of the event about to occur. *The thought of me drinking again? Impossible! Nothing was going to slow my momentum.*

April 6, 1986

About 7:50 p.m. on Wednesday, the second of April, I walked down into the baptismal waters wearing my white temple jumpsuit. It had been with a heavy heart that, years earlier, I had folded my temple garments and jumpsuit and placed them into Grandpa Haycock's little, green temple suitcase. I had wondered then if I would ever open the case again. But a miracle has occurred—*I have been rebaptized!*

Before entering the font, I said a few words to the group who had come to support me. With tears in my eyes and with the Spirit in my heart, I shared my thankfulness for having arrived back home after having wandered so long in the wilderness—a miracle I thought could never happen, was happening. The tears in Mom's and Vickie's eyes testified of their gratitude for this event. How I love them both. No one has known my struggles and supported and loved me more than these two precious women.

Standing in the warm water, thoughts filled my mind: *I am about to become a member of God's kingdom on earth again. I will be able to take the sacrament, the holy emblems of re-covenant. I will be able to say a prayer in Church, teach a class, and speak in a sacrament meeting. Most of all, my old friend and Comforter, the Holy Ghost, will again be my companion.*

There, in the font, before my friends and family, I felt humble and vulnerable as a small child. Tears ran down my cheeks and splashed into the warm water as the bishop called me by name, stated his sacred authority and then buried me beneath the water's surface.[5]

Following my baptism, the bishopric laid their hands upon my head and the bishop confirmed me a *member* of The Church of Jesus Christ of Latter-day Saints and said, *"Receive the Holy Ghost."*

NOTES

1. *Home Teachers.* Home teachers, assigned in pairs from ward priesthood quorums, represent the bishop in visiting and supporting each family in the ward. Home teachers usually visit two or three families monthly to determine special needs and deliver a message from the bishop. Following the monthly visit, home teachers report to their quorum leaders, who then convey any special needs or concerns to the bishop.

2. *Wickedness Not Happiness.* "Do not suppose, because it has been spoken concerning restoration, that ye shall be restored from sin to happiness. Behold, I say unto you, wickedness never was happiness" (Book of Mormon, Alma 41:10).

3. *Past Feeling.*

> Ye are swift to do iniquity but slow to remember the Lord your God. Ye have seen an angel, and he spake unto you; yea, ye have heard his voice from time to time; and he hath spoken unto you in a still small voice, but ye were past feeling, that ye could not feel his words; wherefore, he has spoken unto you like unto the voice of thunder, which did cause the earth to shake as if it were to divide asunder. (Book of Mormon, 2 Nephi 17:45)

4. Boyd K. Packer, "Feed My Sheep," *Ensign*, May 1984, 41.

5. *Baptism.*

> Baptism is to be administered in the following manner unto all those who repent—The person who is called of God and has authority from Jesus Christ to baptize, shall go down into the water with the person who has presented himself or herself for baptism, and shall say, calling him or her by name: Having been commissioned of Jesus Christ, I baptize you in the name of the Father, and of the Son, and of the Holy Ghost. Amen. Then shall he immerse him or her in the water, and come forth again out of the water. (Doctrine and Covenants 20:72–74)

Neither did they receive any unto baptism save they came forth with a broken heart and a contrite spirit, and witnessed unto the church that they truly repented of all their sins.

And none were received unto baptism save they took upon them the name of Christ, having a determination to serve him to the end.

And after they had been received unto baptism, and were wrought upon and cleansed by the power of the Holy Ghost, they were numbered among the people of the church of Christ; and their names were taken, that they might be remembered and nourished by the good word of God, to keep them in the right way, to keep them continually watchful unto prayer, relying alone upon the merits of Christ, who was the author and the finisher of their faith. (Moroni 6:2–4)

$\mathcal{I}$ STOOD AT THE TURNING POINT

Even so I would that ye should remember, and always retain in remembrance, the greatness of God, and your own nothingness . . . and humble yourselves even in the depths of humility. . . . For behold, are we not all beggars?

—Mosiah 4:11, 19

HAVING STOPPED SMOKING AND DRINKING, MY CRAVINGS shifted to chocolate. My weight soared to over two hundred pounds. At five feet, eight inches, I felt as wide as I was tall. Determined to reverse this sudden increase in body fat, I began jogging. At first, I could barely run a block. I stayed at it until I could run a mile without stopping. By mid-summer 1986, I was running ten miles most evenings and fifteen miles on weekends. The fat had disappeared.

I managed to stay sober nearly six months before I started drinking and smoking again. It was not a binge or a major fall off the sobriety wagon, rather the rationalization of an alcoholic's "stinkin' thinkin'." My alcoholic mind believed that I could reward my running effort with a beer and a smoke in the evening. It seems incomprehensible now, but I was running dozens of miles a week to justify having a few beers. AA had taught me that I had to become willing to go to any length to stay sober. Now it seemed I was willing to run any distance to drink. My bishop's words were proving ever so prophetic! My baptism had given me Church membership, but it had not removed my medical tag for alcoholism.

Using a nearby canyon as a training area, I would run for hours without stopping. Then, drenched with perspiration, I would relax in my truck with a beer in one hand and a smoke in the other. But, in spite of the negative habits, my running regimen was having an overall good effect. My body was becoming healthier, and my self-discipline was increasing. I seldom drank to drunkenness. My desire to run began to give me more power to combat my negative habits. In addition, my spirit had been strengthened with baptism and the gift of the Holy Ghost.

September 1986

When I get feeling low and thinking I've made no progress, I look back over the year and see much positive change. Yes, there is still a lot of conflict. I'm struggling again with beer and cigarettes. But my testimony is returning, little by little, and my determination to be prepared for whatever the Lord requires, continues. I am not giving up.

Having the day off yesterday, I drove up Hobble Creek Canyon and clocked out a fifteen-mile course. Beginning at Jolley's Ranch, I ran to the end of the asphalt in Right Hand Canyon. Then, without stopping, I turned around and ran all the way back. Fifteen miles in two hours and eighteen minutes. I wanted desperately to quit after twelve miles. It hurt badly but I kept running until I finished the fifteen. It was as painful as any physical experience I can remember, except withdrawal from alcohol. But this was a far different pain. I controlled it. I could simply stop running to stop hurting. I had a choice. With alcohol withdrawal, all I could do was wait until the physical and mental anguish subsided.

I know that I will run again and much longer distances and will probably hurt more than yesterday. But I can do it. Although I ran today, I still struggle with old habits that haunt me. I guess I'm just melancholy reflecting on the day, the past week, a twelve-mile run up the back side of Mt. Timp on Labor Day . . . the wonder of God's mountainous earth stretching out far above and below me.

I have many other thoughts, feelings of unworthiness for the callings now coming to me. I remember what my bishop said about staying active. I am not giving up, in spite of my Word of Wisdom failings.

I need to end now, but want to record that on Saturday I attended

Josh's baptism and on Sunday witnessed his confirmation. The tears ran off my cheeks as I watched my precious little boy, dressed in a white shirt and bow tie, being confirmed a member of the Church and given the Holy Ghost by a complete stranger. I know I deserved it—but only those who have experienced this, can understand the pain. It's *not* the kind you stop.

An unusual event was about to occur that would provide a much-needed boost. A counselor in the stake presidency, President Christensen, had requested a meeting with me. At the appointment, I explained to him that I had been drinking alcohol earlier that evening. Ignoring my confession, he made a surprising request. Would I address the stake general priesthood meeting in one week? Shocked, I respectfully asked if he had understood what I had just revealed. I didn't even hold the priesthood. Was he sure? He said he was aware of my priesthood standing but had not anticipated the alcohol on my breath. Still he said he felt impressed that I should speak. He again extended the invitation. Who was I to question his sanity? I gave him my unenthusiastic consent. Then he called in the stake clerk, and together they laid their hands upon my head. President Christensen gave me a powerful priesthood blessing. I left the church feeling the influences of two strong, opposing powers: the first one dark and destructive—alcohol—and the second, brilliant and life-giving—the priesthood of God.

A few months previous, Vickie and I had spoken in our ward's sacrament meeting. But then, I had been sober four months and enjoyed a tiny bit of self-confidence. For the stake priesthood meeting, if I could manage, I would have just one week's sobriety and a whole bunch of fear.

The tears ran off my cheeks as I watched my precious little boy, dressed in a white shirt and bow tie, being confirmed a member of the Church and given the Holy Ghost by a complete stranger.

129

The assignment to speak at stake priesthood meeting came at a pivotal time for my encouragement. I have since wondered if the stake presidency was somehow aware of how close I was to slipping back into full-blown alcoholism and had purposely designed this challenge for me. One thing I was certain—my invitation to speak, considering my Word of Wisdom problem, was *not* Church protocol. Someone must have been inspired to bend the rules.

President Christensen's blessing, my experience speaking, and the thank-you note I received following the Priesthood meeting had a marvelous effect on me. A most credible source—the stake presidency—believed in me. Although I was still using alcohol, to them, my behavior did not classify me as a leper.

September 23, 1986 (Journal Record—Letter from the Stake President)

Dear Brother Simkins,

May I take this time to thank you for your work in preparing and speaking in our stake general priesthood meeting. Your testimony of the Priesthood and of the gospel is greatly appreciated. Those who came were fed greatly by the spirit of our Father in Heaven. It takes great courage to stand and bear your testimony the way you did.

I want you to know how much you are loved by us and by the Lord. The spirit at this meeting was strong and well received. You were a great part in making this meeting a success and we thank you for it. May the Lord bless you and be with you in your needs. Thanks again!

Sincerely,

President Snyder

Having trained all summer, I became serious about running a marathon. I ran 168 miles in the final month of preparation. On the first Friday of October in 1986, I drove alone to St. George, Utah, to participate in their well-known marathon. Arising early on Saturday morning, I drove to the park where buses were supposed to be waiting to convey runners to the race. To my dismay, I had confused the time of departure. The buses had already left! I could drive to the starting point, but my truck was out of gas and I had left my wallet at the motel. In addition, I had no idea where the race began. I only knew that it started at 6:00 a.m. and was at least twenty-six miles away. For me, finishing the marathon was more than running a race. I had been losing for years. Running and finishing the marathon symbolized winning. But I might have already been too late. It was now five thirty.

With each stride, I started repeating, "I can make it. I can make it." And I did! I completed the St. George Marathon in three hours and thirty minutes, a full half hour ahead of my goal.

I rushed to an all-night gas station and explained my circumstances to the attendant. This Good Samaritan woman gave me directions to the starting point, paid for my gasoline, and sent me dashing out the door with her blessing. Traveling at top speed, I used up all of the Gas Lady's blessing to arrive just moments before the race began.

With the sharp crack of the starter's gun, a thousand runners, in a great wave of humanity, lunged forward with a loud shout. I was at the end, but I was in the pack. As the miles ticked off, my legs began to feel like dead stumps. By the last few miles, I had no energy left. A deep ache began to envelope my body. With each stride, I started repeating, "I can make it. I can make it." And I did! I completed the St. George Marathon in three hours and thirty minutes, a full half-hour ahead of my goal.

But the high I had experienced in running the marathon was short-lived. Gravity set in.

November 17, 1986

I have felt super depressed the last few weeks. I am drinking more in the evenings and eating Valium like it's candy. The Troop Medical Clinic prescribes it for me. I think they believe it helps me drink less. It is easy to see why this drug has become so popular, especially with Church members. I learned this in the LDS Substance Abuse Program. [Dr. McFarland from the VA Hospital introduced Vickie and me to this pilot Church-sponsored program. We had attended a few meetings at a stake center in West Jordan, Utah.] Valium has no smell. Hard for anyone to know you are taking it, especially in Church; except that sometimes you fall asleep in the middle of a sentence. The drug is fairly easy to get since it is prescribed for nerves. There seems to be a lot of that going around these days.

The Christmas season didn't help my mood or my addiction.

December 27, 1986

On Christmas Eve, I picked up Josh [now 8]. We went to the drugstore to buy a present for his Mom. I felt such a deep helplessness and sadness as I watched my little boy search for something that might be special. Walking around the store, I tried to enjoy just being close to him. But it hurt seeing his Christmas Eve excitement knowing I wouldn't be with him the next morning.

After taking him home, I drove back home in the cold winter night. An overwhelming power of darkness and pain filled my soul—more than I could bear. I hadn't had a drink in several weeks and had hoped to make it through Christmas. With very little thought, I stopped, bought a six-pack of beer, and drank it all swiftly in a futile attempt to kill the pain. *It didn't make any difference!*

Just after midnight on New Year's Eve, my fifteen-year-old son, Michael, called from a phone booth and asked if I would come and get him. He explained that, earlier in the evening, he'd had a serious fight with his Mom. He couldn't go home. For me, every New Year's Eve was a struggle to get through without alcohol. My son's request gave me reason to feel grateful that I had managed this one sober.

Once retrieved and warmed with cocoa, Mike spent hours into the night sharing his feelings with Vickie and me. I had never heard him express himself this way. But then I hadn't been around for years to hear him express much of anything.

The next morning, I called Mike's mom. We agreed that it would be best if he lived with me. Our daughter, Brooke, who had been living with me, would move back with her mother.

I made several trips between cities in my small pickup to switch my two children. My youngest son, Josh, rode along. When the moving was completed, I drove him home. No words spoken. Although I loved him deeply, we were more strangers than father and son.

As the miles passed, my thoughts drifted back to a hot July day, a month before Josh had turned two. I was out of money and at the end of a week-long bout of drunkenness. I had returned to the house to fetch my deer rifle and shotgun to hock. The last of the alcohol was wearing off, and I had only one thing in mind. But my wife met me at the door with divorce papers. We exchanged harsh words, and I went to the basement to get my guns. Leaving the house, I hurried up the street to where a drinking companion was waiting in his truck. Josh had overheard the argument and came running out of the house, bawling, tearing up the street toward me as fast as his little legs would carry him. I turned to see him coming and stood frozen with guns in hand for a moment. Then I realized that if he reached me, I would have to return him to the house and face his mother. I climbed in the truck and told my friend to drive away. The image of my little boy running through the dust toward me as I drove off would never leave me. It would do little good now to say I was sorry for that morning. He most likely wouldn't remember. No matter how badly I wanted to, I would never be able to remove the effect of that incident on either of us. It was just something we would have to live with. As we neared the end of our trip, I knew Josh's and my thoughts were miles apart. He stared out the window into the dark night with his head against his hand. The fact that his brother was gone was beginning to settle in—no more brothers sharing basketball after school; no more wrestling together on the floor; no more sharing bedrooms—no more Michael. There was nothing I could do.

January 15, 1987

My heart aches as I think about my son Michael so caught up in the drug and music culture he has embraced. I hug him and tell him I love him and he hugs me back—but words can't make up for time lost or undo the loneliness and pain he has known since the divorce. Before, while I was part of the family, we were such great pals, always playing and laughing together. Then, one morning he woke up with *no dad*.

Where have the past six years gone? I have been so selfish with my own problems that I haven't realized his life was being sacrificed. I have myself to blame for his seeking relief of loneliness in drugs. After all, he has only been doing what I did, seeking to numb the pain. I have thought about him constantly over the past years, yet I have not thought about what he has been going through—maybe I just couldn't.

Through no fault of his, he was suddenly made abnormal through the divorce. When all of his friends were going with their dads on Scouting activities and other occasions, he had to be "adopted" to participate. I guess he only did what was natural, turning to those who would accept him and offer the friendship he lost. Looking back, I ponder—*would it have made any difference had I known how his life would be so terribly altered on the day I drank the cooking sherry?* But knowing what I now know about addiction, I doubt it. Like the line in *Against The Wind*, "I wish I didn't know now what I didn't know then.'

I spoke with Jenny [Mike's mom] on the phone tonight. She cried, saying that, since he had been gone, it felt as if a death had occurred in the family. I spoke with Josh. He just wanted his brother back. I couldn't tell him but I knew his brother would never be back.

That winter, Vickie and I often attended AA and Al-Anon meetings. Vickie usually went to Al-Anon, the twelve-step program giving support to those living with alcoholics. I was managing to stay sober except for a few minor slips. By the late spring, however, my sporadic drinking turned into a major field-testing expedition.

Before this binge, I had been doing fairly well—sober over three months—and living by the Twelve Steps. But an unusual circumstance set me up for a major fall off the sobriety wagon.

My wife and I had acquired an unusual hobby. Because we had

little money, we often went "dumpster diving." On Sunday mornings, we would seek out large refuse containers that might produce discarded items such as furniture or other useful things for the house. One Sunday morning, I was digging through a large container when to my amazement I found a small barrel filled with a half dozen unopened bottles of liquor. I yelled to Vickie to come and check out my unexpected find. We concluded that some drunk had failed his latest field test. Most likely, he had been hauled away to the hospital or the morgue. We surmised that someone had placed his remaining supply of booze into the small barrel and tossed it in the dumpster. To prevent youths from discovering the liquor, we emptied the bottles. Well, almost all them. Still remaining was a full bottle of tequila packed neatly in a red, velvet-lined box. It was too tempting. The packaging gave no clue of its contents. It looked so appealing, especially to me. The thought occurred that, unless I spared it, we would have no way of proving this dumpster diving novelty. (Talk about stinkin' thinkin'!) I gave Vickie my lame motive for keeping the bottle and tucked it away.

Back home, I placed the boxed-up bottle at the top of our bedroom closet and forgot about it—almost. But, like a kid at the candy store with a coin burning in his pocket, not many days passed before I began my final field test. I "spent" the fifth of tequila. The binge lasted a while. I emerged from my bedroom only to get more "testing materials." Otherwise, I just slept and drank. Having had extensive experience with my binges, Vickie could only open the door to see if I was still breathing.

After a week, unwilling to witness my slow suicide any longer, she decided intervention was necessary. She made a deal with the people at the Troop Medical Clinic where I still worked to support my admittance to one more treatment center. The binge had run its course. I willingly accepted the offer.

Remaining at this facility for a week, I began to feel alive again. The staff had been extraordinary in their encouragement. Leaving treatment "bright-eyed and bushy-tailed," I felt a renewed commitment to my wife, to the clinic, and to myself that I would *never, ever* drink again. My wife told me that, promise or no promise, she would no longer stand by and watch me die. But this time, I was confident.

I was convinced I had reached the lowest bend of the alcoholic pipe-line and was heading up the recovery side.

I was wrong. *"Never, ever"* is too long a time for an alcoholic to commit to. Two months later, I checked back into the same treatment facility.

I was crushed. I was certain there would be no more chances with my wife. I knew there shouldn't be. The fact that I had let her down was one thing, but there was more. The National Guard had relieved me from duty—*permanently*! Then, following a medical exam at the treatment center for a painful hip, I was informed that, at the young age of forty, I had degenerative arthritis. If I wanted to continue walking, I would need a total hip replacement!

"You have to hit *your* bottom," the Old-Timers say. Like the funny little fellow with the big ears at the Alcohol Recovery Center had advised me many years earlier, "You have to be willing to crawl through cut glass to get sober!" Well, shattered glass was all around. I had hit bottom directly in the middle of it.

I knew I had. I hit my bottom like a concrete block plunging down through a twelve-story building, shattering glass as it went. When I hit, I didn't even bounce—I just crunched into a lifeless heap. More than a degenerative hip joint, *I was a degenerative disease*—degenerative addiction, degenerative marriage, degenerative soul. Depression rolled over me like the waves of a dark, stormy ocean. Heavy and suffocating, my condition was more than I could bear. I had no more tries left in me. I despaired. I prayed. My prayers were unlike any I had ever uttered. I didn't ask for anything. Not to stay sober. Not to have my job back. Not for my wife to stay. Not to feel peace. Not to remove my pain. Not for anything! I was conquered. All I could do was mutter words about my total nothingness and cry out for help.

As my prayers continued, something about the way I viewed life began to change. It was not as if I had been struck with sudden brilliance. I was not filled with the burnings of truth or peace. I realized it was futile to say, *"This time* I'm going to stay sober," or "I promise . . ." It was just the opposite. Alcohol had won. I was broken. I knew I couldn't stay sober—no matter what. As this realization settled upon me, for the first time in my life, I honestly and completely admitted my powerlessness and gave my life totally over to a Power greater than myself. With childlike demeanor, I humbly asked for God's protection, direction, and care. As a hopeless beggar, I surrendered all of me into the waiting arms of my Heavenly Father. *"Do with me what you will. I can do nothing."*

I began to feel tiny stirrings within me—a feeling of warmth, barely detectable, as if a tiny penlight had turned on in my bosom. A powerful key turned. Somehow, I knew in my heart that it *could* be over. I stood at that point I had heard described in hundreds of AA meetings—the testimony of myriad alcoholics who had hit bottom and had found the only way up: "Half measures availed us nothing. We stood at the *turning* point. We asked His protection and care with complete abandon."[1]

I knew I didn't possess the ability to manage *all* of my life. I couldn't even manage a small piece of it. I suddenly understood that if I could just focus my energy *on today,* turning the *guilt* of yesterday and the *fear* of tomorrow over to God, then this terrible ordeal could be over. Like finding and putting in place a long lost, last piece of a puzzle, the picture became clear. I understood what to do. My life could be pieced back together—I simply needed to do it in humility and surrender—and *one moment at a time!*

Elder Neal A. Maxwell has taught:

The submission of one's will is really the only uniquely personal thing we have to place on God's altar. The many other things we "give," brothers and sisters, are actually the things He has already given or loaned to us. However, when you and I finally submit ourselves, by letting our individual *wills* be swallowed up in God's will, then we are really giving something to Him! *It is the only possession which is truly ours to give!* Consecration thus constitutes the only unconditional surrender which is also a total victory![2]

Elder Robert D. Hales teaches us that:

The Lord is the ultimate caregiver. *We must surrender ourselves to the Lord. In doing so, we give up whatever is causing our pain and turn everything over to Him.* "Cast thy burden upon the Lord, and he shall sustain thee" (Psalm 55:22). "And then may God grant unto you that your burdens may be light, through the joy of his Son" (Alma 33:23). Through faith and trust in the Lord and obedience to His counsel, we make ourselves eligible to be partakers of the Atonement of Jesus Christ so that one day we may return to live with Him.[3]

NOTES

1.   *Alcoholics Anonymous* (Alcoholics Anonymous World Services Inc., 1976), 58.

2.   Neal A. Maxwell. "Swallowed Up in the Will of the Father," *Ensign*, November 1995, 24, emphasis added.

3.   Robert D. Hales. "Healing Soul and Body," *Ensign*, November 1998, 17, emphasis added.

$\mathcal{H}$ORSESHOES & TESTIMONY

Looking for that blessed hope, and the glorious appearing of the great God and our Savior Jesus Christ, who gave himself for us, that he might redeem us from all iniquity, and purify unto himself a peculiar people, zealous of good works.

—Titus 2:13–14

H ALLOWEEN NIGHT 1987, A STORM FILLED THE VALLEY WITH dark, moisture-laden clouds. Goblin winds harvested autumn leaves, whipping them about sidewalks and streets. Memories of happier times trick-or-treating with my children haunted me. It was a most melancholy evening. From experience, I should have recognized these conditions as a mortal threat to my four months' sobriety.

Vickie had taken the kids to visit friends and left me home to dispense Halloween treats. Early in the evening, a friend of my daughter's stopped by to ask if I would buy her a bottle of Annie Green Springs wine for a Halloween toast. I had already had a white-knuckled day. Ignoring nagging alerts from my conscience, I gave in to the favor.

I had learned in AA that anyone sliding down the pipeline of alcoholism could hit bottom and reverse directions by surrendering; or in other words, admitting that he is powerless over alcohol and then turning his will and life over to God. The point at which one hits bottom varies by person, but the key to recovery is certain: *Complete and honest surrender to God.*

I believed I had hit my bottom, surrendered, and was on my way up. I was so sure of this fact that, upon leaving the last treatment center, I went into AA's central office and purchased, in advance, my own sobriety chips. An AA sobriety chip is a small, coin-like medallion used to reward individuals for achieving periods of successful sobriety. A person's AA sponsor[1] usually awards each chip as it is earned in sobriety. I bought a chip for the first, third, sixth and ninth months of continuous sobriety and the coveted "one-year chip." On September 27, I had accomplished three months of sobriety, and Vickie had given me my three-month chip in a AA meeting. But by Halloween, my six-month chip was in peril.

As I drove to the liquor store to buy the wine for my daughter's friend, I rationalized that this particular wine was more like a fruit-juicy soda than alcohol. It was no big deal. It wasn't like I was buying her hard liquor. And for sure, I wasn't buying anything for myself. As I walked into the store, the Old-Timers' caution flashed through my mind, "If you don't want to get bitten, don't go where there are snakes!" I passed by the rows of colorful bottles, looking for the wine. Then, suddenly all of my old favorite brands began to beckon, *Come to me on this lonely evening. I'm your friend. I'll take care of your pain.*

Stinkin' thinkin', as the Old-Timers call it, took over. The memory of previous drinking episodes and the throwing up, aching, sick to death, filled with remorse, defeated, depressed, and hopeless state faded into the background. All that mattered most was being seduced away by what mattered least—the seemingly animate bottles. I had walked directly into a huge, writhing snake pit.

My stinkin' thinkin' brain churned. *Maybe I can have just one tiny drink on this sad, windy, filled with memories of my children and yesteryear, night.* Although the past months had held some new hope, they had been difficult, painful, and nearly overwhelming at times. Now, standing in the liquor store surrounded by my old friends, inviting and enticing, I began to ponder which one I might drink *safely*.

Then, my eyes fell upon the sparkling bottles of Annie Green Springs. Suddenly, I was jolted back to reality. *Whoa, Phil, wait a minute! What do you think you're doing? Do you really want to throw away all of your hard-fought-for sobriety months?* My stinkin' thinkin' began to turn. *How could I get out of this predicament? What did the Old-Timers advise?* I remembered, "If you're over the edge, you've decided to drink, and nothing is going stop you, call your sponsor or another sober drunk. If that's not possible, start saying the Serenity Prayer as fast as you can. It works like a miracle. It's the one thing that can save you."

Part of me resisted; it wanted a drink—badly. But the words of the prayer began to form in my mind: *God grant me the serenity to accept the things I cannot change*—images of friends holding hands in AA meetings came into my mind—*courage to change the things I can*—get out of there—*and the wisdom to know the difference.*

November 4, 1987

I am unsure of what happened in the liquor store Halloween night. I *am sure* that I had chosen to drink. Somehow, I was able to *think through the drink to the consequences.* This is the first time I have been able to predict the certainty of the future based on past experience and *then* make the *sane* choice.

By saying the Serenity Prayer, strength entered my body. I turned and left the store without the Halloween toast, *or anything else.* I still don't understand how I escaped. That little prayer must have summoned a guardian angel or two.

Reflecting tonight, I gratefully thank a Higher Power for my safe emergence from the rattlesnake pit. I thank whoever wrote that wonderful little prayer packed with so much power. I humbly thank my Father in Heaven for answering it. No doubt—He did!

Late that autumn, an unplanned event added a needed boost to my recovery. What began as another routine day of unemployment turned into a remarkable experience. A warm fall morning had made conditions perfect for a trip to the park to read and write. I arrived at my favorite place, a comfortable table facing the mountains, and began writing. Glancing up now and then, I feasted on the golden and red colors that were beginning to blanket the eastern mountains.

Shortly, an elderly man dressed in bib overalls rode up on a bicycle. He was toting a set of horseshoes. Parking his bike, he walked to a nearby pit and began tossing the game pieces. One after the other, each piece floated through the air in a slow circling motion and landed, nearly every time, encircled about the narrow steel target. *This man is no beginner,* I thought. I soon lost interest in my writing and began to observe the skill on display. Several minutes passed. The man gathered up his horseshoes and, taking a course past my table, walked toward the bicycle he arrived on. I was sure to offer a greeting would risk a lengthy conversation. I couldn't resist. "Good morning," I said.

My greeting prompted the man to explain that the horseshoes were trophies for having won first place in a state championship *forty years* earlier. I knew the telling of this yarn would not be spun in the few minutes I hadn't allotted for this conversation. Still, I was intrigued. I sensed a deep character in this man. I liked him immediately. I was sure I could learn more than the proper technique for throwing a horseshoe—and I knew why. He continued to be warm and friendly even after noticing my pack of cigarettes on the table. (I had started and stopped smoking cigarettes a half dozen times over the past year.) As I spoke with him I thought, *Maybe this man is a true Christian.*

Now introduced, Lawrence asked what I was writing about. To answer truthfully would guarantee an increased length to our conversation, but his attitude had me curious. "Alcoholism," I replied.

"Who's the alcoholic?" he asked.

Now I would test his real charity. "Me," I answered.

"I've known some awfully good people who are alcoholics," he said. "I used to work with one at a car dealership a few years ago. No better man than a sober alcoholic," was Lawrence's casual observation.

This was not the comment I expected.

"Do you know Ray C.?" he asked.

Not waiting for an answer, he continued, "Ray C., now there was a fine man in spite of his weakness with the liquor."

The truth was I did know Ray C. He had befriended me more than once. I had heard his story many time in AA. He had been sober many years—another miracle story of someone who had found God through AA.

I was beginning to understand why this fellow hadn't made some *Mormal Norman* wisecrack about my cigarettes. My experience with

Lawrence was far different from the one I'd had a few days earlier. I had just finished unloading leaves from my pickup in a vacant field near my home and was smoking a cigarette. A lady I knew from my ward walked by and interrupted my break. Without any greeting, she uttered, "Looks like you got a "coffin nail" there to pollute *my* fresh air." She might as well have said, "You're the stupidest man I've ever seen. I hope you die a terrible, horrible death from smoking those putrid vile things." Her comment, and the way she said it, had made me want to continue polluting "her air" forever. (In defense of this good woman, I found out later that her husband had died from cigarette caused lung cancer.) The emotions Lawrence created within me that morning were the exact opposite. His kindness made me a bit ashamed. I *wanted* to throw my cigarettes away.

Before we parted, my new friend explained that he was an ordinance worker in the Provo Utah Temple. He spoke of his joy in this labor. He told me that he had helped many men obtain the Melchizedek Priesthood and go to the temple. He described his happiness when each one did. I knew his motive, but it didn't matter. He had qualified to testify of the truths of the temple. In a quiet manner, Lawrence exemplified the pure love of Christ. He didn't have to bear

In a quiet manner, Lawrence exemplified the pure love of Christ. He didn't have to bear his testimony. He was his testimony!

his testimony. He *was* his testimony! My "good morning" had been richly rewarded. Our visit supercharged my desire to become worthy to return to the house of the Lord.

The year ended without compromise to my sobriety. Unemployed and with much time for thought, each day was difficult but not impossible. It took strength and vigilance, but I managed to keep my thinking out of yesterday's guilt and tomorrow's fear. Surrendering my will, moment by moment, to God, I tried to live "one day at a time." Because this is a difficult concept for a non-addict to understand, I will illustrate.

It is human nature to want to be alone in the driver's seat; to control events and other people. But this desire is a luxury the recovering alcoholic *cannot* afford. "*I* need to get a job." "*I* need to pay the bills." "*I* need to give my son a college education." "*I* need my children to behave." All these are important needs, but for the recovering addict, the word *I* signals that, in his self-talk, he is no longer allowing God to help him. He is relying *upon himself and his own strength* for the things he must do. The addict's history gives concrete proof that relying upon himself results in disaster. In AA's Step Three, we turn our will and our life over to a higher power. For the addict, this must involve *complete surrender;* otherwise, our faith in the future is supplanted by fear. Our ego, or in other words, our willpower, our insistence on maintaining control takes over and invalidates our surrender to God. Likewise, we find that, focusing on the guilt of the past, we cannot deal with all of the wreckage that has built up through our drinking. We repair what we can, but the rest of the wreckage we surrender to God. Then we live in the present, one day at a time. If we don't, sooner or later *we will drink again.* (See Appendix I, Part 2.)

Applying daily surrender in my life made it possible for Vickie to award me a six-month chip at the Friday night group AA meeting late in December. I had been elected chairperson for this particular group several months earlier. Participating in AA, living by the Twelve Steps, praying, turning my will over to God, reading the scriptures, and helping friends were all keys to my staying sober through the end of the year. I began thinking about taking the next steps.

January 2, 1988

Rather than belabor any lengthy attempts to write about 1987, I
will make a quick statement about this year of personal struggle.
The most important thing I can record is that on December 27, I
celebrated six months of continuous sobriety. Doing a lot of white-
knuckled nail-biting, I made it through the holidays. I'm sure I don't
recognize the importance of this accomplishment. I pray that on
June 27 I will celebrate that elusive One-Year Sober.

I also pray that at this time next year, I will feel more of Christ's
love and know more of His peace. Perhaps I will be able to report
being closer to having my Priesthood blessings restored.[2]

Although I was staying sober, I had little serenity. I had tried to
work Step Seven—*Humbly ask God to remove my shortcomings*—but
I was pretty sure, even with my rebaptism, that this process was
incomplete. My relationship with my Heavenly Father was like that
of a wayward teenager who, after having a falling out with his father,
never reconciles. It wasn't that I didn't want to. It was just that I had
gone so far astray, I was sure He was still "put-out at me." Even if He
had forgiven me, I hadn't forgiven myself.[3]

Early that next year, this major stumbling block was removed
miraculously. The day following this experience, I quit smoking for
good and began in earnest to prepare and return to the temple.

January 15, 1988

Some time back, I picked up a cigarette and have been smoking, on
and off, for the last three months. I've been trying to quit without
result. I hate it! It is so completely degrading. I have barely been able
to stand myself.

With no insurance, I have been deeply worried about my hip.
It has been hurting a great deal lately. I have generally been feeling
sorry for myself. I keep asking myself (and God, I guess) why this
has happened to me. I can't run anymore, just limp around like the
Hunchback of Notre Dame. I guess that would be okay if I had some
of his charitable qualities. I'm more like an ornery lame troll.

Last evening, especially depressed and melancholy, I went out
for a long ride though the fields to be alone and have a smoke. The
thought occurred to me that, if there was a light at the end of the

tunnel, it was an oncoming train. I heard someone in AA say this. It seems to fit.

Although unplanned, I ended up at the Provo Library to seek solace among my friends, the old religion books hidden away at the end of a long corridor. I pulled a text from the shelf and began reading. I came across a passage talking about caffeine and the Word of Wisdom. I wasn't reading anything new—just stuff about how caffeine causes uric acid buildup and is a major contributor to arthritis.

Suddenly, a totally different emotion began to fill me. Thoughts raced through my mind and hit my heart with an explosion of feeling. They were something like: *I am the only one responsible for my present health. My hip, shoulder pain, everything about me has been a direct result of the tons of poison in the form of caffeine, tobacco and alcohol that I have poured into my body over the past ten years.*

With power, the thoughts continued to flow as if they were pouring out of all the books around me. *Who did I think I was that I should be exempt from the consequences of drug abuse? Neither God, nor anyone else, is responsible for my present physical and spiritual condition. God is NOT responsible for the mess I have made of my life. I am!*

Suddenly, there was no way to rationalize. This feeling hit me with the power of the train I had thought was coming earlier, but it *was* the light at the end of the tunnel—the light of truth![4]

The self-revelation continued. *Phil, you got yourself exactly where you are. Your choices did it! Stop feeling sorry for yourself.*

For the first time in my life, I accepted responsibility for who I was and where I was. A profound feeling of self-forgiveness began to fill me. Every sinful, painful, heavy thing I had been holding on to lifted—or *I let go of.*

Within these few moments, I realized that if God was not responsible for my situation, then He could be, and should be *trusted as a friend.* I hadn't been giving Him a fair chance! No wonder He couldn't remove my shortcomings. I had been clinging tightly to them as if I could punish myself for my own sins. What arrogance and stupidity!

As the truths continued to distill upon me, my sins, mingled with mists of darkness, seemed to fall away. I felt as if a brilliant light was shinning down upon me. My Heavenly Father loved me. Jesus loved me. I knew it. I felt it! But Phil hadn't loved Phil. How terribly unfair I had been to myself, *and to God.*

Crouching at the end of the dim corridor, light continued to flow into me. Tears fell freely as this new awareness grew. All of my defenses fell away. *If I were to blame, not God, then it was up to me to do something about it—something as simple as waking up and saying, "I'm sorry, I've been blaming the wrong Person."*

Leaving the library, I walked out into the dark, crisp, winter night with light in my mind and a new strength in my heart. The advice repeated in *every* AA meeting I had ever attended occupied my thoughts. *You must be willing to go to any lengths to get sober.* I knew that in order to recover I had to sacrifice all of my sins on the altar of striving. I thought I'd been trying but I had been committing a most grievous sin in light of what Jesus had done for me. I had not been forgiving myself. The moment I let go of my defects of character, *my Heavenly Father took them, root and branch, and became my friend and ally*—truly a Power Greater Than Myself.[5] [Another major piece of the recovery puzzle fell in place.]

The night following my "Provo Library Awakening," I went into my basement study and, after praying, selected a book to read from the many I had collected over the years of teaching seminary. Earlier in the week, I had received a referral from the state employment office to interview for a job at Stephen R. Covey and Associates. Seeking to learn a little more about Dr. Covey, I opened the book *Spiritual Roots of Human Relations*, and randomly selected a passage. What I read was no coincidence.

> One of the finest and highest ways we can demonstrate our faith in the Lord Jesus Christ is to make an unqualified pledge or covenant with him to do one thing or another that *we know must be done*, particularly when it is something that we know *we cannot do by ourselves.* Thereby, we demonstrate we have faith in His integrity to honor his promise to us and also *in His power to enable us to do things far beyond our own capacities.* Unless you promise what you will do (in specific words), you have no contract that will be valid. The Lord promises only when you promise. In other words, if you don't promise, you have no promise. When you do promise, then you have all His promises.[6]

This was the precise counsel I needed. I had been white-knuckle sober and miserable for six and half months and I was anything but a sure bet to make seven. I needed to make a personal covenant with my Savior. Later that evening, I wrote:

I feel like making a promise to myself and to God that I believe I can keep. Although I know better than anyone the danger of making a promise, something profound has happened. My self-pity, excuses, self-loathing, and guilt have disappeared. I want to make this promise, but not a one-way deal. I want to give up tobacco for good. This isn't the first time I've tried the old "I'll-throw-em-away-and-that'll-get-rid-of-em-fer-good" method only to buy another pack the next day. Well, this time my promise is only for tonight. Tomorrow is not here. When it is, I'll promise again and then go forward making my promise anew each day, one day at time.

I know that, as I make this promise between my Heavenly Father and myself, success will depend upon my willingness to live one day at a time and allow His help.

Five days later, I wrote:

January 21, 1988

On January 16, I made a covenant between God and myself to quit smoking. Taking it one day at a time, the result is that today is my fifth day without a smoke and I also have been caffeine free. The difference in how I feel is dramatic. I wake up more alert and feel more energy in the evening rather than just enduring until bedtime. Before, I just felt sick and tired each night after spending the day pouring a gallon of soda pop into my body and smoking a dozen cigarettes.

I have been working on my, "me—the victim," attitude. Some major changes are taking place. Of most importance is the feeling that, for some reason, and believe me I can't figure it out, I don't have to worry about the future. I made some promises to God. I know if I keep my part of the bargain, turning my will and life over to Him daily, He will keep His part.

I have felt an overpowering urge these first few days to break my promise and smoke a cigarette. I just haven't yielded to it.[7] I've worn out my guardian angel and the Serenity Prayer.

I am still out of work with many major creditors who are demanding payment. I can only do the footwork, limping at that, and trust in God. I pray, now that I am becoming free from caffeine, tobacco, and alcohol, I am ready for something more than menial work. Somewhere out there is a job God would have me do.

Once I begin working, contributing a full tithing, and catch up my child support, I can petition to have my Priesthood blessings restored. I am hopeful of returning to the temple someday. Before I petition, I need some stable time in my life.

Please Father, help me find the job I need. I'll do everything I can to keep my part of the bargain.

cNOTES

1. *AA Sponsor.* An AA sponsor is a member of the AA fellowship with at least one year's sobriety and who exhibits exceptional wisdom in living AA's Twelve Steps. Persons new in AA are advised to choose a personal sponsor early in their program of recovery. When a person feels tempted to drink, or is facing other serious life problems, they are told to contact their sponsor for advice.

2. *Priesthood Blessings Restored.* When a person is excommunicated from the LDS Church, all evidence of that individual's membership is erased from Church records. Membership can only be restored when a person shows evidence of worthiness and is rebaptized. If the person was previously temple endowed, after a specified period of time following rebaptism (usually one year), if worthy, the person can petition to have his temple blessings restored. If all qualifications are met and the individual is temple worthy, the restoring of temple blessings is accomplished through the Restoration of Blessings Ordinance. Only a General Authority of the Church holds the priesthood keys to perform this ordinance. In the case of a male member, the Melchizidek Priesthood is also restored.

3. *Forgiving Oneself.* A modern apostle of the Lord, Elder Boyd K. Packer, taught:

> For some reason, we think the Atonement of Christ applies only at the end of mortal life to redemption from the fall, from spiritual death. It is much more than that. It is an ever-present power to call upon in everyday life. When we are racked or harrowed up or tormented by guilt or burdened with grief, He can heal us. While we do not fully understand how the Atonement of Christ was made, we can experience the peace of God, which passeth all understanding." ("The Touch of the Master's Hand," *Ensign*, May 2001, 23)

Another modern apostle, Elder Richard G. Scott, taught on this subject:

Can't you see that to continue to suffer for sins, when there has been proper repentance and forgiveness of the Lord, is not prompted by the Savior but by the master of deceit, whose goal has always been to bind and enslave the children of our Father in Heaven? Satan would encourage you to continue to relive the details of past mistakes, knowing that such thoughts make progress, growth, and service difficult to attain. It is as though Satan ties strings to the mind and body so that he can manipulate one like a puppet, discouraging personal achievement. I testify that Jesus Christ paid the price and satisfied the demands of justice for all who are obedient to His teachings. Thus, full forgiveness is granted, and the distressing effects of sin need no longer persist in one's life. Indeed, they cannot persist if one truly understands the meaning of Christ's Atonement. ("We Love You—Please Come Back," *Ensign*, May 1986, 11)

4. *Christ as light at the end of the tunnel.* Elder Jeffrey R. Holland elaborates on this subject:

My declaration is that this is precisely what the gospel of Jesus Christ offers us, especially in times of need. There is help. There is happiness. There really is light at the end of the tunnel. It is the Light of the World, the Bright and Morning Star, the "light that is endless, that can never be darkened." It is the very Son of God Himself. In loving praise far beyond Romeo's reach, we say, "What light through yonder window breaks?" It is the return of hope, and Jesus is the Sun. To any who may be struggling to see that light and find that hope, I say: Hold on. Keep trying. God loves you. Things will improve. Christ comes to you in His "more excellent ministry" with a future of "better promises." He is your "high priest of good things to come." ("An High Priest of Good Things to Come" *Ensign*, November 1999, 36)

5. *Letting go of sin.* Elder Neal A. Maxell has taught:

No part of walking by faith is more difficult than walking the road of repentance. However, with "faith unto repentance," we can push roadblocks out of the way, moving forward to beg God for mercy. (Alma 34:16) True contrition brings full capitulation. One simply surrenders, caring only about what God thinks, not what "they" think, while meekly offering, "O God, . . . make thyself known unto me, and I will give away all my sins to know thee." (Alma 22:18.) Giving away all our sins is the only way we can come to know God.

("Repentance," *Ensign*, November 1991, 30, emphasis added)

6. Stephen R. Covey, *Spiritual Roots of Human Relations* (Salt Lake: Deseret Book, 1976), 302–3, emphasis added.

7. Yielding To The Spirit of Evil. President Brigham Young taught:

> Many think that the devil has rule and power over both body and spirit. Now, I want to tell you that he does not hold any power over man, only so far as the body overcomes the spirit that is in man, through yielding to the spirit of evil . . . if the spirit yields to the body, the devil then has power to overcome both the body and the spirit of that man.
>
> When you are full of evil passion, and wish to yield to it, then stop and let the spirit, which God has put into your tabernacles, take the lead. If you do that, I will promise that you will overcome all evil, and obtain eternal lives. But many, very many, let the spirit yield to the body, and are overcome and destroyed. (*Journal of Discourses* 2:255)

CHAPTER TEN

*T*HOUGH YOUR SINS BE AS SCARLET

Come now, and let us reason together, saith the Lord: though your sins be as scarlet, they shall be as white as snow; though they be red like crimson, they shall be as wool.

—Isaiah 1:18

March 10, 1988

It is encouraging to review my progress over the past six months. Back in October, I followed my daily unemployment routine of dropping my son off at school, then going to the 7-Eleven for a cup of Java. With nothing to do, I sought out a place, usually behind the 7-Eleven, to sit in the warm sun, smoke a cigarette, and drink coffee. For the most part, I felt hopeless and quite sorry for myself.

Now sober nine months, I have been smoke-free for three months and have had an enjoyable and respectable job for the same length of time. I have my own little office with a place for pictures, plants, and the things I love. It was fun arranging and decorating.

After getting moved in and situated, I held a private celebration for a significant event. Having prepared a dark wooden frame for my Ballet Lady poster, I resurrected her from her cardboard tomb and placed her in the frame for display. As I positioned her on the wall, my thoughts went back to that broken-hearted day eight years earlier when I had spared her the garbage can death suffered by her poster mates. Having regained some hope in life, I am most grateful to have saved her. Gazing at her on the wall, her delicate beauty reminds me of my sweet wife. The words printed at the bottom of her dancing feet inspire me: *If you can imagine it, you can achieve it. If you can dream it, you can become it.*

I now had a decent job with potential and was paying tithing, child support, and back taxes. I had been sober ten months–a respectable period. I had been tobacco-free four months. I felt ready to begin the petition to Church authorities for restoration of my priesthood and temple blessings.

April 13, 1988

Dear Bishop Steed,

It has been over two years since my rebaptism. It has taken time to recover, grow, commit, and feel worthy of this petition. I am not repeating trite words when I say that my recovery, repentance, and any degree of righteousness have not come easy. This has been a terrible struggle, but I believe I am worthy to petition to have my Priesthood blessings restored. I have found some peace in my heart, and, although life is still a struggle and a challenge, in my daily prayers I feel God's presence. I know that I am far from perfect but I feel better about my life.

Gazing at her on the wall, her delicate beauty reminds me of my sweet wife. The words printed at the bottom of her dancing feet inspire me: If you can imagine it, you can achieve it. If you can dream it, you can become it.

My wife and I have a special and loving relationship, one that I feel can and will be eternal. It is deeply sad to me that my former wife and children suffered the tragedy of divorce. I have labored to be as good a father as possible under the circumstances and to help support my former wife and children, as well as my present wife's four children. I have paid full child support for the last four years, and I am slowly paying my debt to Utah Social Services for the support they provided to my former wife when I was unable to contribute.

I was a seminary teacher for the Church for seven years before my alcoholism and troubles began. As a full-time religion teacher, I loved the restored gospel with all my heart. I loved the young people I taught. My love for the gospel has never diminished. There have been times of great despair when I just wished not to exist. At one point, I believed there was no hope.

I struggled with alcoholism for many years following my experiences as a seminary teacher. Someone just reading this might find this fact incomprehensible. The fact is, it happened. Since finding sobriety through the fellowship of Alcoholics Anonymous, I have had the opportunity to tell my story and bear my testimony. I am grateful I have something to share from my experience. As I share, others learn and better understand the plight of the addict.

Bishop, I have felt over the years of teaching the gospel, fasting to teach, fasting on fast Sundays and for other special purposes, the goodness of my Heavenly Father. I have never doubted that He exists. I just believed that, after my mistakes and blunders, He couldn't possibly love me. I had burned with His love and known that precious peace and warmth towards all of my fellowmen, having no desire to do evil. But, after all this, I did fail, mostly because of my addiction to alcohol, not because I purposely sought to be immoral.

President Kimball taught that big sin doesn't come into our lives overnight. Rather it comes through small sins, "Hidden Wedges" he called them, slowly prying our lives and our souls apart until the big sin can enter. This happened to me, and I fell.

Through my experience, I have learned of the hidden wedges or Satan's traps. I have approached this request cautiously, thoughtfully, and prayerfully.

I yearn to feel once again the beauty and peace of the temple; to feel the white clothing about me; the fellowship of precious souls filled with light; the joy of going to the Lord's house. I look up at the temple and long to be permitted within its walls. I hope it is the Lord's will that I am acceptable to enter therein someday.

I love my Heavenly Father and bear my witness of His reality and of the reality of His Son. I know repentance can rid me of past sin because of what Christ did. Without His Atonement, my repentance would be without effect.

I have not meant to ramble so, but pray what I have written is a small token of what I have known and what I now feel. I gratefully wait upon whatever the Lord would have me do and be.

Sincerely,

Brother Phil Simkins

My wife was also asked to provide a letter.

April 26, 1988

Dear Bishop,

I would like to express my support for my husband during this time of petition for restoration of blessings. This will be an important step for us to obtain the eternal blessings of our Father in Heaven.

There are many attributes that I admire about Phil: his enthusiasm when attending to his church callings and the positive support he gives me in whatever I do; his sensitive, sweet, loving nature to everyone. One of the reasons I was attracted to him in the first place was that, even though he was struggling with life's problems, I felt his sincere love of the gospel and his deep testimony of Jesus Christ, the Book of Mormon, and the Prophet Joseph Smith.

Since we first met, I have seen him grow spiritually. He has allowed and helped me to grow also. We are hoping to achieve the same goals in life and in the eternities. It will be a dream come true to marry him in the temple. It will be a blessing to finally have the Priesthood in my home.

I love Phil completely. We have a happy, workable marriage now, and can have forever. We are able to work out our problems as they come up. There have been hard times but mostly good ones. I wouldn't trade any of it. My husband is my best friend as well as my sweetheart. He is a joy and a blessing to my family and me.

Sincerely,

Vickie Lee

These letters, along with ones from my bishop and former wife, were forwarded to LDS Church headquarters. We waited.

Two months had passed when the bishop informed me that

a further statement regarding the status of my child support was needed. I had been honest and current in my monthly child support and alimony. I was making regular payments to the state government to erase my remaining debt. I was supporting my former wife in every request. I stated these facts in a letter to the First Presidency that ended with this statement: "My desire is to have my blessings restored only if I am found worthy. I look forward to again being clothed with the peace, joy, and power of the priesthood. God willing, someday that privilege will be mine."

With nothing left to do but wait on the request, I focused on the day I would celebrate my first year of continuous sobriety—June 27, 1988.

June 9, 1988

> It is a precious, summer evening as I work on the computer at the stake offices. [I was assisting the stake president in secretarial work.] I am basically happy. I am deeply grateful approaching my one-year AA birthday—one year clean and sober! I haven't been perfectly clean. I still use caffeine occasionally, but no alcohol has entered my body in eleven months and 12 days. Just 15 days to go!
>
> I recall those dismal days living in the motel. Just a moment's thought sends me back to the dark depression and hopelessness I lived with daily. That I survived is amazing, no, it is Amazing Grace; it is a miracle.
>
> My soul is full of gratitude to my God. I have a constant prayer in my heart of thanksgiving for His goodness. He has been so very merciful and, *Oh it is wonderful, so wonderful to me.*[1]

My One-Year-Sober AA birthday arrived. For ten years, I had watched others who had become eligible respond to the chairman's announcement: "Anyone celebrating one year's sobriety, come forward and receive your one-year chip." I had finally qualified to answer the call!

Applause erupted as Vickie handed me the coveted chip and gave me a warm hug. As is traditional, I shared my feelings about reaching this milestone. Mom and Dad had traveled from southern Utah and were seated in the audience. My thoughts went back to that special Sunday, eleven years earlier. It had been the day following a three-day hiking trip into the mountains. I had spoken with the influence of the Spirit in their sacrament meeting. My parents had been most proud of me.

On this night, in a smoke-filled room and under vastly different circumstances, I again spoke with the feelings of the Holy Spirit. Gratitude filled me as I caught Mom and Dad's eyes. Their tears said they were proud of me. I was giving another kind of speech about hiking another kind of mountain. But in my words, I took no credit for my success. I knew exactly who was responsible—a Power Greater than Myself.

I wrote about reaching this milestone in a letter to my daughter on her twentieth birthday.

August 2, 1988

Dear Sunshine,

An important note of news, on June 27, I received my one-year AA chip. Mom and Dad were in the meeting. Mom said a few words and I spoke. It was very special to me. I had just about lost hope of ever completing that difficult first year sober. I can't believe how swiftly life has improved for me since becoming free of alcohol.

There are many feelings I hope to share with you someday. You may not remember, or not want to, but I was so close to you as a little girl. I hope that someday you will read my journals. Maybe you will understand how deeply I loved you and cherished your life. It is a tragedy that probably all you remember is the pain that alcoholism brought into our family's life. We have all hurt so much over the past ten years.

In AA, we are taught that we should not regret the past because we can't change it, and spending time there only takes away energy to live in the present. But whether this statement is true or not, I realize how terribly unfair the past has been. I regret deeply what this experience has cost my family. I regret what happened in your teenage years, the pain I caused you, your brothers, and your Mom.

I hope someday, Sunshine, you will forgive me. I know I can never make up what we could have had, if things had been different. I sure don't understand why this happened, but please know I love you and appreciate your struggles. You are precious to me!

Love Ya Lots,

Dad

In a return letter, my daughter revealed that what I had perceived, as an unhappy time for her, wasn't as bad as I thought. She wrote, "I remember that time in Wyoming when we ate in those teepees. It was really fun. I didn't know anything about your sneaking off to buy booze. I remember, of course, that the food was yummy. I'm grateful that I had a happy childhood."

By the end of the summer, the doctor informed me that I would need an immediate hip replacement. Two years earlier, I had run a marathon. The previous year, I had climbed to the summit of the twelve-thousand-foot high Mt. Timpanogos three times in one month. Now at forty-one, I needed to have my hip replaced with artificial parts. The thought of losing my active life hurt more than the ache in my side from the grinding bones.

The lengthy recovery period following my hip surgery distracted me from my petition to the First Presidency regarding my priesthood blessings. Nine months from the date I submitted my request, my bishop informed me an appointment was being arranged to meet with a General Authority. I received in the mail a single-day parking permit to the LDS Church headquarters in Salt Lake City. I taped the parking permit, like a precious document, next to a lengthy entry in my journal—proof that this significant event had really happened.

My appointment with this well-known General Authority was for the purpose of being interviewed, and if found worthy, to have my priesthood and temple blessings restored through the restoration of blessings ordinance. As Vickie and I were seated in front of this good man, thoughts filled my mind.

February 13, 1989

Oh good brother, can you know how much this means to me? I heard you speak in the Golden Stake house in Logan on my birthday nearly twenty years ago. I was a young seminary teacher, filled with enthusiasm. How powerful you were! How you touched my spirit and filled my being with love.

You talked about setting goals. With youth's naïve optimism, I believed I could do anything. I went home after your speech and wrote down important, almost impossible goals—goals I am still striving to achieve. How could I have known that night eighteen years ago that someday I would speak with you in person—to be interviewed for such a thing! Yes, as you say, I could not have known then that I would have to go through so much.

As the interview began, this special man commented that he had participated in thousands of interviews to restore blessings. My heart pounded with anticipation. I thought, *You mean you are really going to do it, now, today?* I could hardly believe this was going to happen. Eight years earlier, with heavy heart, I had packed into a suitcase my temple clothes and garments, and locked the lid. I had wondered then if I would ever open it again. Just before going to Salt Lake, City I went to the basement and retrieved the little green suitcase, which had been my grandfather's temple case, from behind several rows of bottled fruit. Unlocking the rusty latches, I opened the case and, in the event I would be given back the privilege of wearing them, I removed a temple garment to take with me.

Speaking with the General Authority, my thoughts continued,

February 13, 1989 (continued)

How grateful I am to be here—especially with you. You say this is the sweet part, that the hard part is out in the courts—that's where the real pain is.

As the interview continued, I mentioned that Vickie and I had started an AA Twelve Step group at the Provo High Seminary building to help Church members with addictions. We talked about AA. He seemed intrigued by something Vickie said about the spirit in AA meetings being as strong as in sacrament meetings. He paused and made a note. This gentle conversation helped me relax before he focused on the main purpose of our meeting.

Thoughts continued to race through my mind. *Now comes the biggie. Am I really worthy to be here? Am I perfect in my repentance? What is he going to ask?*

He had only one question—but it was most important. "Brother Phil, have you forgiven yourself?"

That's it? Only one question? I thought, reflecting on my Provo Library Awakening experience. I knew the exact day, time, and place of this event. "Yes," I replied. "I have forgiven myself."

He smiled. He asked me how, after teaching seminary, I had fallen into alcoholism? I related my story briefly about the hidden wedges, my rationalizing, and my making small concessions that eventually led to serious transgres-

THE CHURCH OF JESUS CHRIST OF LATTER-DAY SAINTS

Single Day Permit
LDS Parking Plaza

Display this permit on the dash so it can be seen through the windshield.

☑ Employee parking ☐ Red reserved parking
☐ Service ☐ Delivery (15 min.)

Good for this date only: 2-10-89

Name: *Phil Simpkins*

Department or destination: *Elder*

Company:

Officer: *958*

Time: *1:45 pm*

WHITE—Vehicle CANARY—Security FMSE1591 6/85 Printed in USA

sion. He listened intently. He nodded that he understood. My story was not unique. He had probably heard a similar version each time he had restored priesthood blessings.

How precious was this gentle man. Each time he smiled, his face lit up with pure light, and my heart was lifted a little more. I felt his goodness, his love, and his spirit, the familiar testimony of the Spirit . . . and I felt a deep love for him. He informed me that once my blessings were restored, the records of the Church would contain no indication that I had lost my membership. I thought of the scripture from Isaiah, *Though your sins be as scarlet, they shall be as white as snow [Isaiah 1:18].*

He placed his hands on my head and restored my priesthood and temple blessings and gave me a powerful blessing of comfort and counsel. I listened carefully, intent on remembering as much as possible to record in my journal. As the blessing progressed, I began to feel a profound transformation. I felt God's power through the priesthood flowing into me. I felt this power radiating down through the hands of this pure man and into my body. I know that the priesthood and the temple endowment has tangible properties. I felt their reality at that moment. I felt renewed. I recognized this feeling like the companionship of an old friend, the wonderful witness from the Holy Ghost giving ultimate proof of the truth. I felt within *me* the power of the Priesthood of God—it was now mine again! I had my temple blessings back! I again had the promise that I could receive *all God has* if I continued faithful.[2]

Immediately following this experience, Vickie and I drove to the VA hospital to meet Mom and Dad, who were there for one of dad's many medical appointments. My parents had known previously that I was to interview with a General Authority. However, when we arrived at the hospital, they were not aware the interview had taken place. A week later, Mom wrote me of the joy she felt in the return of her prodigal son.

February 17, 1989

When I saw a man coming through the front door of the hospital dressed in a suit and white shirt, my heart leaped within me. I knew immediately it was you. As you approached, there was a glow all about you, but especially about your head—almost like a halo. I didn't have to ask if your priesthood and temple blessings had been restored. From a distance, I knew they had! I felt it with assurance as you hugged me.

There is no greater joy for a mother than to have a child who was lost, return Home. With the same measure of despair that I shared the darkness and sorrow of your life over the past years of struggle, my soul now rejoices in the light of your return. I share your joy, for it is mine also!

Loving You Forever,

Mom

At the hospital, I showed my parents the restoration of blessings document. It recorded the glad news that my temple blessings had been restored. But it contained one piece of bad news: "There is a restriction on sealing to present spouse." Our temple marriage would have to wait.

Thereafter, although my priesthood blessings had been restored, I wanted to be doubly sure that I was spiritually prepared for the temple. It was September before I interviewed with my bishop and stake president to obtain a personal temple recommend. During these interviews, I was able to affirm my worthiness.

As surely as I believed as a young religion teacher in Idaho that I would never drink alcohol again, and then it happened, I had believed that I would never hear again the words, *"You are worthy to enter the temple."* Following my visit with the stake president, he handed me the small, but priceless, recommend, shook my hand vigorously and said, "Good brother, enjoy your trip back to the temple! *You are a worthy man!*"

*N*OTES

1. *Hymn—I Stand All Amazed.* "I stand all amazed at the love Jesus offers me, Confused at the graced that so fully he proffers me. I tremble to know that for me he was crucified, that for me, a sinner, he suffered, he bled and died. Oh it is wonderful that he should care for me enough to die for me! Oh, it is wonderful, wonderful to me!" (*Hymns of The Church of Jesus Christ of Latter-day Saints*, 1985, no. 193)

2. *All that my Father has.*

> And he that receiveth my Father receiveth my Father's kingdom; therefore all that my Father hath shall be given unto him. And this is according to the oath and covenant which belongeth to the priesthood. Therefore, all those who receive the priesthood, receive this oath and covenant of my Father, which he cannot break, neither can it be moved. (Doctrine and Covenants 84:38–40)

$\mathscr{F}$OR TIME &
ALL ETERNITY

*And establish a house, even a house of prayer, a house of fasting,
a house of faith, a house of learning, a house of glory, a house of
order, a house of God.*

—Doctrine and Covenants 109:8

N A WARM, AUTUMN DAY IN SEPTEMBER 1989, I PACKED MY
temple clothes in my grandpa's little green suitcase and drove
toward the eastern mountains—my destination, the temple of the
Most High God—my purpose, to serve as proxy[1] in doing ordinance
work for a deceased brother. Enjoying the sweet fragrance and bright
colors of flower beds that lined the long sidewalk, I approached the
entrance of the Provo Utah Temple. The peace and beauty of the
building hinted of the experience waiting inside. Over ten years had
passed since my last visit. During this decade, the formidable structure had always provoked feelings of guilt mingled with a melancholy
longing. Now, gazing upon the loveliness of the sacred building, I
felt welcomed.

Stepping through the tall doors, the ambiance of the house of the
Lord enveloped me. I was filled with the familiar warmth of truth
and virtue vibrating through everything and everyone. The constant
battering from the world's pride, greed, and wickedness were locked
out. Here was true shelter from the storm.

After dressing in white, I went to the chapel on the temple's second floor to wait for the next endowment session (see chapter 1, note 3). Before entering the chapel, I paused in the hallway and pulled back the curtains covering the tall windows to the west. I had performed this ritual many years earlier with each visit to the Provo Utah Temple. The view of the outside world from this lofty perch was always inspiring. Now, as I peeked out from behind the curtains, there revealed before me was a magnificent vista. Soft white clouds filled the dark-blue sky. A green carpet of earth stretched out for miles toward Utah Lake, which lay glistening in the setting sun. For years, the memory of viewing this incredible panorama from high in the temple had been frozen within me. A moment's glimpse thawed the memory replacing it with spiritual warmth—evidence that I had returned home.

The sacred hours passed. The words of the endowment flooded back into my mind with familiarity. I remembered and my bosom burned. The spiritual substance that surrounded me was undeniable. I thought, *What I am about is my Father's business. This is His house. I am in His presence.* During my years of active alcoholism, I had lived in memory of this feeling. But on this morning, I burned with the Spirit! I *was* about my Heavenly Father's business–saving my kindred dead—and saving myself. I felt it! I knew it! I loved it!

Following the endowment session, I again paused by a window in the hallway with the hope of obtaining another glimpse of the valley. As I pulled back the curtains, I discovered I was on the mountainous eastern side of the circular temple. I looked down upon a feast of flowers planted in spoke-like arrangement, extending outward as if the temple's eastern doors were the hub. My gaze lifted up the steep ridges of the autumn-colored mountains that towered above the temple. Rather than looking down on the valley, I was looking up toward heaven! I felt hope as I had never felt before that I might someday live there.

Turning from the window, I paused in the empty, quiet hallway. Then, into my mind came the image of my grandmother, the one who had rescued me as an infant from the canal. At the time of her death, she and Grandpa had been temple workers in the St. George Temple. It was as if I could see her walking toward me in the peaceful corridor. She was smiling with that special twinkle in her eyes that had always been a precious part of my memory. I seemed to feel her arms around me. I felt her love. I sensed her gratitude for my return. My bosom burned with joy and tears fell onto the soft carpet floor. I knew I was standing in a most holy habitation where angels and mortals mingle.

Over the next years, I returned to the temple often. Living in sobriety, my life was improving on all fronts. I continued going to AA meetings and working diligently at my employment. I was called to be a Sunday School teacher for a youth class. Once more, I was teaching the gospel to young people!

In June 1990, I received my three-year AA chip. Alcohol no longer seemed a threat. But an experience late that summer reminded me of just how fragile my sobriety was. Friends from work had organized a rafting trip to the Little Salmon River in Idaho. I had been invited along with my two older children and two of their friends. My wife chose to remain home, and my children and friends wanted to travel by themselves. So, rising early in the morning to avoid the summer heat, I departed by myself on the ten-hour trip.

My truck had no air conditioning. By midday, the hot wind battered me through the open windows, forcing more and more pit stops for cold sodas at gas station oases. I had plenty of time alone in my thoughts. It was late evening when I arrived at camp near the Little Salmon. With an unfriendly horde of mosquitoes for company, I settled down to wait for my children. They finally arrived around midnight.

The next morning started out hot as we hurried to make the rendezvous for the river trip. I took along my mountain bike, planning to ride back to camp after rafting. At the river, we piled onto large rubber rafts and pushed off. After an hour or so, I escaped the crowded boats by riding in a one-man rubber canoe. Relaxing, I basked in the sun's rays. When rapids approached, I would paddle to avoid the more risky section and drift free out onto the dark green river. Eventually, the rapids won out as I capsized into turbulent water. Everyone thought my abrupt baptism amusing, but I experienced a tense moment as my artificial hip banged against the rocks in the swift water. Fortunately, I was carried into calmer water. I thought the perils of the day were over.

When the rafting ended, I left the kids to return with the truck at their leisure and began the bike trek for camp. I estimated the distance around ten miles—about right for a good workout. Peddling hard the first hour, the dusty canyon road was much steeper and longer than I had thought. I had finished off the pint of water in the bike carrier much earlier and was now eager for the cold sodas waiting in the ice chest at camp. However, I was unaware that, earlier that morning, others in camp had placed several cans of *beer* in the cooler.

If Satan has power to manipulate events to destroy a man, surely he orchestrated the next few moments. I had already let my guard down with two days of stinkin' thinkin'. The previous long day of driving alone had roused in me memories of the more carefree days when I used alcohol. Rafting on the river had been a struggle not to envy those who seemed to be having a lot of beer-driven fun. Two days of stinkin'-thinkin.' Two hours and fifteen miles biking in the hot sun. Terribly thirsty and naïve to the events developing, I was about to ride straight into the gaping jaws of Demon Alcohol.

Pedaling faster the last few hundred yards, I reached the campsite, dismounted, yanked the cooler from under the picnic table, and shoved my hand into the icy water searching for a soda. I grasped the first can encountered, withdrew it, popped the lid, and lifted it to my lips in one motion. A split second before the liquid entered my mouth, the rich smell of hops filled my nostrils like the familiar perfume of an old love. The trap was sprung. An explosion of memories filled my mind. Euphoria. Rationalization. Everything combined to make perfect sense. *The tiny amount of alcohol in beer can't hurt . . . I'm so thirsty. I can have just one. Drink it, drink it, drink it!*

It was as though time suspended and I hung powerless against the drug. My life balanced precariously, ready to tip to either misery or joy with the weight of one little gulp. The alcohol was already on my lips. I could taste it. With no effort I could let it into my mouth, swallow—and the feeling!

Then suddenly, the protection I had prayed for early that morning kicked in. It was as though I heard Old-Timers screaming: *You are powerless against the first drink! If you reach that point, say the prayer. Say it!* With the can of beer pressed against my lips, I forced the words in my mind: *God grant me the serenity to accept the things I cannot change, courage to change the things I can, and the wisdom to know the difference.*

Guardian angels were summoned. Spiritual energy entered my body. The feeling of powerlessness caved in. I hurled the foaming can of poison into the bushes and spit the taste from my lips. Reaching back into the chest, I quickly guzzled three Dr Peppers, one after the other. A sudden gut-ache, rather than the numbing effects of alcohol, brought the stark realization that I had just survived a significant life test.

Later, during the long drive home, I had ample time to reflect. I had been progressing well. My self-respect had been increasing through continuous employment, restored priesthood and temple blessings, and repaired family relationships. Then, I had nearly erased it all in a millisecond with one swallow of beer. There was no doubt, I was still an alcoholic—and *always would be*. I could never become complacent or think that I was ultimately strong enough. *I was still powerless*. But I knew I could draw on a higher power. I knew it was *that* power—the power of my Heavenly Father—and not *my* power that had prevented a tragedy infinitely worse than had I broken some bones in the Salmon River rapids.

Summer became autumn, and my wife and I still waited for permission to be married in the temple. While we waited, Vickie, now forty-three, went to the temple to receive her endowment.

September 29, 1991

Early on a crisp, autumn-painted mountain morning, Vickie, her Mom, and I traveled to the Manti Utah Temple for a sacred and special event. My wife was being endowed.

Vickie was anxious as we walked up the long hill toward the great, granite structure. I too shared in her excitement, knowing the precious, life-altering events about to occur. I knew she would be calmed as we entered this holy home on earth.

It is difficult to describe the feelings that come when one enters a temple of God. Every aspect of the structure, from its tall spires pointing heavenward to the magnificent celestial room, testifies of the Most High God and His Son, Jesus Christ. Peace that can't be dismissed as coincidence, comes into one's being. Every trouble lifts.

I have no doubt—*It is the safest, most trusted feeling on earth.*

We presented ourselves in worthiness at the front desk to an elderly brother, who, while inspecting our recommends, welcomed us with a soft voice and a special love. A friendly matron appeared and escorted Vickie away.

After dressing in white, we met in the small chapel to wait for the endowment session. Vickie's eyes sparkled. Her soft brown hair contrasted against the white gown she wore. How beautiful and pure she looked. How she deserved this day. Joy filled my soul as I looked upon this precious daughter of God. Finally, I was together with my best friend and home in the House of the Lord.

Following Vickie's endowment, we returned weekly to the temple to serve and continue learning. On the third anniversary of my receiving my restoration of blessings, we received a letter from our bishop.

February 13, 1992

Dear Brother Simkins,

I am pleased to inform you that as of January 30, 1992, the restriction on your sealing to your wife, Vickie Lee, has been lifted. Under the direction of the First Presidency, I am instructed to invite you and your wife to obtain the necessary temple recommends from myself and the stake president.

I express my appreciation for your faithfulness and patience in this matter and convey the appreciation of the First Presidency for having made the efforts necessary in your life to accomplish this goal.

Sincerely,

Bishop Steed

April 3, 1992, was the day Vickie and I chose to be sealed in the temple. When the day dawned, a brilliant blue sky appeared through the previous night's spring rain. I sensed this day's contrast to the dark, despairing days we had known in alcoholism. Today would be a day of light and celebration.

Mom, Dad, and my sister, together with Vickie's parents,

brothers, and many friends filled one of the larger sealing rooms in the Provo Utah Temple. Light radiated from the face of the elderly man who possessed the priesthood authority to seal us together for time and eternity.[2] Prior to his pronouncing the incredible promises of the eternal marriage ordinance, first I, and then Vickie, responded affirmatively to the sealer's question about our willingness to receive each other as eternal companions.

Power filled the room—priesthood power. I felt the Holy Ghost. I recalled my experience the first time I had returned back to the temple. It was the same feeling of testimony, the same thoughts: *This is God's power. This is his appointed servant who holds the keys. This man has the sealing authority. This will be binding upon us forever.* I had no doubt. If we lived worthily, the priceless blessings pronounced upon us by the sealer would be ours: *Eternal life—together—forever.*

My wife recorded this event in her journal.

April 6, 1992

I was filled with excitement for this blessed event to arrive. All of the women close to me and that I loved had gathered together to honor me (and us) in this long-awaited and special event of my life. Mom and Dad, my brother and his wife, my friends, all who had been pulling for me, came to join us. I was sure others, whom I couldn't see, from the other side, were present.

Before going up to the sealing room, the temple matron delivered the precious information pertaining to the ceremony that was about to unfold. I couldn't believe I was actually there. All of my life I had waited to be sealed in the temple to a worthy husband. This day had finally arrived.

The Spirit was strong within me, testifying that it was right to be there, right to be marrying Phil, forever. I felt through my entire being the sweet presence of my Heavenly Parents, their joy for me, for us, and for this moment.

Entering the large sealing room, I was surprised at how many people had come to witness this sacred ordinance. Light filled the room and light filled their faces. My dad and Phil's dad were seated in the witness chairs in front of the altar.

In the quiet room, I wondered if I listened hard enough, I might hear the sound of angels' pens recording in the book of life, the details of our union. Dressed in temple white, my husband was

beautiful inside and out.

Kneeling at the altar, I felt as if time ceased—as if the entire hosts of heaven were holding their breath—as if I were suspended in a time vacuum. There are some doors in life I have passed through by myself. At those moments, as at this eternal marriage portal, I have had the unearthly feeling that time slowed, nearly stopping on its course. If events moved at all, they were in slow motion—intervals of space, like giving birth to my children or lying in an operating room when my life hung in the balance. In these moments, everyone and everything was removed. Only my Heavenly Father and I remained together, motionless and timeless.

The Sealer's face shone as if there was a sun inside him. With Priesthood authority given of God, he pronounced the sealing ordinance. Did I accept Phil to be my lawfully wedded husband forever? Yes! Oh yes! Oh yes!

That's how our forever marriage was. Though my sweetheart was there, I knew that, as much as this was for the two of us, it was also between God and me. It was as if this event lasted forever—is still lasting—a moment frozen in time.

Phil and I knelt holding hands across the altar. The image of the two of us looking into each other's eyes reflected in the two large mirrors that hung on opposing walls. They seemed to reflect us back and forth forever—image, after image, after image. The Sealer's face shone as if there was a sun inside him. With Priesthood authority given of God,[3] he pronounced the sealing ordinance. *Did I accept Phil to be my lawfully wedded husband forever? Yes! Oh yes! Oh yes!*

𝒩OTES

1. *Proxy.* In Latter-day Saint temples, worthy Church members serve as substitutes, or proxies, for family members and others who have

departed mortality and whose spirits dwell in a spirit realm or *spirit world.* This process affords the opportunity for every person who has lived upon the earth, and so desires, to satisfy the earthly or mortal requirements of being baptized, endowed and sealed in eternal marriages. This process also allows living Church members to revisit the temple. "Else what shall they do which are baptized for the dead, if the dead rise not at all? Why are they then baptized for the dead?" (1 Corinthians 15:29).

Bruce R. McConkie describes this vicarious work, linking it to Christ's Atonement:

> Through his suffering, death, and resurrection, immortality comes to all men and eternal life to those who obey the full gospel law. He acted on man's behalf, that is, vicariously, paying the penalty for our sins on condition of repentance, ransoming us from the effects of Adam's fall. In conformity with this pattern of vicarious service, the gospel law enables worthy members of the Church to act on behalf of their dead ancestors in the performance of the ordinances of salvation and exaltation. Baptism is essential to salvation in the celestial kingdom, endowments and sealings to an exaltation therein. The living saints, acting on a proxy basis, perform these ordinances for and in behalf of those who have died and who did not have an opportunity while in this life to receive the ordinances personally. (*Mormon Doctrine* [Salt Lake City: Bookcraft, 1966], 822)

James E Talmage adds:

> The Latter-day Saints affirm that their vicarious work in behalf of the dead is required of them by the call of the Lord through direct revelation; and that it becomes the duty and privilege of every individual who accepts the Gospel and enters the Church to labor for the salvation of his dead. He is expected and required by the obligations and responsibility he has assumed as a member of the Church of Jesus Christ, so to live as to be a worthy representative of his departed ancestors, in holy ordinance, and to be of clean life, that he may not forfeit his right to enter the sacred confines of the Lord's House, where alone he may officiate in that privileged capacity. (*The House of the Lord* [Salt Lake City: Deseret Book, 1971], 68)

2. *Eternal Marriage.*

And again, verily I say unto you, if a man marry a wife by my word, which is my law, and by the new and everlasting covenant, and it is sealed unto them by the Holy Spirit of promise, by him who is anointed, unto whom I have appointed this power and the keys of this priesthood; and it shall be said unto them—Ye shall come forth in the first resurrection; and if it be after the first resurrection, in the next resurrection; and shall inherit thrones, kingdoms, principalities, and powers, dominions, all heights and depths—then shall it be written in the Lamb's Book of Life, that he shall commit no murder whereby to shed innocent blood, and if ye abide in my covenant, and commit no murder whereby to shed innocent blood, it shall be done unto them in all things whatsoever my servant hath put upon them, in time, and through all eternity; and shall be of full force when they are out of the world; and they shall pass by the angels, and the gods, which are set there, to their exaltation and glory in all things, as hath been sealed upon their heads, which glory shall be a fulness and a continuation of the seeds forever and ever. (Doctrine and Covenants 132:19)

3. *Priesthood Authority*: Temple sealers receive the authority or *keys* to seal couples in eternal marriages directly from the First Presidency of The Church of Jesus Christ of Latter-day Saints. These sealing keys have been passed, through ordination, from prophet to prophet beginning with Joseph Smith, first Prophet of the LDS Church. Joseph Smith describes receiving the keys of the priesthood and the power to seal in the following manner. This remarkable occurrence, recorded in the *Doctrine and Covenants*, happened to Joseph Smith and Oliver Cowdery in the Kirtland Ohio Temple on Sunday, April 3, 1836:

After this vision had closed, another great and glorious vision burst upon us; for Elijah the prophet, who was taken to heaven without tasting death, stood before us, and said: "Behold, the time has fully come, which was spoken of by the mouth of Malachi—testifying that he [Elijah] should be sent, before the great and dreadful day of the Lord come—To turn the hearts of the fathers to the children, and the children to the fathers, lest the whole earth be smitten with a curse—Therefore, *the keys of this dispensation are committed into your hands*; and by this ye may know that the great and dreadful day of the Lord is near, even at the doors. (Doctrine and Covenants 110:13–16.)

$\mathcal{T}$HE PERFECT BRIGHTNESS OF HOPE

Wherefore, ye must press forward with a steadfastness in Christ, having a perfect brightness of hope, and a love of God and of all men. Wherefore, if ye shall press forward, feasting upon the word of Christ, and endure to the end, behold, thus saith the Father: Ye shall have eternal life.

—2 Nephi 31:20

July 17, 2000

It was a hot, muggy Sunday afternoon—not a day for lying around in a cheap motel room. Empty beer cans littered the floor. A full six-pack lay on a small nightstand. The air stank of stale cigarette smoke and moldy carpet. The odor of spray paint along with occasional cursing from a woman painting an old truck just outside the open window drifted through the screen.

My knock on the door had brought a gruff "Come-in." I entered the small room and stood just inside the door a moment while my eyes adjusted to the dimness. As the small room focused, I saw a man lying on the bed. For a moment, memories of the despair of being that man flooded my mind with such clarity that it startled me. Struggling back to the present, a silent prayer passed through my mind, *Dear Father, but for the grace of Thee, there go I.*

This journal entry recorded an AA Twelve Step visit that I made at the request of a bishop. It was written eight years after Vickie and I were married in the Provo Utah Temple. During those years, life had steadily improved. We had dedicated ourselves to living in harmony with true principles.

Striving daily to practice AA's Tenth Step, Vickie and I "Continued to take personal inventory and when we were wrong, promptly admitted it." Preparing to take the Lord's sacrament each Sabbath provided a special opportunity to work this step. While the deacons walked through the congregation with the emblems of covenant, we reviewed our behavior for the previous week. Then, in silent prayer, we sought forgiveness from our Heavenly Father for our shortcomings. Through this exercise, we could let go of yesterday's guilt and look forward to a new week with lightened hearts. Also, the philosophy "promptly admitting when we were wrong" contributed to a healthy marriage. Resentment and bruised feelings were quickly resolved through communication and sincere apologies.

We knelt daily in prayer, together and individually, to implement AA's Eleventh Step: "Sought through prayer and meditation to improve our conscious contact with God, as we understood Him, praying only for knowledge of His will for us and the power to carry that out." Prayer, coupled with striving to live the Twelve Steps and gospel principles, opened the windows of heaven.[1] We received blessings beyond what we thought possible. We repaid debt, repaired credit, and purchased a nice home in the country. We served concurrently as our ward's Young Men and Young Women presidents. We became legal guardians of our granddaughter and supported my son Josh's full-time mission. Instead of having only a bike for transportation, as was the case during part of our early-married life, we now had two automobiles and a bunch of bikes. As part of my employment, I was able to visit many of America's largest cities. Often Vickie accompanied me. We came to believe that all things *are* possible with the Lord.

But some things could not be repaired. I could not wipe away the damage alcoholism had had on my original family. Undoing the past was impossible. My children had missed enjoying a "normal" childhood. Each family member had suffered the social stigma that comes with divorce. Although I sought their forgiveness formally, and informally through consistent caring, I learned an unequivocal fact: *Broken Families = Broken Hearts! Always!* I had to accept that fact and accept living with a permanent heartache.

But blessings continued. Four years after Vickie's and my temple sealing, I was called as an ordinance worker in the Provo Utah Temple.

June 2, 1996

Each Friday after work, I make the hurried trip from my home in the country, through rush hour traffic and up to the Provo Utah Temple. Locating a parking place, I hurriedly limp up the long side-walk as fast as my pseudo hip will carry me. Entering the temple, I am detained only for a moment as a brother scrutinizes my temple recommend. Skipping down the soft (yes, my hip can skip), carpeted stairs to the basement locker rooms, I change from street clothes into my white suit. Checking my neatness in the mirror, I hurry down the corridor to the meeting room and relax in a soft chair.

Our shift's correlation meeting begins as I join with forty other white-clad brothers in singing a deep, bass rendition of a hymn that reverences Jesus. While we sing, an inspiring experience occurs as sister workers singing in an adjacent room provide an echo. They sound like an choir of angels. The stress of the business day begins to fade. My body shifts down as my spiritual surrounding evaporates tension.

Following meeting, I ascend the temple stairs to a higher floor for the evening's first assignment. Fragments of our recently sung hymn still linger in my mind, "Peace be still . . . Peace, Peace be still."[2]

The joy of leaving the world and entering the Lord's house fills me once again. A quickening Spirit permeates the corridors, paintings, chandeliers, rooms, people, and me. My soul is filled to its center with Christ's light and love.

I loved being a home teacher and a temple worker. I was content in these callings, but now a new version of an old program would surface and intrigue me. A dozen years earlier, Vickie and I had been introduced to a pilot program for Latter-day Saint addicts and alcoholics. I recorded one of our experiences with that program in a 1985 journal entry.

March 6, 1985

At the invitation of Dr. McFarland [my friend from the VA Hospital], Vic and I have been attending LDS drug and alcohol recovery group meetings in the West Jordan Stake high council room. Similar to AA meetings, the Lord's Spirit is in abundance. Participants share their struggles with alcohol as well as illegal and legal drugs.

Vic and I share our experience and try to offer strength and hope by referring to the scriptures and often to the AA "Big Book." We talk about the critical role the Twelve Steps play in our emotional and spiritual recovery.

Driving home, we have discussed our concern as to why our references and encouragement toward the Twelve Steps have not been more welcomed. We know that Bill W. and Dr. Bob [cofounders of AA] were inspired by Heavenly Father to develop the Twelve Steps so that addicts can recover. We know they are *true Christian principles*. Yet there is obvious resistance in discussing them.

My testimony from attending hundreds of AA meetings is that shared experience in recovery is important, but it only gets you half way there. There must be a spiritual program of recovery—the Twelve Steps. The program is: *Unless you have walked in my shoes, don't try to tell me how to get sober. If you have walked in them, tell me your experience, give me your strength, and offer me hope in living the Twelve Steps. Then, and only then, will I listen.*

Our hearts told us that this Church program was a sincere and commendable effort. It could "lead a horse to water." But without the Twelve Steps, the trough was at least half empty. Now, twelve years later, we saw the trough was beginning to fill.

August 22, 1997

Vickie and I received welcomed news. LDS Family Services has instituted an *official* Latter-day Saint Substance Abuse Recovery Program based on gospel principles *and the Twelve Steps* (which are one and the same). Couple missionaries are being called to administer this new program. Facilitators, *with experience in recovery,* are being called to conduct group meetings.

We attended a meeting to see for ourselves if this new program was what we had hoped for.

September 21, 1997

Last evening, Vickie and I went to one of the new LDS Substance Abuse Recovery Group meetings. As we entered the stake high council room, the sharing part of the meeting had already begun. A lady in her thirties was speaking. Referring to the man beside her, she shared that, although they were Latter-day Saints, they had made the mistake, early in their marriage, of running with a party crowd. Over time, and three children later, her husband had gotten heavily into drugs and a divorce ensued. She had remarried and tried to forget him, but couldn't. Her second marriage ended in divorce. Now, she was back tentatively supporting her first husband who had entered a Twelve Step program to overcome his addiction.

The man she was referring to shared next. Based upon my AA experience, I felt he was pretty much saying the *right things* from his heart. Speaking in humility, acknowledging his powerlessness, he stated that he had been clean and sober several months.

Sharing continued around the table until it was my turn. I knew I could just introduce myself as a recovering alcoholic and pass. I was fatigued from a hectic business day. But I also knew that my experience as a Church member and my AA background might help someone. I decided to say a few words.

As I began speaking, my heart lightened and the stress of the day fell away. Then, a feeling burst into my bosom that this was the Lord's *official* Substance Abuse Recovery Program for addicted Latter-day Saints.

My wife shared next. With tears of gratitude Vickie related some of her experiences as an alcoholic and as the wife of an alcoholic. Referring to the Eleventh Step and theme for the meeting, she spoke of improving her conscious contact with God through prayer, and how, as she drew closer to Him and surrendered, power had been given her to overcome many of life's serious trials.

The meeting lasted nearly two hours. The Savior's love was rich and abundant. Being "caught up in the spirit," I was surprised when the facilitator announced it was time to wrap up. Following the meeting, we visited with the couple missionaries and expressed our enthusiasm.

A month later, I was contacted by the missionaries and invited to facilitate a weekly meeting at an LDS stake center near my home. At first elated by the invitation, I then realized that the meetings were held on Friday evenings, my temple night.

October 21, 1997 (My 50th birthday!)

After a year and a half of wonderful labor, I have asked to be released as an ordinance worker in the Provo Utah Temple. In its place, I have accepted an invitation from Church Family Services to facilitate an LDS Substance Abuse Recovery Group. Although I will miss working in the temple, I have found Christ's light and love abundant in this program.

As I prepared to facilitate my first meeting, the high council room filled to near capacity. My stomach also filled to capacity with large butterflies. But soon, the calming presence of the Physician beckoning people to come to His Hospital, filled the room. My butterflies shrunk into tiny, soft, spiritually fluttering ones.

Jesus taught that through His children He would do His work. They would become His Hands, His Voice, and express His Love. Here is the power and the miracle that happens in Twelve Step meetings: *One humble person sharing from his heart, without judgment or guile, to another.* Through their mouths, the Savior points the way home. Each humble expression speaks to our hearts; and our hearts, and hope, and strength go out to others.

Humility and understanding through experience, mingled with the Lord's sweet spirit and His atoning sacrifice—that's the magic!

Alcoholics Anonymous's Twelfth Step states, "Having had a spiritual awakening as the result of these steps, I tried to carry this message to alcoholics, and to practice these principles in all my affairs." It was in obedience to this last all-encompassing step that I found myself visiting another drunk on that hot Sunday afternoon in the summer of 2000.

July 17, 2000 (Journal Entry Continued)

Still dressed in white shirt and tie from attending church, I introduced myself to the man on the bed, "Hi, I'm Phil. I'm an alcoholic. Your bishop asked me to drop by."

Lynn, a man in his early fifties, but looking much older, was now sitting on the edge of the bed. "The bishop sent you? Are you sure? Are you really an alcoholic? You sure don't look like one!"

I responded, "I've been sober quite a few years, but you can be sure I am an alcoholic. I think I understand some of what you're feeling. Would you like to talk?"

Lynn asked me several more questions to assure himself that I was really an alcoholic, then began sharing.

Nothing new here, just another alcoholic's story. He was once married and had enjoyed a prosperous life. Then his wife had left with another man and alcohol got the better of him. Leaving California, he had returned to his roots in Utah hoping to find a better way. In AA, we call this a *geographical* solution. It *never* works because spiritual and emotional illness is the root of the problem, not a person's physical location.

Depressed and unable to find work, Lynn had located the LDS bishop in charge of transient Church members, and asked for help. He received assistance and was aided in obtaining temporary work, but it would end soon. He didn't know what he would do after that.

Through personal experience and based upon what he told me, I knew what he should do—*accept defeat at the hands of alcohol and surrender himself to God.*

He said he had gone *through* AA (like it was a treatment center) and was familiar with the Twelve Steps. He then stated that if he could just get a break and get back on his feet, he was sure he could *control* his drinking. I knew from this statement that AA hadn't gone *through* him—no surrender here. My heart ached for him. I knew he hadn't reached his bottom. But he was sincere and honest, a good man—still trying.

We talked at length. I told him I was a temple ordinance worker and had been for several years. Looking steadily into his eyes, I told him that I could easily envision him dressed in white and sitting in a temple endowment room, a worthy member of the Church. Tears filled his eyes as he said, "Do you really believe that?"

I gently affirmed my answer, "Yes, Lynn, with all my heart I know you can go to the temple. You simply must be willing to take certain steps."

I asked him if he would like to kneel in prayer. He accepted. Light entered my heart and seemed to fill the dismal room as two sons of God knelt together and sought their Heavenly Father's help. As our prayer continued, I felt the wonderful and familiar peace that testified our Father had picked up the receiver. Tears flowed down Lynn's cheeks as we stood and embraced. I knew he had also felt this feeling, perhaps for the first time in a long time.

I invited Lynn to join me at a Substance Abuse meeting. I explained that this new program incorporated gospel principles and an LDS approach to AA's Twelve Steps. He accepted.

My mom died in the summer of 2000. Although her passing left a huge emptiness, I was thankful that our relationship had been fully repaired. Her last note to me was one of her most special. On this occasion, we had spent what would turn out to be our last Mother's Day weekend together. We had cleaned yards, planted spring flowers, and attended church. In church I had been asked to say the closing prayer in sacrament meeting. In that prayer, I expressed my love for Mom.

May 3, 2000 (Note from Mom retained in my journal.)

Dearest Will, My Babe,

I know you know how much I truly love and appreciate all you do for me, just as I know how good it makes you feel to come down and help out. But, I just want you to know how special it was yesterday to work side-by-side with you, enjoying just the two of us as always! Another unforgettable day to store away with all the other precious memories we've made. It really gave me a big lift, both emotionally and physically.

I am so very thankful for you—your loving, caring, thoughtfulness; your expertise, etc. It seems like we've been trimming, working, hiking, biking, moving bushes, dragging huge tree stumps around, building chicken roosts, and whatever I've wanted done around The Ranch, just forever and ever. I pray that it will continue for many years and on into eternity.

I thank God for all of my many blessings. I am very thankful for you and want you to know that. I know that you do—I've told you enough times. But I wouldn't trade you for anyone, or anything. Thank you for the beautiful prayer of yesterday. I'll never forget it. We do now, and have always had, a rare and precious relationship, mother and son. I value it and treasure it. I am more proud of you than words can express.

I'll love you forever,

Mom

Mom's note brings my journey full circle. I had traveled back to where it all began. But I was not the same person. Twenty-seven years earlier as a young seminary teacher in Idaho, my wildest imaginations could not have conjured the life I would yet live. Eight years later, I would be separated from my God, untethered and adrift, tortured by the consequences of violating true principles. Then the miracle of rescue and healing began, not an overnight miracle, but a process. The AA Old-Timers, a group of crusty, wise men and women, tossed me a rope. This rope consisted of several strands, each one critical to my recovery from alcoholism and return to Church activity. The strands were: The Twelve Steps; the spoken wisdom of recovering addicts; the support and understanding of compassionate friends and family; the scriptures; faith; hope; and prayer. All of these strands wound about a central cord—*the Perfect Brightness of Hope*—the Atonement of Jesus Christ.

There were times I let go of the rope and abandoned myself to the world. But then I re-grasped it and pulled myself up to living in better harmony with true principles. The rope often slipped through my hands and burned painful wounds into my spiritual flesh. But I have been able to hang on. I have learned to not look back dwelling on past mistakes or anticipating the future with fear. I use this rope to pull myself through the challenge of each moment. This process continues daily, one minute at a time; and, I believe, *will forever.* I have learned that I must press forward with a steadfastness in Christ, having a perfect brightness of hope, and a

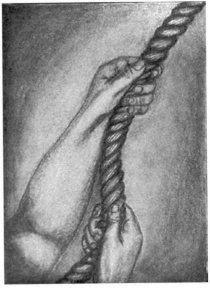

The Old-Timers tossed me a rope. I use this rope to pull myself though the challenge of each moment. This process continues daily, one minute at a time, and, I believe, will forever.

love of God and of all men. I know that if I do press forward, feasting upon the words of Christ, and endure to the end, my Father promises that I will have eternal life (2 Nephi 31:20).

While in the temple, I occasionally kneel at the altar with my wife in a sealing session. I look into the soft eyes of my sweetheart. Her loving gaze and warm smile return. The sealer pronounces the eternal marriage vows in behalf of the deceased couple we represent. We feel their presence. We feel the priesthood power by which they become sealed together forever. We feel peace, light, and joy. With the passing of time, our hope increases for that precious day when we will bow in reverence before the Lord Jesus Christ and hear him say, "Welcome home my good and faithful servants. Of me, thou hast not been ashamed" (Romans 1:16).

The final paragraph from Alcoholics Anonymous says it best: "Abandon yourself to God as you understand God. Admit your faults to Him and to your fellows. Clear away the wreckage of your past. Give freely of what you find and join us. We shall be with you in the Fellowship of the Spirit, and you will surely meet some of us as you trudge the Road of Happy Destiny. May God bless you and keep you—until then." [3]

✐OTES

1. *Blessings poured out.* "Bring ye all the tithes into the storehouse, that there may be meat in mine house, and prove me now herewith, saith the Lord of hosts, if I will not open you the windows of heaven, and pour you out a blessing, that there shall not be room enough to receive it" (Malachi 3:10).

2. *Hymn—Dear To The Heart of the Shepherd.* "Dear to the heart of the Shepherd, Dear are the sheep of his fold; Dear is the love that he gives them, Dearer than silver or gold. Dear to the heart of the Shepherd, Dear are his "other" lost sheep; Over the mountain she follows, Over

the waters so deep. Out in the desert they wander, Hungry and helpless and cold; Off to the rescue he hastens, Bringing them back to the fold."
—*Hymns of The Church of Jesus Christ of Latter-day Saints*, 1985 no. 221.

3. *Alcoholics Anonymous.* Alcoholics Anonymous World Services Inc., 164.

$\mathcal{E}$PILOGUE

Sixty years ago, Matthew Cowley, an Apostle of the LDS Church, said, "I don't think there is a family in the United States . . . who isn't affected by a relative or a close friend who is addicted to some of these habits (tobacco, alcohol, and drugs) . . . *It is up to you and to me to reach out to these men and* women."[1] (See Appendix II.)

This statement was made a half century *before* the gates holding back a flood of street and prescription drugs opened. Today, addiction and alcoholism have swelled to reach tidal wave proportions. The need for those *not addicted* to understand and reach out to those individuals who *are addicted* is urgent. The Savior gave this challenge: "How think ye? If a man have an hundred sheep, and one of them be gone astray, doth he not leave the ninety and nine, and goeth into the mountains, and seeketh that which is gone astray? And if so be that he find it, verily I say unto you, *he rejoiceth more of that sheep*, than of the ninety and nine which went not astray" (Matthew 18:12–13).

We are to *seek out* those who have gone astray—*not criticize them*. In these latter days, the Lord has told us: "Wherefore I say unto you that ye ought to forgive one another; for he that forgiveth not his brother his trespasses standeth condemned before the Lord, *for there remaineth in him the greater sin*" (Doctrine & Covenants 64:9; emphasis added).

One hundred sixty years ago, President Brigham Young taught

regarding our obligation to fellowship those who struggle with human failings:

> Who has the greatest reason to be thankful to his God–the man that has no strong passion or evil appetite to overcome, or the one that tries day by day to overcome, and yet is overtaken in a fault?
>
> Who has reason to be the most thankful? The being that has comparatively no strong passion to overcome ought constantly to walk in the vale of humility, *rather than boast of his righteousness over his brother.* We are under obligation, through the filial feeling and ties of humanity, to more or less fellowship those who do evil . . . If brethren and sisters are overtaken in fault, your hearts should be filled with kindness—with brotherly, angelic feeling—to overlook their faults as far as possible.[2]

President Gordon B. Hinkley echoed this counsel:

> There are those who were once warm in the faith, but whose faith has grown cold. Many of them wish to come back but *do not know quite how to do it. They need friendly hands reaching out to them.* With a little effort, many of them can be brought back to feast again at the table of the Lord.[3]

Many can be brought back. I know because that "little effort" of understanding, compassion, and fellowshipping brought me back. It doesn't take much—just a friendly hand extended.

If you are an addict traveling in the opposite direction of happiness, you can turn about. Elder Richard G. Scott, a modern apostle of Jesus Christ, testifies that transgression can be turned into a climbing tool toward happiness.

> I know that every difficulty we face in life, even those that come from our own negligence *or even transgression,* can be turned by the Lord into growth experiences, a virtual ladder upward. I certainly do not recommend transgression as a path to growth. It is painful, difficult, and so totally unnecessary. It is far wiser and so much easier to move forward in righteousness. But through proper repentance, faith in the Lord Jesus Christ, and obedience to His commandments, *even the disappointment that comes from transgression can be converted into a return to happiness.*[4]

Nor do I recommend transgression as a means to gain experience. I echo Elder Scott's statement: *Transgression is painful, difficult, and so totally unnecessary!* I will never regain time lost through transgression. I will never undo the pain I brought into the lives of others. But I would make my situation worse if I did not use my experience to climb to a better life. As I have done this, I have been able to affect the lives of others for good. If you are an addict, or care for an addict, you can do it as well! Begin *this moment* by admitting to yourself: *I recognize my life is unmanageable because of addiction or because I am powerless over someone else's addiction*; and then *turn your will and your life over to a Power Greater Than Yourself—your Heavenly Father!* Do it now! You don't have to remain locked in the sin-guilt cycle of self destruction, or continue suffering because of some other person's actions. Another modern Apostle of Jesus Christ, President Boyd K. Packer testifies this is so.

> The gospel teaches us that relief from torment and guilt can be earned through repentance . . . *There is no habit, no addiction, no rebellion, no transgression, no offense exempted from the promise of complete forgiveness* . . . It is contrary to the order of heaven for any soul to be locked into compulsive immoral behavior with no way out.[5]

Once you admit your problem, you will have taken the first step toward repentance and recovery. The next step is easier. If you are LDS, ask your bishop about the LDS Substance Abuse Recovery Program or, if not LDS, find a meeting of Alcoholics Anonymous or some other Twelve Step group. Then, don't wait—go to the meeting—and continue going to meetings! Do it today! *It will be the most important decision of your life.*

One purpose in sharing my story was to provide information to addicts, alcoholics, spouses, friends, families, employers, clergy and all seeking answers to the problem of addiction. In Appendix I and Appendix II, I provide more information about alcoholism, addiction, and attitude. This information cannot replace the understanding that comes from attending Twelve Step meetings, but it is a place to begin. Please *do not set this book aside* until you have considered this vital knowledge.

*N*OTES

1.   Matthew Cowley, *Matthew Cowley Speaks*. (Salt Lake City: Deseret Book, 1954), 345, emphasis added.

2.   *Teachings of the Presidents of the Church: Brigham Young* (Salt Lake City: The Church of Jesus Christ of Latter-day Saints, 1997), 180.

3.   Gordon B. Hinkley, "Reach with a Rescuing Hand," *Ensign*, November 1996, 85, emphasis added.

4.   Richard G. Scott, "Finding Joy in Life," *Ensign*, May 1996, 24, emphasis added.

5.   Boyd K. Packer, "The Brilliant Morning of Forgiveness," *Ensign*, November 1995, 18, emphasis added.

$\mathcal{R}$ECOVERY & THE TWELVE–STEP PROGRAM

NOTE: IN THIS APPENDIX, THE TERM "ADDICT" APPLIES TO alcoholics, drug addicts and all others with *destructive*, compulsive behaviors.

Recovery for anyone affected by compulsive-addictive behavior begins by *gaining awareness* and *getting information!* The addict gains information by listening to those in recovery. For the addict's codependents (a parent, spouse, child, or friend living in a close relationship with an addict), recovery begins by getting information through literature, programs, and other codependents in recovery. Both the addict and the codependent must become aware that, unless arrested, drug or alcohol addiction *is terminal.* This understanding must then be followed by a *spiritual* plan of action.

There are many programs offering treatment for addiction. From my experience, those most effective are based upon Alcoholics Anonymous's Twelve Steps of Recovery. Because they work, the Twelve Steps have been adopted into various programs such as Narcotics Anonymous, Overeaters Anonymous, Smokers Anonymous, and the LDS Substance Abuse Recovery Program.

Part One of this appendix provides a historical sketch of Alcoholics Anonymous. Part Two reviews the Twelve Steps and key principles of AA. Part Three provides information for the codependent. Part Four gives insight into the peculiar relationship between addiction and Christian cultures that have specific health codes (such as the LDS Church). Part Five contains a review and a promise.

PART 1

Alcoholics Anonymous—
A Brief History

Alcoholics Anonymous originated in the 1930s mostly from the efforts of two men, Bill W. and Dr. Bob[1] now referred to as the cofounders of AA. After many years of alcohol abuse, doctors had pronounced Bill incurable from alcoholism. He describes his condition this way:

> The frightful day came when I drank once more. The curve of my declining moral and bodily health fell off like a ski-jump. After a time I returned to the hospital. This was the finish, the curtain, it seemed to me. My weary and despairing wife was informed that it would all end with heart failure during delirium tremens, or I would develop a wet brain, perhaps within a year. She would soon have to give me over to the undertaker or the asylum. They did not need to tell me. I knew, and almost welcomed the idea.[2]

But then a friend, who'd had a spiritual experience, visited Bill:

> But my friend sat before me, and he made the point-blank declaration that God had done for him what he could not do for himself. His human will had failed. Doctors had pronounced him incurable. Society was about to lock him up. Like myself, he had admitted complete defeat. Then he had, in effect, been raised from the dead, suddenly taken from the scrap heap to a level of life better than the best he had ever known. Had this power originated in him? Obviously it

had not. There had been no more power in him than there was in me at that minute; and this was none at all.[3]

Bill describes how deeply he was affected when his friend recommended that he appeal to *his own* concept of God.

That statement hit me hard. It melted the icy intellectual mountain in whose shadow I had lived and shivered many years. I stood in the sunlight at last. It was only a matter of being willing to believe in a Power greater than I was. Nothing more was required of me to make my beginning.[4]

Following one more relapse, Bill wrote:

At the hospital I was separated from alcohol for the last time. Treatment seemed wise, for I showed signs of delirium tremens. There I humbly offered myself to God, as I then understood Him, to do with me as He would. I placed myself unreservedly under his care and direction. I admitted for the first time that of myself I was nothing; that without Him I was lost. I ruthlessly faced my sins and became willing to have my newfound Friend take them away, root and branch. I have not had a drink since.[5]

Bill describes more intimately the spiritual experience that occurred during his last stay in the hospital.

My depression deepened unbearably, and finally it seemed to me as though I were at the very bottom of the pit. For the moment, the last vestige of my proud obstinacy was crushed. All at once I found myself crying out, "If there is a God, let Him show Himself! I am ready to do anything, anything."

Suddenly the room lit up with a great white light. It seemed to me, in the mind's eye, that I was on a mountain and that a wind, not of air but of spirit, was blowing. And then it (the idea) burst upon me that I was a free man. Slowly the ecstasy subsided. I lay on the bed, but now for a time I was in another world, a new world of consciousness. All about me and through me there was a wonderful feeling of Presence, and I thought to myself, "So this is the God of the preachers."[6]

Bill lived in continuous sobriety from his 1931 hospital experience with God until his death in 1971.

Alcoholics' sharing their experience in recovery is the hinge pin of AA. Dr. Bob shares his recollection of his initial meeting with Bill.

> He gave me information about the subject of alcoholism which was undoubtedly helpful. Of far more importance was the fact that he was the first living human with whom I had ever talked *who knew what he was talking about in regard to alcoholism from actual experience.* In other words, he talked my language. He knew all the answers, and certainly not because he had picked them up in his reading.[7]

Dr. Bob's first day of permanent sobriety was June 10, 1935. By 1950, the year of his death, "he had carried the AA message to over five thousand alcoholic men and women, and to all these he gave his medical services without thought of charge."[8]

Bill W. and Dr. Bob collaborated with other alcoholics to capture their knowledge and experience about recovering from alcoholism. This effort resulted in the foundational book *Alcoholics Anonymous,* first published in 1939. With an official platform, AA began a legacy that would restore millions of hopeless addicts and their families to productive and happy lives.[9]

"Alcoholics Anonymous is a fellowship of men and women who have a *sincere* desire to stop drinking and who meet together often to share their experience, strength and hope with each other in order to solve their common problems."[10] It is with this common purpose that AA brings together men and women of all age groups, education, and backgrounds to share their experiences in living The Twelve Steps.

PART 2

Alcoholics Anonymous—Twelve Steps and Key Principles

At the beginning of every AA meeting, a member is invited to read a portion of Chapter Five from *Alcoholics Anonymous*. Members then use the bulk of the meeting to share their experience, strength, and hope. It is through this sharing that understanding comes. At the meeting's conclusion, all join hands and recite in unison either the Serenity Prayer or the Lord's Prayer. In many cases, the prayer is followed by the unison chant, "Keep coming back. It works if you work it!" Nothing describes better what addicts and codependents must *work* than those passages from Chapter Five read in *every* AA meeting. Recovering addicts repeat these words so often that they become deeply rooted in our minds. As daily challenges occur, this text surfaces from memory to deliver needed answers, strength, and hope.

How It Works

Excerpted from Chapter Five of Alcoholics Anonymous

Rarely have we seen a person fail who has thoroughly followed our path. Those who do not recover are people who cannot or will not completely give themselves to this simple program, usually men and women who are constitutionally incapable of being honest with themselves. There are such unfortunates. They are not at fault; they seem to have been born that way. They are naturally incapable of grasping and developing a manner of living which demands rigorous honesty. Their chances are less than average. There are those, too, who suffer from grave emotional and mental disorders, but many of them do recover if they have the capacity to be honest.

Our stories disclose in a general way what we used to be like, what happened, and what we are like now. If you have decided you want what we have and *are willing to go to any length to get it*—then you are ready to take certain steps.

At some of these we balked. We thought we could find *an easier, softer way*. But we could not. With all the earnestness at our command, we beg of you to be thorough and fearless from the very start. Some of us have tried to hold on to our old ideas and *the result was nil until we let go absolutely.*

Remember, we deal with alcohol [or other compulsive behaviors]—cunning, baffling, powerful. Without help it is too much for us. But there is One who has all power—that One is God. May you find Him now!

Half measures availed us nothing. We stood at the turning point. *We asked His protection and care with complete abandon.*

Here are the steps we took, which are suggested as a program of recovery:

1. We admitted we were powerless over alcohol—that our lives had become unmanageable.

2. Came to believe that a Power greater than ourselves could restore us to Sanity.

3. Made a decision to turn our will and our lives over to the care of God, as we understood Him.

4. Made a searching and fearless moral inventory of ourselves

5. Admitted to God, to ourselves, and to another human being the exact nature of our wrongs.

6. Were entirely ready to have God remove all these defects of character.

7. Humbly asked Him to remove our shortcomings.

8. Made a list of all persons we had harmed, and became willing to make amends to them all.

9. Made direct amends to such people wherever possible, except when to do so would injure them or others.

10. Continued to take personal inventory and when we were wrong promptly admitted it.

11. Sought through prayer and meditation to improve our conscious contact with God, as we understood Him, praying only for knowledge of His will for us and the power to carry that out.

12. Having had a spiritual awakening as the result of these steps, we tried to carry this message to alcoholics, and to practice these principles in all our affairs.

Many of us exclaimed, "What an order! I can't go through with it." Do not be discouraged. No one among us has been able to maintain anything like perfect adherence to these principles. *We are not saints. The point is, that we are willing to grow along spiritual lines.* The principles we have set down are guides to progress. We claim spiritual progress rather than spiritual perfection.

Our description of the alcoholic, the chapter to the agnostic, and our personal adventures before and after makes clear three pertinent ideas:

That we were alcoholic and could not manage our own lives.

That probably no human power could have relieved our alcoholism.

That God could and would if He were sought.[11]

Much of the power to arrest addiction, as described in Twelve Step programs, comes as people honestly share (in generalities, not specifics) their common weaknesses and experiences in recovery. Key knowledge is dispensed when the AA Old-Timers share. Newcomers to AA, still in the hell of active addiction, remind older members that no one in recovery is more than a drink away from once more becoming an active drunk, or addict.

The American Medical Association recognizes alcoholism as a disease, which, if not arrested, will result in insanity or death. How a person obtained the disease is no longer important. Whether the disease is immoral or not becomes meaningless. Addicts cannot deal with the immoral nature of their disease and repent until it is arrested. Addicts should be considered as people who are suffering from a terminal disease, much like sufferers of cancer or diabetes. Without a remedy, they will die from their illness. Whereas judgment and condemnation feed the disease, compassion and understanding help arrest it. As we build trusting relationships with addicts through compassionate behavior, we increase our chances of success in advising and helping the addict to join programs that will provide the antidote.

Being compassionate does *not* mean removing the natural consequences of an addict's behavior. This is a crucial principle to understand: *The more we remove the natural consequences of addictive behavior from our loved ones and friends, the more we ensure that they will remain irresponsible and unable to recognize their need for help.* If understood, this fact alone can save parents and loved ones from squandering fortunes in failed attempts to remove the consequences from their alcoholic or addict. Such a paradox. The cheapest way, allowing consequences to fall, is the best way. As my mom used to say, "It's like pounding sand down a rat hole." It is the accumulative physical and emotional pain of alcohol or drug abuse that *forces* the addict into the solution—surrender. *Don't take away their pain!* They will eventually respond. In the Old Timer's words, "We just got sick and tired of being sick and tired."

Although I experienced numerous treatment programs, pain still got my attention best. Somewhere within myself, I understood that I had to suffer the consequences of my choices in order to learn to not make those choices. I even reached a point where I gave explicit instructions to those who were consistently helping me avoid consequences—to stop! Only after numerous failings did I learn that "half measures availed me nothing." I had to be literally clubbed into making correct choices and into a serious dedication to live The Twelve Steps.

The more we addicts deny our own accountability *by shifting the consequences of our actions to others*, the more we lock ourselves in guilt and addiction. This fact is critical to both addict and codependent: Regardless of our circumstances, if we want to stop hurting and begin recovering, *we must come to an absolute acceptance that no one is responsible for the misery and unmanageability of our lives except ourselves.* No one did it to us! If we continue to insist on focusing outward, blaming others and external circumstances, we will remain powerless in the one thing we *can* change—ourselves! I learned this fact slowly—drinking binges followed by AA meetings filled with more tidbits of truth from the Old-Timers.

The pathway to recovery became clearer over time. The first time I heard an old-timer say, "A belly full of booze and a head full of AA don't mix," I didn't understand. But as my head filled with the principles of recovery, I began to understand. It became more difficult to rationalize my drinking. For a long time I went in and out of AA as if caught in a revolving door, but had no success until I let AA go *through me.*

During my early AA years, I would hear the Old-Timers speak about self-will, or willpower, as *enemies* to the addict! This was another difficult concept to grasp. After all, wasn't it willpower that would keep me from drinking? I had believed all of my life that willpower was the *only* power. A close relative had once told me, "I know you could stop drinking if you just had enough willpower—if you wanted to bad enough!" This person had no idea how badly I wanted to stop or how many times and ways I had tried. What sane person would continue torturing himself the way I had? I exerted megatons of willpower but always with the same negative results.

The addict's coming to believe that self-will or willpower is the opposite of *God's Power* is an absolute to recovery. The addict must learn not to be willful, controlling, insistent that my will, not *Thy* will be done. Until the addict realizes that he is powerless, he will continue to try to control his addiction through willpower—and he *will* continue his addiction. Willpower is not enough power. No power *on earth* is enough power to stop addiction once it is firmly established.

Once a person admits he has a problem, "comes to believe that he is powerless over alcohol (or drugs or pornography) and his life is unmanageable," and is willing to believe there is a God—"comes to realize that a power greater than himself can restore him to sanity,"— he must then *surrender his will to God*—"turn his will and his life over to the care of God, as he understands Him."

This philosophy should not be new to Latter-day Saints. Elder Neal A. Maxwell has taught:

> The submission of one's will is really the only uniquely personal thing we have to place on God's altar. The many other things we "give," brothers and sisters, are actually the things He has already given or loaned to us. However, when you and I finally submit ourselves, *by letting our individual wills be swallowed up in God's will*, then we are really giving something to Him! *It is the only possession which is truly ours to give!* Consecration thus constitutes the only *unconditional surrender* which is also *a total victory!* [12]

Elder Robert D. Hales taught:

> The Lord is the ultimate caregiver. *We must surrender ourselves to the Lord. In doing so, we give up whatever is causing our pain and turn everything over to Him.* "Cast thy burden upon the Lord, and he shall sustain thee" (Psalm. 55:22). "And then may God grant unto you that your burdens may be light, through the joy of his Son" (Alma 33:23). Through faith and trust in the Lord and obedience to His counsel, we make ourselves eligible to be partakers of the Atonement of Jesus Christ so that one day we may return to live with Him. [13]

The addict's "soul battle" is a paradox. Victory comes through surrendering one's will to God. Until this happens, our pride or self-will remains in constant struggle or *enmity* with God. President Ezra Taft Bensen describes this enmity:

> The central feature of pride is enmity—enmity toward God and enmity toward our fellowmen. Enmity means "hatred toward, hostility to, or a state of opposition." It is the power by which Satan wishes to reign over us. Pride is essentially competitive in nature. We pit our will against God's. When we direct our pride toward God, it is in the spirit of "my will and not thine be done." Our will in competition to God's will *allows desires, appetites, and passions to go unbridled.* [14]

I discovered through my experience that pride—self-will, will-power, selfishness—lies at the heart of addiction. Fed on pride, my selfish addictions grew out of control. When I persistently surrendered my will to God, I was able to starve them into extinction. Learning this philosophy was a process. I came to realize, through repeated experience, that surrendering my self-will to God *brought me immediate peace.* This did not, however, absolve me of responsibility for my actions. Similarly, we must surrender our will to God each day in prayer, then we must go forward with all of our might trying to *make choices that harmonize with His will for us.* Bill W. taught this principle:

> It is when we try to make our will conform with God's that we begin to use it rightly. To all of us, this was a most wonderful revelation. Our whole trouble had been the *misuse* of willpower. We had tried to bombard our problems with it instead of attempting to *bring it into agreement with God's intention for us.*[15]

In Chapter Five of *Alcoholics Anonymous* we read:

> The first requirement is that we be convinced that any life run on self-will can hardly be a success. On that basis we are almost always in collision with something or somebody, *even though our motives are good.* Most people try to live by *self-propulsion.* Each person is like an actor who wants to run the whole show; is forever trying to arrange the lights, the ballet, the scenery and the rest of the players in his own way. If his arrangements would only stay put, if only people would do as he wished, the show would be great.
>
> Selfishness–self-centeredness! That, we think, is the root of our troubles. Driven by a hundred forms of fear, self-delusion, self-seeking, and self-pity, we step on the toes of our fellows and they retaliate. Sometimes they hurt us, seemingly without provocation, but we invariably find that *at some time in the past we have made decisions based on self,* which later placed us in a position to be hurt.
>
> So our troubles, we think, are basically of our own making. They arise out of ourselves, and the alcoholic is an extreme example of *self-will run riot,* though he usually doesn't think so.[16]

As long as the addict believes that through his own power he can control the events and characters of his life, he will fail to overcome addiction. *Realizing that I am in a powerless situation must occur in order for me to feel the need to surrender to God.* This may happen through intervention or through personal awareness brought about by pain—*but it must happen.*

Colleen Harrison, author of *He Did Deliver Me from Bondage*, illustrates the Twelve Steps with principles from the Book of Mormon. She describes her arriving at the point of surrender.

> And thus I "dieted" my way up the scale instead of down, ending up in the summer of 1981 at about 315 pounds . . . I stepped off the scale and dropped to my knees.
>
> This time, in this prayer, there was to be no weeping and wailing on my part, no whining and justifying and rationalizing and bargaining. I was down for the count, and I knew it. I knew it because I had finally done all that I could do. I had sewn, canned, cleaned, quilted, made babies, served husband and children past a righteous balance and had held four church positions at the same time. I had stayed up late and gotten up early. I had gone to Education Week classes, read books, made charts, made pledges, gone to every "quick-weight (money) loss" program I could afford. There was nothing left. Nothing. I couldn't even pray—at least not out loud. I felt a little like Joseph in the grove, oppressed under a great cloud of darkness; only mine had not appeared in seconds—mine had taken years to build up.
>
> I literally crawled to my bedside and crumpled there, and the tears finally came—*tears of complete surrender to God.* No words, no excuses, no pleadings, no answers—just tears. These were not tears of "poor-me" or "why-me." These were tears of "not my will—but Thine be done." Today, I know those tears were, at least in spirit, mingled with blood–Jesus Christ's own atoning blood; for from that hour my deliverance began . . .[17]

In *The Unseen Enemy*, another Latter-day Saint, Robert Gray, describes his arrival at the point of powerlessness:

> To sum it all up—and no doubt about it—I was in a real hell. Total fear and hopelessness. It seemed that I had lost all hope of ever putting my life back together again. I couldn't see any light shining through. . . .
>
> I don't know how many miles I paced back and forth that night, but being totally exhausted and in the greatest anguish, I went to my room to lie down. There on the table by the bed was something that

had been following me my whole life long, a Book of Mormon. It was an old, battered up book with the cover torn right off. I would guess that it had been more abused than used. The pages were stained from heaven knows what.

I looked away. The sight of it scorched me. You see, I was raised a Mormon and quit going to church as soon as my parents got tired of making me go. But there were things I was taught as a little boy that were written in my heart. And no matter how hard I tried to drink it away, deny it, or ignore it, it just wouldn't go away.

I made a choice that day that saved my life. What the heck, I had tried everything else. I wasn't expecting too much, not having much hope at all. I read a few pages, and then did something that had become strange to me—I said a prayer.

This prayer was different from all the rest of my prayers. It came from my heart. Alcohol had won! It had ravaged my body and soul. I couldn't take anymore. I would do anything to stop drinking. I had finally reached the point where I humbled myself enough to ask for some big-time help. I was too dazed to realize it at the time, but it really was the best day of my life.[18]

As addicts, we must come to understand that all attempts to control our addictive behavior through self-will, *will fail* in the long run. The launching pad for recovery is admitting personal powerlessness and humility—this invites a Higher Power into our lives.

Although *simple*, the Twelve Steps are not *easy* principles to apply in one's life. I attempted to live them, more or less, for over *ten years* accomplished little more than breaking myself against them. *Breaking* is descriptive of what happened. My self-will, selfishness, and ego were chipped away, piece by piece, by the truth of the Twelve Steps. I became more childlike, finally submissive, ready to learn and do. The seeds of my recovery were sown in the soil of humility and surrender.

PART 3

Understanding Alcoholism, Addiction, and Codependent Behavior

Note: This section contains a number of quotations from the pamphlet, *Understanding Ourselves and Alcoholism*. I am grateful to Al-Anon Family Group Headquarters, Inc., for permission to quote this material. Although the passages cited refer specifically to alcoholism, the effects and behaviors of addiction are universal. For this reason, the quotes provided have application to all compulsive and addictive behaviors.

The American Medical Association describes alcoholism as a disease that can be arrested *but not cured*. Alcoholics have an uncontrollable desire to drink which becomes progressively worse over time. Without treatment and arrest, this disease usually ends in early death or insanity. For all alcoholics, the only effective treatment is *complete abstinence* throughout the rest of their lives. *At no point can the alcoholic begin drinking again without falling swiftly back into uncontrollable addiction.* The notion that most alcoholics are skid row, hopeless bums is a myth.

All kinds of people are alcoholics . . . only about three to five percent of alcoholics are "bums" or skid-row types. The rest have families, friends and jobs, and are functioning fairly well. But their drinking affects some part of their lives. Their family life, their social life, or their job life may suffer. It might be all three. *An alcoholic is someone whose drinking causes a continuing and growing problem in any department of his/her life.*[19]

We alcoholics drink because *we believe* we have to. We are in emotional pain and use alcohol to mask our pain. Over time and with continued use, we become convinced that we cannot live without a drink. This is our *obsession.*

> When some alcoholics try to do without alcohol, the withdrawal symptoms are so overwhelming that they go back to drinking because drinking seems to be the only way to get rid of the agony. This is *addiction.*[20]

It is the dream of every alcoholic who has crossed the line into addiction that he will someday be able to return to "good-time" drinking and join the old party crowd. We use every conceivable argument to convince ourselves that we are not alcoholic.

> Here are some of the methods we have tried: Drinking beer only, limiting the number of drinks, never drinking alone, never drinking in the morning, drinking only at home, never having it in the house, never drinking during business hours, drinking only at parties, switching from scotch to brandy, drinking only natural wines, agreeing to resign if ever drunk on the job, taking a trip, not taking a trip, swearing off forever (with and without a solemn oath), taking more physical exercise, reading inspirational books.[21]

Regardless of the methods tried or promises made, sooner or later, we end up getting drunk. This is our *compulsion.*

Alcoholism is a baffling disease because those who have it are usually the last to realize it. This is our *denial.* Recovery is only possible when we arrive at a point where we truly desire to stop drinking, when we recognize our need for help, and when we admit we cannot overcome our addiction alone.

Alcoholism is a family disease. Those individuals who live closest to the alcoholic are affected the most. The term "codependent" refers to these individuals, usually a parent, spouse, child, or friend, who are living in a close relationship with an alcoholic. The codependent's behavior becomes intertwined or dependent on the behavior of the addicted person. These individuals attempt to control the irrational behavior of the alcoholic. Unable to do so, they begin to believe they—the codependents—are to blame. Unable to separate their own emotions from the alcoholic's, codependents feel the alcoholic's hurt, fear, guilt, and pain. They, too, become emotionally ill as they take on ever-increasing worries and fears about important family issues that the alcoholic neglects.

> These well-meaning people begin to count the number of drinks another person is having. They pour expensive liquor down drains, search the house for hidden bottles, listen for the sound of opening cans. *All their thinking is directed at what the alcoholic is doing or not doing* and how to get the drinker to stop drinking. This is their *obsession.*[22]

Over a short period, a codependent's mood can swing from anger, to resentment, to guilt, to anxiety, to elation, to despair—all based upon the behavior of the alcoholic. Ultimately, codependents become so fixated on the other's behavior, they lose their own identity. They spiral downward and deeper into their own emotional *and* physical illness. And, just like the alcoholic, they deny their own illness.

> Those who are close to the alcoholic begin to pretend. They accept promises, they believe, they want to believe the problem has gone away each time there is a sober period. When every good sense tells them there is something wrong with the alcoholic's drinking and thinking, they still hide how they feel and what they know. This is their *denial.*[23]

The most damaging aspect of alcoholism for the codependent is *guilt.*

> Perhaps the most severe damage to those who have shared some part of life with an alcoholic comes in the form of the nagging belief that they are somehow at fault; they were not up to it all, not attractive enough, not clever enough to have solved this problem for the one they love. They think it was something they did or did not do. These are *their feelings of guilt.*[24]

The flaw in codependents' thinking is that they have centered all of their attention on the *alcoholic's behavior* and trying to control them. In doing this, they lose sight of what they *can* control. This paradigm can only be remedied when a codependent shifts his thinking focus from outward—what he can't control, the alcoholic's behavior—to inward—what he has some control over, himself. The codependent must come to realize that, in order to save himself, he has to stop focusing on and *trying to control* the alcoholic. If he doesn't, his own future is at terrible risk.

> We soon come to know that our own thinking has to change before we can make a new and successful approach to the problem of living. It is in Al-Anon (and other Twelve Step groups) that we learn to deal with our obsession, our anxiety, our anger, our denial, and our feelings of guilt . . . Little by little we come to realize . . .that much of our discomfort comes from our attitudes. We try to change these attitudes, learn about our responsibilities to ourselves, discover feelings of self-worth, love, and grow spiritually. *The emphasis begins to be lifted from the alcoholic and placed where we do have some power—over our own lives.*[25]

PART 4

Addiction & Christian Cultures with Stringent Health Codes

Note: This section refers specifically to my experiences as a member of The Church of Jesus Christ of Latter-day Saints. However, this information applies to members of any religious organization that places emphasis on living a health code that advises against the use of addictive substances or indulging in other obsessive-compulsive habits.

In the area where I attended AA meetings, there was a pronounced and often *announced* resentment by AA members toward the area's predominant faith—The Church of Jesus-Christ of Latter-day Saints. Much of this resentment came as a result of Church member's tendency to place persons who use coffee and tobacco high on the list of moral transgressors. Early in recovery, most addicts use coffee and tobacco to help them deal with their cravings for alcohol and drugs. Coffee has been the official beverage of AA from the beginning.

> They went out into the city's lower edges, the city of Akron, and gathered together a group of drunks, and they started talking and drinking coffee. Bob's wife told me she had never made as much coffee as she did in the next two weeks. And they stayed there drinking coffee

and starting this group of one helping the other, and that was the way AA developed.[26]

I used both coffee and tobacco as crutches, albeit unhealthy ones, to help me fight the more life-threatening and life-altering drug, alcohol. I am in no way advocating their use, rather, simply stating that their use is routine for the alcoholic and should not be judged too harshly. Once the alcoholism is under control, the other vices can be tamed. Alcoholics and drug addicts are teetering between life and death. Their use of tobacco or coffee, although addictive substances, is not as destructive as are mind-altering drugs and alcohol. Thus, during the early recovery period, tobacco and coffee use are *not* the primary concern.

AA recommends that, as people recover, they seek out a religion or faith and become active therein. Alcoholics who find sobriety through twelve-step programs gain a desire to improve their lives. Often, they are able to overcome their dependence on coffee and tobacco. Recovering alcoholics become prime candidates for reactivation into their faith or religion because they have painfully learned that only reliance on God has pulled them through. Church fellowship, without condemning judgment (especially for their use of tobacco and coffee) is the magnet that draws recovering alcoholics into religious activity.

The words *alcoholic* and *Latter-day Saint* are seldom spoken in the same phrase. Latter-day Saints who use alcohol or drugs do so in defiance of clearly stated ecclesiastical teachings and strong cultural sanctions. For me, violating Church counsel, going against the norm, and ignoring my own conscience resulted in strong feelings of guilt. From those feelings of guilt came increased alcohol and drug abuse, which resulted in more guilt. And thus the cycle went on. My not being able to live up to my former values, my all-or-nothing perfectionism, and my unwillingness to forgive myself, resulted in guilt so painful that using the substance that created the guilt became the remedy.

Many Latter-day Saints place the Word of Wisdom offender at the top of their list of Serious Sinners. The attitude, *God wouldn't have anything to do with these sinners,* is often reflected in not-so-subtle ways. Member alcoholics can become bitter toward their faith when, what they hoped for—a hand of fellowship—becomes a pointing finger of judgment. Although in desperate need, the sufferer is often alienated from his faith. Latter-day Saint alcoholics, already laden with guilt, are super-sensitive to the judgments of others, especially Church members. Intimately aware of their own defects, they compare how they feel on the inside—polluted and dirty—with the apparently perfect appearance of those around them. To compensate, addicts build barriers: shame, self-judgment, paranoia, an *I-don't-care* attitude, and a false ego. They shield themselves from everyone except those who are the most persistent and understanding—those who do not portray a *holier-than-thou* attitude.

Some active Church members build barriers against the alcoholic through a self-righteous attitude and judgment. *Walls of attitude* are built around the chapels discouraging the *sinner* from entering. The bishop who rebaptized me once remarked in a sacrament meeting something like, "Many members believe it is a sin for Word of Wisdom breakers to come to church, when the real sin lies in the fact that part of the reason they don't come is because they don't feel welcome."

My experience supports this bishop's statement. Because I smelled of alcohol and tobacco, many Church members shunned me. I can appreciate how lepers in olden times must have felt. With the exception of a few persistent Christians, I experienced little welcome. But I was determined to attend church regardless of what others thought. I would sometimes smoke a cigarette in the church parking lot, take a drink of whiskey, and then go into the chapel like a fire-breathing dragon. I didn't do this to impress or annoy anyone. Knowing I was unworthy and as an excommunicated member, I never partook of the sacrament. This behavior was simply me during that part of my life. I received many nonverbal, and a few verbal, rebukes from the Saints sitting near me. But I was spiritually starving to death. I wanted to feel the inner peace associated with a life in harmony with the gospel. I knew if I waited until I smelled better, I would never get back my spiritual health.

Matthew Cowley, the Apostle known as "The Patron Saint of the Alcoholic" (see Appendix II), states the problem and the challenge:

The good man—no matter how bad he is, how low he has sunk—is the man who starts coming up. The bad man is the man who, no matter how high he has reached in his goodness and morality, begins to come down.[27]

PART 5

Review and a Promise

Recovery is a process. Those persons who (1) admit they have a problem; (2) believe in a God and trust in His power; (3) surrender themselves to God for deliverance; (4) review their wrongs; (5) make amends to others; (6) take daily personal moral inventory and promptly admit fault; (7) pray continually to improve their relationship with God; and (8) consistently help others *will overcome addiction.*

I believe the majority of alcoholic and addicted people have the honesty and courage to take these steps. If you are an alcoholic or an addict, or know someone who is, consider the consequences of not taking these steps. Professional workers, medical associations, and AA members unanimously agree that the single pathway alcoholics and addicts follow always leads to one of three eventual ends. In AA, the pathway is known as "The Four Horsemen"—*Terror, Bewilderment, Frustration, and Despair.*[28] The pathway always ends in *incarceration, insanity,* or *early death.*

But there is great hope. Twelve Step programs throughout the world promise that a new way of life awaits those willing to be thorough and fearless from the start.

> We are going to know a new freedom and a new happiness. We will not regret the past nor wish to shut the door on it. We will comprehend the word serenity and we will know peace. No matter how far down the scale we have gone, we will see how our experience can

benefit others. That feeling of uselessness and self-pity will disappear. We will lose interest in selfish things and gain interest in our fellows. Self-seeking will slip away. Our whole attitude and outlook upon life will change. Fear of people and of economic insecurity will leave us. We will intuitively know how to handle situations which used to baffle us. We will suddenly realize that God is doing for us what we could not do for ourselves.[29]

I add my testimony to myriad recovered alcoholics and addicts who live by the Twelve Steps and who are realizing these promises daily. I know these promises are true. They are evidenced every day of my life. God is doing for me what I could not do for myself.

Notes

1. *Anonymity.* When individuals in AA refer to themselves, or are referred to at the level of press, radio and films, they use their first name followed by the first initial of their last name. This procedure complies with AA's Eleventh and Twelfth Traditions: (11) "Our public relations policy is based on attraction rather than promotion; we need always maintain personal anonymity at the level of press, radio, and films; (12) Anonymity is the spiritual foundation of all our traditions, ever reminding us to place principles before personalities." *Twelve Steps and Twelve Traditions* (Alcoholics Anonymous World Services Inc., 1981), 180.

2. *Alcoholics Anonymous* (Alcoholics Anonymous World Services Inc., 1976), 7.

3. Ibid., 11.

4. Ibid., 12.

5. Ibid., 13.

6. *As Bill Sees It*, Alcoholics Anonymous World Services Inc., 1967), 2.

7. *Dr. Bob and the Good Old-Timers* (Alcoholics Anonymous World Services Inc., 1980), 68, emphasis added.

8. Ibid. 171.

9. Alcoholics Anonymous World Services Inc. reports that, as of

January 1, 2001, membership in AA was estimated at 2,160,013 with over 100,766 groups (www.alcoholics-anonymous.org).

10. "Understanding Anonymity." AA pamphlet (Alcoholics Anonymous World Services, Inc., 1981). Original copyright by The A.A. Grapevine, Inc.

11. *Alcoholics Anonymous*. (Alcoholics Anonymous World Services Inc., 1976), 58–60.

12. Neal A. Maxwell. "Swallowed Up in the Will of the Father," *Ensign*, November 1995, 24.

13. Robert D. Hales, "Healing Soul and Body," *Ensign*, November 1998, 17, emphasis added.

14. Ezra Taft Benson, "Beware of Pride," *Ensign*, May 1989, 4, emphasis added.

15. *As Bill Sees It* (Alcoholics Anonymous World Services Inc., 1967), 42, emphasis added.

16. *Alcoholics Anonymous* (Alcoholics Anonymous World Services Inc., 1976), 61–62, emphasis added.

17. Colleen C. Harrison, *He Did Deliver Me From Bondage.* (Hyrum, Utah: Windhaven Publishing and Productions, 2000), iii, emphasis added.

18. Robert Gray, *The Unseen Enemy* (Windhaven Publishing and Productions, 2003), 17.

19. From *Understanding Ourselves and Alcoholism* (Al-Anon Family Group Headquarters, Inc., 1979), 2, emphasis added. Reprinted by permission of Al-Anon Family Group Headquarters, Inc.

20. Ibid., 2–3, emphasis added.

21. *Alcoholics Anonymous* (Alcoholics Anonymous World Services Inc., 1976), 31.

22. From *Understanding Ourselves and Alcoholism* (Al-Anon Family Group Headquarters, Inc., 1979), 4, emphasis added. Reprinted by permission of Al-Anon Family Group Headquarters, Inc.

23. Ibid.

24. Ibid.

25. Ibid., 5., emphasis added.

26. *Dr. Bob and the Good Old-Timers* (Alcoholics Anonymous World Services Inc., 1980), 67.

27. Cowley, *Matthew Cowley—Man of Faith*, 147, emphasis added.

28. *Alcoholics Anonymous*, 151.

29. Ibid., 84.

$\mathcal{U}$NDERSTAND THE LESS FORTUNATE

MATTHEW COWLEY WAS A MEMBER OF THE QUORUM OF THE Twelve Apostles of The Church of Jesus Christ of Latter-day Saints from 1945 until his death in 1953. During his calling as a special witness to Jesus Christ, Elder Cowley became well known for his long and dedicated Church and humanitarian service to the Maori people of the Pacific Islands. These people claimed him as their personal apostle. To them, he became known as "Tumuaki," which means great leader, big chief, or president.[1]

What is less known of this special man is that, in the many chapters of Alcoholics Anonymous in the Intermountain Region, he was referred to as the "patron saint" to the alcoholic. They also claimed Elder Cowley as their own special apostle. In January 1954, the Utah Alcoholism Review said of Matthew Cowley:

> His love and devotion to his fellow men, his faith in the good which he found in all men, not only inspired those in high circles but gave to the lost and forgotten man a renewed feeling of strength and courage. What greater tribute could be paid any man than the words spoken of him by such as one of these, who said, "I was friendless, lost, and wanton. I went to him in my darkest hour, and he received me; he asked naught of me nor did he judge; but he gave of himself to me. He understood and had faith, he inspired me with the courage and determination that led to the new and happy way of life that I now live."[2]

Elder Cowley expressed his special philosophy as follows:

We are in the business of saving souls, not condemning them—even though we condemn the thing which makes them weak. We must not condemn the souls. There is no man who lives, under the gospel of Jesus Christ, but who can overcome his weaknesses—and then follow the principle of repentance and forgiveness. We must forgive all men . . . I hate the thing called self-righteousness; that has no place in God's plan . . . Let us all remember we are God's children and be loving and appreciative of his other children, that we may reach out and touch their lives.[3]

The following experience illustrates Brother Cowley's unique view on the power of the human relationship.

He [Elder Cowley] once told a woman who came to his office and said she had divorced her drunken husband whom she had married in the temple, "Your companion is no longer your husband in the eyes of the law, but now he is your brother, and there is no law under heaven which can destroy that relationship. Now, work with him as your brother, and I have suggestions which may help you." Of this experience he said, "I still know that the influence of that woman will lead her husband into sobriety, and under the goodness and mercy of God there will return the clasp of the hand."[4]

This appendix provides some of the words and experiences of this remarkable man as they pertain to alcoholism and addiction. Matthew Cowley said:

I went to an AA meeting one night in Salt Lake City and I heard the finest testimony on that saying of Lorenzo Snow's [Fifth President of the LDS Church 1898–1901], "As man now is, God once was, and as God now is, man may become" that I have ever heard. Now this fellow got up in his working clothes, overalls. He is a mechanic I think and he said, "It is my turn to speak. I am going to give a talk tonight on something I have heard all my life and didn't know what it meant until recently and that is this saying. I never knew what that meant, but I know now. Five years ago I was in the gutter. I was degenerate, demoralized, and had been drunk for ages. My wife left me, got the custody of my four children. She got our home and she was entitled to it all, and I was just turned loose, and I was just down in the gutter. Then you fellows (AA) got hold of me, and for five years I haven't had a drink. You know what has happened. I've got my wife back. I've converted her. She is baptized. The children have all been baptized. Last week I was ordained an elder, and the bishop said a year from now I can go to the temple of God and all be sealed to each other. Fellows, from the gutter to the temple of God in six years. You are looking at a God. As God now is, many may become." [5]

So brothers and sisters, let's be very kind to one another. None of us has lived his life yet. We don't know what the morrow is going to bring, you know. Men who haven't touched a drop (of alcohol) today may next year be alcoholics. Men who are alcoholics today may in a couple of years from now be bishops of the South 18th Ward. You can never tell. That's the Gospel of Jesus Christ. We should always keep in mind that two of the most glorious principles in this Church are repentance and forgiveness. [6]

Brothers and sisters in this Church, the last words President Smith said to me when I visited him in the hospital, and he could scarcely speak, were, "My boy, you will always find good in everyone if you look for it."

Remember that when you see these young men and women in your ward, remember that if they are drunk Saturday night, maybe a year from now one of them will be the bishop of the ward, or two years from now. I know a man not far from here who was a chain smoker for fifty years, who didn't go to church much. He is a bishop now—a wonderful bishop because he speaks the language of those who need help. That's an important thing in this business we are in, too—trying to understand the other fellow's viewpoint, trying to find out what caused him to do this. Maybe it was family background. Maybe you and I have just been luckier than he. To us Providence has been kind as we read in that hymn, "Let Each Man Learn to Know Himself." To us has Providence been kind. Consider all of those things. [7]

We have an Alcohol Rehabilitation Center in Salt Lake City, you know, and every few months I go to the welfare committee, and I insist on their sending food over to that Alcoholic Rehabilitation Center, and we feed those "drunks." Do you know why we do it? Because sixty-five percent of them belong to us! They're our people. They may be "drunks," but they're our "drunks." Why, you don't know what good you're doing, brothers and sisters, in this welfare work. You just can't imagine. Now, as a result, I'm the best friend the drunks have in Salt Lake City. They come to me for counsel. But I don't talk to them unless they're sober, because they're not there, and I can't waste my time. But my, we're all God's children. He wants us all to have security—to sit "under our own vines, our own fig trees" . . . I thank God for those who are in need. I thank God for the poor; I thank God for the downtrodden, for the sinners, because it's a challenge. It's a challenge to all of us who are fortunate, and we should be close to those who are in need.[8]

(Excerpts from an address given to members of Alcoholics Anonymous, Logan, Utah, November 24, 1953):

Maybe I shouldn't say, "We of Alcoholics Anonymous." The other day I heard from a sister who belongs to the Church, and she said, "If you can belong to Alcoholics Anonymous, I am going to stay with my drunken husband."

I first came in contact with this organization in 1945. I had been away for about eight years, and I was walking down the street in Salt Lake City. I met one of my friends whom I grew up with—not a member of my Church. He came up and shook hands with me and welcomed me home. He said, "When you have a few minutes, I would like to visit with you and talk to you about true religion." I thought he was going to bear his testimony to me about the church he belonged to. I never thought anymore of it until on one occasion I heard something about Alcoholics Anonymous. I had a very dear friend who was drinking, and I thought maybe Alcoholics Anonymous could do something for him. I got in touch with a member of the AA and was invited to come to one of their closed meetings. At that time they were holding them in the Newhouse Hotel. I got hold of my friend and took him down to the AA meeting, and at the AA meeting I saw this man that I had met on the street, who told me that he wanted to tell me something about true religion. After that meeting, I knew what he meant because he had been the town bum for many years—one of the worst drinkers I have ever known, and he had now been a member of Alcoholics Anonymous for several years and hadn't touched a drop.

I was very much inspired with that meeting. I didn't understand all there was to understand about it that night, and I had some misgivings. At the time I was suffering with a little breaking out [on the face], and that is sometimes [like] the breaking out of alcohol on the face. Of course, I knew that wasn't the cause of mine. I had been on a mission for eight years, and that was what was causing it. When I came out of there with my friend, he started to laugh. I said, "What's the matter with you?" He said, "You were the only one in there that looked like an alcoholic." I am sure glad I am not an alcoholic. He had been drunk for twenty-seven years, that I knew about, and had gone through $400,000.

Well, I decided that I was in the business of saving souls, and I saw in this group of men, many men whom I had known all of my life. Several of them had been my neighbors. I never will forget one fellow who was there. I used to run on the other side of the street when I would see him coming. He was an alcoholic if there ever was one. When I was county attorney in Salt Lake County and I couldn't find anyone else to prosecute, he would always show up and accommodate me. He not only drank alcohol, but he would also take this canned heat—I used to see him open a can, take his knife, dig it out, and put it in his handkerchief. Then he would squeeze the handkerchief and lick out that ooze from that canned heat, containing alcohol. He took goof balls, too. Well I saw him there. That fellow hasn't had a drink now for a number of years. I always said if there was any organization in the world that could sober that man, it was a great organization. His wife had left him. He has his wife back again now and a lovely home. He is in business. He calls in to see me regularly. In fact, he wants to be a good Latter-day Saint. He is having quite a time at it. I said to him one day, "How are you getting along with smoking?" He said, "Well, I smoke Kools, and I think anybody that can smoke Kools can beat the tobacco habit." One day I asked him how he was getting along, and he said, "Well, I'm not doing so bad.

I started to drink Postum. Isn't that the nastiest darn stuff you have ever tasted?" He is making a great effort—wonderful man.

There is one thing that I have learned from these men—they don't sanctify themselves. There is no self-righteousness in them. They are a bunch of screwballs. Well, that's about what they are, I suppose. A lot of others that are screwballs have never touched a drink. This humility and sincerity appeals to me in this organization. That is what the world needs today, the language of sincerity. These men and women have to be sincere. I sometimes have people in the Church think that there may be some ulterior motive in this organization. Some of them have told me that they thought the liquor interests were financing them, and I think the liquor interest would be smart to finance some organization like this. I have had a great deal of pride in going around and discussing the little problems of AA with our own people. Sometimes our own people get the idea that AA is a religion. That if you join AA you may be taken out of your own Church. Oh, no. No, when a Mormon joins AA, he becomes the best Mormon he has been for many years. When a Catholic joins AA, he becomes the best Catholic he has been for a long while—or a Methodist, or a Presbyterian.

Nothing controversial enters into their deliberations or their discussions. They never discuss the matter of sectarian religion. They never discuss political matters. They sometimes will say, "Well, if you want to be a moderate drinker, that's all right with us." But at the same time they don't drink. They are all concerned with one problem and that is staying on this raft of sobriety—their only goal, their only objective. All other things are just secondary to them.

As I go around the Church, I generally mention AA. Recently I was in Oakland, and I said something about the AA organization. After the meeting up come some of our Church members and quietly whispered in my ear, "We belong." One of them was the superintendent of the Sunday School down there, and a member of AA.

They do the things we would like to do in our Church. Of course, I want to talk about our Church. If you don't belong to our Church, just forgive me because I can't talk to you about your church. All I know is about my Church, and I don't know enough about that. I can see that within our Church activities, where we are vitally interested in helping these men and women who are alcoholics, we find it very difficult because we don't have understanding; for instance, if I should see a man drunk out on the street tonight, and I recognized him as a brother in the Church—and we have a lot of brothers in the Church who are drunk tonight—if I walked up to him and put my arm around him and said, "Bill, why don't you cut this out? It is no good for you." Well, he might be respectful, and he might not. But anyway, when he would get away from me, he would say, "He ought to go and get on a bender himself. He doesn't know what it is all about." As long as he thinks I don't understand him, it is just the same as if I didn't understand him, even if I do. But these men understand each other. You see when one of these men goes to the bedside of an alcoholic and talks to him or to her, they are kindred spirits. There is an understanding—a common understanding. There is a willingness to receive the help, and they do receive it. It is a thing they call group therapy—a wonderful way of helping each other in their groups.

I used to think that our Church had more meetings than any other Church or organization on earth. The Alcoholics Anonymous has us beaten. They are meeting all the time. If you get tired of going to fast meeting and attending long testimony meetings, you ought to go to these closed AA meetings, and then you would be very happy to go back to fast meeting and hear the testimonies of the brothers and sisters of the Church. That is all they do is hold meetings—stick together, stay together on this great program. It is a simple program, only twenty-four hours a day. They stay sober for only twenty-four hours a day. They get up in the morning—no drinks for the next twenty-four hours! That's easier than saying, "I am not going to take a drink in [for the rest of] my whole life." Twenty-four hours is much shorter than a lifetime. So it makes the program much easier.

They believe in prayer. They believe in the efficacy of prayer. There is no question about that. Many of these men have tried everything else. They have been in institutions; they have been to psychiatrists, they have been to medical doctors; and they have came away still alcoholics.

So, I would like to say to you people who are members of the Church, you who are officials of the Church, you don't make a mistake if you avail yourselves of this organization to assist you with these problems, and there are genuine problems.

I was in Honolulu, and I went to the AA meeting there. I went to this meeting because I noticed it in the paper. It was a public meeting, so I went. The special guests that night were from the nurses from the Queen's Hospital in Honolulu. I got a real kick out of watching those nurses when they came in and started walking around and mingling with these alcoholics. One of them would go up to a man and say, "I had wondered where you had been. You haven't been in the hospital for months. I haven't seen you for a couple of years. This is the reason. You belong to AA." Yes, they belong to AA. I'll never forget the testimony of a woman in that meeting. She was one of those who had nothing further to do—the end had come. She was hopeless and helpless, had lost all power of resistance. She went to her room, intoxicated, and when she reached her little room, she turned on the light, and in her drunken stupor she just fell to her knees—this is her story—before a chair, and there as clearly as she could utter any words she told God that she was through. She told him to take her life. She said, "I have come to the end of things. There isn't anything I can do." When she finally opened her eyes, she noticed on the chair a newspaper and her eyes immediately saw the letters AA and a telephone number—AA for Alcoholics Anonymous. She went to the telephone and called the number, and she has never touched a drink from that day until the day she was telling the story. That had been three or four years.

I mentioned in our leadership meeting one day a little about the Alcoholics Anonymous. The next morning the president of the Rotary Club called me up. He was a member of the Church and had been to the meeting. He said, "I wonder if there is a chapter of AA here in Honolulu?" That was before I knew that there was one, before I had attended that meeting. I said, "There must be. Why, do you want to join?" He said, "No. Last Tuesday the speaker at Rotary didn't show up. I called him up and asked him what was the idea. He had promised to come and speak—a very influential man in Honolulu. When I called him, he was drunk, and he told me over the telephone, "Fred, I am all washed up. I am going to lose my business. I am going to lose my family. I am just a drunken bum, and there isn't anything I can do about it." So Fred called me and asked me if there was a branch [of AA] there or a chapter. I said, "The newspapers will know," so we went up to see Mr. Riley Allen, the editor of the Honolulu Star Bulletin. He says, "Yes, there is a chapter of AA here," and he went to his desk and got out a phone number. He said, "You have your friends or whoever it is that wants to get in touch with AA call that number and make an appointment with the man who will answer the phone." It has been seven years now. That man made the phone call. He still has his business. He still has his family, and he keeps his speaking appointments with Rotary and all other organizations. He belongs to AA, and he hasn't had a drop.

There isn't anything I can say that is too good about this great organization. I have attended the meetings. I am always glad to give whatever support I can. Now, of course, we should always help the alcoholic whether we belong to AA or not. You won't find any Communists in Alcoholics Anonymous. They are all real, patriotic, God fearing Americans—men and women who are not afraid to get down on their knees and pray to God, not only for their own sanity, but also for the well-being of humanity and for the good institutions of this great nation.

Now, there is one thing I have learned, and it has been a wonderful thing for me as a religionist in my present position. I've learned from these men that there isn't a man living who isn't greater than his sins, who isn't greater than his weaknesses. That's a wonderful thing to know. It is a wonderful thing to know that, even though a man may sink so low that he is at the bottom of the gutter, yet within him there is a greatness that can regenerate him if he will submit himself to the right influences and to the power above and beyond himself. When science fails and medicine has to lay the burden down, those who are afflicted with alcoholism can reach out to God, and he takes over and that is what science, medicine, fails to do. So I say, God bless these men in their great undertaking. They are their brothers" keepers. They are engaged in the business of rehabilitating the unfortunate, and they rehabilitate each other.

Now, of course, in our Church we don't believe in the use of alcohol in any form. There is a reverend somebody—I've forgotten his name right now—who writes to me regularly from South Carolina. He doesn't believe in any kind of non-drinking organizations. He is quite annoyed with me because I believe in AA. He is a strong prohibitionist, this man. Well, the other day I wrote him a note, and I said, "Well, Reverend Sir, if all the drinkers in the United States belong to AA there wouldn't be any liquor business left in this country. If every drinker would become a member of AA, there wouldn't be any need of any prohibition movement or any other temperance movement because the AA member never takes a drink." It has been said here, "One is too many and a billion is not enough, so he doesn't take the one."

Now, in conclusion may I say, too, that we do not drink. Don't think that we are not alcoholics because we don't drink. At least one out of sixteen of us is alcoholic; and if we started to drink, we would be alcoholics.

I ask God to bless them and bless us, especially in our endeavors to help one another, to be our brothers' keepers and realize that we are all God's children and as his children we should be in the business, all of us, of saving one another, not only spiritually, but also materially, physically, and every other way. I want to join in thanking those who have made this building available to us tonight. It has been time well spent. I have enjoyed these testimonies of these members of AA, and I appreciate the lessons I have learned from them. They bring into my heart a spirit of humility and a spirit of sincerity.

God bless us all, I pray in the name of Jesus Christ. Amen.[9]

If all men and women were like unto to Matthew Cowley,[10] imagine how the smell of alcohol and tobacco in our places of worship *would increase*. Then imagine how that smell would lessen and lessen until it vanished altogether, as we loved our brothers and sisters back into the Gospel of Jesus Christ.

Notes

1. Cowley, *Matthew Cowley—Man of Faith*, 109.

2. Ibid., 147.

3. Ibid., 146.

4. Ibid., 151.

5. Cowley, *Matthew Cowley Speaks*, 340–341, emphasis added.

6. Ibid., 155.

7. Ibid. 135.

8. Ibid. 315–6.

9. Ibid. 212–9.

10. *Like unto Moroni.* "Yea, verily, verily I say unto you, if all men had been, and were, and ever would be, like unto Moroni, behold, the very powers of hell would have been shaken forever; yea, the devil would never have power over the hearts of the children of men" (Alma 48:17).

$\mathcal{A}$BOUT
the AUTHOR

THE YOUNGEST OF THREE CHILDREN, PHIL GREW UP IN RURAL
Southern Utah, served two years with the US Army in Panama,
and eventually earned a bachelor's degree in English from Utah State
University. Employed by the LDS Church Educational System, Phil
taught seminary for the next seven years. Between seminary assign-
ments in Idaho and Wyoming, he completed three years of graduate
studies at BYU in family life education.

In September 1978, still a seminary teacher but also a hopeless
alcoholic, Phil attended his first meeting of Alcoholics Anonymous.
The next decade, he was educated at the "University of Hard Knocks."
In addition to copious hours at AA and LDS Twelve Step Meetings,
he studied self-help gurus, books on thinking and meditation, Eastern and Western religions, and learned from those in sobriety. But
he remained hopelessly addicted. Painfully slow, knock-by-knock,

he learned the Steps to sober living. Longer periods of sobriety were achieved but not without costs. Bankruptcy, divorce, family lost, and excommunication were but some of the wreckage strewn along the way. On July 27, 1987, Phil pushed the stop button on the down elevator and got off the merry-go-round of alcoholism. Living one moment at a time, he has not needed to take a drink since that day. Although still learning, Phil has earned his PhD—in Alcoholism.

In 1988, Phil was employed by Stephen R. Covey and Associates (later to become FranklinCovey). Following a successful career, in 2000 Phil created Perfect Brightness LLC and published *The Perfect Brightness of Hope: A Latter-Day Saint's Journey Through Alcoholism and Addiction*. As a life coach, Phil currently offers his unique approach to living a peaceful and successful life through his original curriculum: Living @5: A Spiritual Course in Thought & Time.

Phil and his wife Vickie Lee are the parents of seven children, twenty-one grandchildren, and four great grandchildren.